Between Myth and Morning

WOMEN AWAKENING

Also by Elizabeth Janeway

The Walsh Girls
Daisy Kenyon
The Question of Gregory
Leaving Home
The Third Choice
Accident
Man's World, Woman's Place

Between Myth and Morning

WOMEN AWAKENING

by ELIZABETH JANEWAY

WILLIAM MORROW & COMPANY, INC.
NEW YORK 1974

Grateful acknowledgment is made for permission to reprint the following:

"Reflections on the History of Women" from *Women: Their Changing Roles*, edited by Elizabeth Janeway, Copyright © 1973 by The New York Times Company. Reprinted by permission of Arno Press, Inc.
"Women in Business" from *Boardroom Reports*, July 17, 1972. Copyright © 1972, Boardroom Reports, Inc. Reprinted by permission of Boardroom Reports, Inc.
"The Question Is, What Is a Family, Anyway?" from the Op. Ed. page of *The New York Times* of April 1, 1972. Copyright © 1972 by The New York Times Company. Reprinted by permission of *The New York Times*.
"Raising Children in the Year 2000" from *The Saturday Review for Education*, March, 1973, Copyright © 1973 by *The Saturday Review for Education*. Reprinted by permission of *Saturday Review/World*.
"Freud's View of Female Sexuality," from *Women & Analysis*, edited by Jean Strouse, Copyright © 1974 by Jean Strouse. Reprinted by permission of Grossman Publishers.
"Realizing Human Potential," from *Educational Horizons*, Winter, 1973-74. Reprinted by permission of *Educational Horizons*.
"Breaking the Age Barrier," from *Ms.*, April, 1973, Copyright © Ms. Magazine 1973. Reprinted by permission of Ms. Magazine.
"Images of Woman," from *Arts in Society*, Volume VII, Number 1, "Women and the Arts," Copyright © University of Wisconsin Regents, 1974. Reprinted by permission of *Arts in Society*.
"A Woman Examines Dr. Kinsey," from *The New Leader*, November 16, 1953, Copyright © 1953 by The American Labor Conference on International Affairs, Inc. Reprinted by permission of *The New Leader*.
"A Woman's Role," from *The New York Times Book Review*, August 1, 1965, Copyright © 1965 by The New York Times Company. Reprinted by permission of *The New York Times*.
"The Lives of Four Women," from *Harper's*, November, 1967, Copyright © 1967 by Harper's Magazine. Reprinted by special permission of Harper's Magazine.
"Meg, Jo, Beth, Amy and Louisa," from *The New York Times Book Review*, September 29, 1968. Copyright © 1968 by The New York Times Company. Reprinted by permission of *The New York Times*.
"The Subordinate Sex," from *The Saturday Review*, October 11, 1969. Copyright © 1969 by *The Saturday Review*. Reprinted by permission of *Saturday Review/World*.
"About Women," from *Civil Liberties*, Issue 2, Spring, 1974. Copyright © 1974 by The American Civil Liberties Union, Inc.

Grateful acknowledgment is made for permission to quote from the following:

The Life and Work of Sigmund Freud by Ernest Jones, Volume III, Copyright © 1955 by Ernest Jones, New York: Basic Books, and Copyright © Katherine Jones 1957, London: The Hogarth Press. Quoted by permission of Mrs. Katherine Jones, The Hogarth Press, Ltd. and Basic Books, Inc.
Nine lines from "For the Time Being" from *Collected Longer Poems*, by W. H. Auden, Copyright 1944 and renewed 1972 by W. H. Auden. Quoted by permission of Random House, Inc.

Printed in the United States of America.
1 2 3 4 5 78 77 76 75 74
Design by Helen Roberts

Library of Congress Cataloging in Publication Data

Janeway, Elizabeth.
    Between myth and morning; women awakening.

    1. Women in the United States. 2. Woman—History and condition of women. 3. Woman (Psychology)
4. Women's liberation movement—United States.
I. Title.
HQ1426.J35   301.41'2'0973   74-7166
ISBN 0-688-00311-7

Contents

Between Myth and Morning

WOMEN AWAKENING

1

The last ten years have seen so many changes in the world that we who have lived through them all may well feel—and fear—that we are getting numb. "Future shock" has replaced "The Sense of the Past," which Henry James celebrated and which does indeed have great value when it nurtures an awareness of life as a continuing process, an awareness that assumes a relationship of some kind, not necessarily a simple linear one, between prior and present events. Of course, traditions must be judged singly; some are valuable, some are irrelevant. Crises of the past lose their force as they lose their pertinence and tragedies soften into bittersweet pathos. Thus, our current enjoyment of nostalgia can be seen as no more than a way of acknowledging the occasion for penitence without having to do anything about it. To wear fashions of the 1940's or hum tunes from the 1930's is a way of relinquishing the past by minimizing its significance, until it is reduced to a mere adornment and amusement of the all-important present. That may pain (or exasperate) the old, but in a world of great and continuing change we must prevent the past from ruling the present and tying our hands and our brains.

Nonetheless, the variety and rapidity with which change has overtaken us do dazzle the mind and by so doing create their own dangers. At times we seem to be making a whole ideology out of leaping from wave to wave, with anything and everything novel taken to be worth our serious attention. We want to be where the action is. Instead of shuddering away from the buffets of future shock, we embrace the excitement it brings. But excitement is a treacherous emotion because indiscriminate. If we go

1

by what's exciting we will find all emotions increasingly similar, a buzzing of the nerves at any stimulus, and we will lose our ability to distinguish between one stimulus and the next.

So I want to preface this preface with the flat-footed, obvious statement that some changes are bigger than others. You can, if you want, call a revolution a fad—in fact, that's a normal human reaction to revolution. But calling it a fad won't make it go away. Among the multifarious novelties of the last decade can be found a few which are major and permanent.

One grand change, perhaps the grandest, is our growing awareness that a presence which had been knocking for a century or more on the door of consciousness has entered the world and shows no sign of leaving. God knows it's been given a cool enough welcome, the awkward creature, and no wonder. Balky and shy at times, it's unnervingly indiscreet at others and will disturb the most sophisticated by its habit of talking too much or laughing at unexpected moments. Worse still, no one can be sure when it may burst into outrageous threats or dissolve in tears of rage for no clear reason. Older inhabitants, who have resigned themselves philosophically to man's fate and curbed their own desires, often find it greedy, and even those who declare they are open-minded object to the way it mutters to itself instead of speaking up in forthright, understandable terms. Its demands have been declared by experts to be contradictory and overweening, quite out of the question for any well-ordered system to live with. And yet—

It is still here. Neither mockery nor attack has banished it, and paying lip service to its wishes, the next political step, seems merely to encourage it to formulate more. Like a fragment of nightmare, like a character from Beckett or Ionesco, the creature has not only moved in, it keeps growing. It hardly has a name, for it runs uncontrollably over the bounds of any neat definition. Women's Lib? Worn out at the beginning by its pejorative intent. This creature doesn't *care* if it's laughed at and opposition is only what it expects. Feminism? Yes, but humanism too. The Women's Movement? Better, but still too structured. "Movement" implies direction, and this being has no more articulated, coherent view of its goals than a baby does. Its goals and its acts are the same— growth, realization, discovery. Yet here it is, named or not. It is consciousness, it is presence, it is woman wakened from a millennial slumber and looking around at a world in which, astonishingly, one might be at home: Galatea without Pygmalion, dreaming herself out of the stone by her own force of creation.

To say that this presence is new is an understatement. When, a hundred-odd years ago, the pioneers of the Feminist Movement began to declare that women actually had rights of their own, when they attacked and painfully breached the walls surrounding "Woman's Place," they were inaugurating an action which, as far as can be told, had never before been undertaken in human history. Out of the relics of thirty thousand years, there is no image of woman that we can point to and say: This was made by women alone, apart from the eyes or the direction of men. Take the earliest images of all, the little "Venuses" of the Old Stone Age which have been found across Europe and Asia from the Atlantic littoral to Siberia. To name them Venuses is to imply that they are goddesses; and so they have been called by many an archaeologist. But look at them with a human eye: they are not goddesses, they are fetishes, lucky pieces for a desperate man, hunter or hunted, starving or wounded, to thumb in time of need; a memory of Mum and Mum's protection and thus not a portrait of woman, but of man's need for her. They have neither faces nor feet, so they are neither present as individuals nor, denied autonomous motion, can they depart by themselves. Unlike the dancing shamans engraved or painted on the cave walls, they need no masks or disguises for they are masked in their own symbolism, fertility, as impenetrable to the mind and as much a part of natural existence as a breeding sow.

Even when the Goddess appears, her image is that of the woman seen by man from outside. She is the Great Mother, feared and adored, both mediator with and representative of necessity. This is not a picture drawn by woman. No girl child would form such an identity for herself, for there is nothing of her inner personal experience in it. What centuries, what millennia it must have required for girl children to accept it as their portrait! What pyrotechnics of training, what useless but ever-renewed rebellion, what reverberant tunnels of despair mocking and echoing the lost lonely voice of oneself as person must have been lived through before the mind came to bow to the knowledge that there was no other sanctioned identity to put on! The Mother Goddess is an image shaped by emotions projected onto women, reflecting the desires and needs of others. In that pattern of making, a woman cannot be allowed to feel or express her own emotions, nor to originate any act, for her purpose is not to create her own life, but to validate the experience of others. *Her* experience isn't and can't be part of the reckoning, for it would confuse it hopelessly. It simply doesn't count and so she is absent from history.

This anonymity is part of her being, in Simone de Beauvoir's word, "other," for if she were not, if she could be seen as similar to men, she would have to be counted in. It is this quality of "otherness" which has engendered the familiar description of woman as enigma. It is, so to speak, a fallback line to be taken up when complete ignoring of her reality becomes impossible. Freud was demonstrating the value of this position in our own historical period when, years after the Feminist Movement had mounted its campaign for women's rights, he asked, "What does a woman want?" Over and over, before then and since, the question has been answered and the answer still goes unheard and unregarded. For to accept it—"A woman wants to be counted as human"—would entail accepting the full validity and equal significance of woman's wanting, woman's needs, woman's human presence; and thereby losing the blank mirror of otherness in which man searches for his face.

So it has been. Now this is ending. Over the last century or two, an instant of human time, women have begun to examine their own experience and to speak of what they find there. First the writers took up their pens. That was reasonably easy to do in niches and crannies of time as the age became literate, and it didn't require much in the way of equipment. A bottle of ink, a bundle of paper and a quill pen were not hard to come by and, as the middle class throve and increased, even women began to have a bit of leisure and privacy; enough to scribble in. Then, too, Romanticism conceived the idea that the individual personality was valuable in itself and though men might fail to assign such value to the female individual, women read the books too and were infected by the idea. Perhaps they had something to say!

Saying it in books had another attraction too. A woman could communicate her experience while invisible from her audience. Instead of being present in all her distracting femininity and disturbing otherness, she disappeared behind the printed page. In addition, the vogue of the novel stood women writers in good stead. No nineteenth-century man could want to be preached at by a woman in a book of sermons, but he would hardly draw the line at being amused by one; entertaining the male had long been an acceptable part of the female role, as Scheherazade knew well. It isn't chance, but the structure of the old role which makes the woman storyteller the first individual artist of her sex; in medieval Japan, too, a time of change produced women novelists, like Lady Murasaki, writing their "entertaining" chronicles in the vernacular while male authors, now forgotten, employed the formal honorific Chinese language. But only in our own recent past have other women artists followed.

The painters were next. Indeed, women painters had appeared as often as women poets, for their work too could be sold or admired without their embarrassing presence. Usually, however, they were apprenticed individually to their trade by painter-fathers who lacked promising sons, and they left no tradition and no protégées. Once more it was the Romantically inspired nineteenth century which found their work sentimentally pleasant and thus gave them a general public. The cult of the home and the family made a place for the recording of women's experience. But how many paintings, even by fine women artists, concentrate on the saleable, limited, *proper* female experience: Mary Cassatt's tea tables, Berthe Morisot's mothers and children. Before Käthe Kollwitz, what woman painted pain, horror or despair? Only the mad. Now, finally, the dramatists and choreographers and film-makers and composers, artists who cannot work alone and have been dependent on the willingness of others (men) to mount their work, are beginning to be seen and heard. At last, at last, our self-portraits are being created across the breadth of art.

It may seem odd to begin a discussion of women's self-image by talking about what the artists have been doing, for our society has cut art off from life and stuffed it into museums. If you say "image-maker" to the average American, he will assume you are referring to some advertising tycoon. And of course some of them *are* artists in their field; but it is a wrong-way-round field, in which the aim is not to respond to life and interpret it but to manipulate it to a given goal, known from the beginning. That can only be done by a shuttered mind, and shuttered minds are a peril both to art and society. For what society requires from art (this is not necessarily what the individual may require) is that it function as an early warning system. We are in trouble because we have forgotten that the artist's job is to react to the world—in a changing world to react especially to change—not for himself only, but for the rest of us. It is the artist alone who can create something besides a straightforward—and therefore clueless—picture of reality, who can supply the symbolic representation of what reality means and how it is to be valued by the human beings who live inside it. Artists do not simply report experience, though they do that too; they define it and name what is new, they connect one aspect of life to another. In short, they make images which help us to know who we are and who others are and how we need to function with these others-like-ourselves. So the appearance of women artists is a strong vital sign of the new presence in the world.

Not that women have never created art before; only that it has always been anonymous. Women's art in the past was folk art: beautiful, moving and communicating a great deal about their lives, but always adapted to functions and purposes set by society. Only in the last few seconds of historical time, last century, this century, have women been allowed to be individual artists speaking with their own voices, soloists apart from the choir.

Consequently the experience of women has not only been structured by men, it has been given its significance by men. Men have said, "This is true and that is false; this is right and that is wrong"; and, most important of all, they have said, "This is important and that is secondary." They have told us even what it is that has happened to us, named the events of our lives. Not all men have had a hand in this, naturally, for such ordering of reality is effected by the powerful, and not all men have a grasp on power. But there is no period we know of in which the powerful have not been men, even when they have made and held to a bargain with the weak. So women have learned to judge their lives and to identify their emotions according to an external determination. It will be a long time yet before we understand all that means, for first we have a great deal to unlearn. We aren't even sure who we are. Barely awake, still rubbing our eyes, we are stunned by the idea that we might say Yes and No because of our own wants and needs, not someone else's. When have we dared to do that without first asking ourselves, "What will they think of me? Isn't it wrong and unwomanly for me to imagine that what I want can be as important as what he wants? Won't I pay for such selfishness, such shameful exposure of my desires, such illicit wants, by bringing down on my head the disapproval of the powerful? And the envy and distrust of other women, who will surely resent any rebel who dares to value herself as the equal of the men they've attached themselves to and are dependent on?" So at the very outset we are tangling with the social imperatives inherent in our society, and with the mythology which justifies them and goes on to direct the fashion in which we live and behave and conceive ourselves.

Thus the awakening and the start on reinterpreting experience, the daring to judge oneself worthy of making judgments and also the coming together with other women as friends and sharers of life instead of as rivals for approval by men—all this is going on at once. That is confusing, but it is a fruitful confusion, in which one aspect of life runs into another. An an example, take this business of sharing, or "bonding," to use Lionel Tiger's phrase. When Tiger declared that men came together into groups and women did not he was, broadly speaking, an accurate reporter of circumstances, though in some societies women find joint action less difficult than in others. Thus, the anthropologist Victor Turner reports of a Zambian people he has studied for many years: "Most Ndembu, both men and women, were members of at least one cult association, and it was hard to find an elderly person who was not an 'expert' in the secret knowledge of more than one cult." Among the Ndembu, too, ceremonies exist in which the whole group of women oppose the men, with each sex singing ribald and jeering songs about the other, though the ambience is one of high good humor: "The whole atmosphere is buoyant and aggressively jovial, as men and women strive to shout one another down."

If women have not joined together for jovial shouting matches more often, the reason does not lie in sex-related genetic coding, for if it did, such variant examples as the Ndembu could hardly exist. Rather it is long-term patterns of living which have isolated women from each other by making them subordinate to men, and thus individually dependent on men. Degrees of subordination differ, and so do degrees of isolation. It might be interesting to ask whether these variations are in any way related: in a purdah society, for instance, women are very much subordinated and are at the same time herded together. At other times and in other places, when they have been less subordinated, they have been isolated by being each encapsulated within a separate nuclear family. Perhaps we are allowed to live in groups when society reckons us weak enough to be no threat! Such a conclusion, though tempting, is much too simple, of course, for it leaves out the variants in men's attitudes, and they are diverse too, influenced by the elaboration of the social structure and the distance it sets between men and women.

Isolation, nonetheless, has been a constant feature of past societies, for women's access to power has always been more or less vicarious, and has had to take a personal route. A woman acts through, or on, a man and her success is ultimately based on her ability to please and persuade. This is not a quality to be belittled, nor is a pleasant and persuasive character to be reprobated, though it need not, surely, be recommended only to women. Pleasant men are pleasant company too. The difficulty comes when the power to please and persuade becomes the *only* road to action, when power must be attained through the show of weakness. If women are called deceptive and not straightforward, it is because of this bind which tells us that if we are going to act at all, we must manipulate the man we are supposed to be pleasing. We know that we have, in the past, pleased most easily when we have accepted, introjected and acted out, *as if spontaneously,* the role in which society cast us. Spontaneity, sincerity, then, become instruments for deception. Virtue itself is smudged by being "useful." And always when the good woman is defined as pleasing others, her own pleasure must come from them, so that everything is reflected and nothing direct.

This is obviously the road to lonely rivalry with other women, not to bonding in sisterhood. Bonding involves a promise to act together and to be responsible with others in action. In turn, this demands that one trust oneself to be that responsible creature. Can we trust ourselves? The way in which women have been disvalued by society has persuaded us to disvalue ourselves. But suddenly, in these last awakening years, the tables have turned. By trusting each other, we find we can trust ourselves. As we value other women more highly we can gain self-confidence. Then bonds begin to form and to strengthen us, for confidence and self-confidence interact powerfully, working together toward greater interior solidity and also toward a kind of comfortable at-homeness in the world. One of the unexpected bonuses of liberation for women is an increased capacity to enjoy oneself in one's own way, to be the pleased person instead of the one who is expected to do the pleasing. If that sounds self-serving, it doesn't work out that way, for the capacity to enjoy oneself is the true basis of generosity. One can't give joy away freely till one feels that one has a store to give it from. To think of oneself constantly as the pleaser instead of the pleased is not only to deny that one is entitled to the elementary human right of enjoyment, but to turn one's own pleasure, meanly, into a hoard that has to be counted and paid out frugally for value received.

In fact, I believe that the societal restraints imposed on women by the stereotypes of our culture have cost us an enormous amount of psychic energy. How much talent and capacity must have been wasted in holding our impulses down, in molding our behavior to match the ideal our consciences held up as appropriate to The Good Woman! How often and how intensely we have quarreled with ourselves when we began to feel the urge to act in some insidious, unwomanly way, just because it would be pleasing to us, instead of being good for others! And such repressions, be it noted, have contributed to the compulsion among women to be private and secret, for these transgressions have seemed like sins, inadmissible even to our dear friends; or, if admitted, forming a private and almost illicit bond: we two evildoers and upholders of subversion. Once again, large bonding for action, easy friendship between free people, is prevented. Only as the stereotypes have

faded and the barriers to enjoyment have gone down have the
barriers to friendships fallen too. Almost automatically the bonding that never happened has begun to form. Nor are such friendships confined to friendships with women, by the way, for being
easy and open with others can mean openness to affectionate
friendship with men too.

What has freed women today is not, of course, the act of any
God or any Goddess either. We have been given a chance at liberation by the workings of historical forces; specifically, by the
disruption and overthrow of old patterns of life through the intervention of profound and long-term economic, technological and
scientific processes. All revolutions come about through the crack-
ing open of social patterns and systems so that previously inhibited
human capacities can come into play. That's as true of a cultural
revolution (the Renaissance) as it is of the overthrow of empires
(the barbarian invasions which finally brought a weakened Rome
to its end). Nor can culture and politics and economics and technology be separated: all work together. The women's revolution,
or movement or liberation—it will find its name one day!—is not
unique, nor is it a thing in itself, set apart in our time from the
other effects of change.

Certainly it was not set in motion originally by women. It is a
response to a whole intermeshed collection of changing pressures
and processes, to other revolutionary social changes, to the decreasing economic function of the family, to schooling outside the
home and to the public images that flood into the home via radio
and television, to the new sort of homes people live in, to the Pill
and what it means for the planning of childbirth, to medical advances that have ended the commonplace death of children in
their first years of life (and so helped both to boom the population
and to produce a reaction to the threat of uncontrolled population growth), to migration and mobility within a society both up
and down and geographically, cross-country, to machines that have
made physical strength unimportant, to higher education for more
than the few—there is really no place to end the list. The modern
world has made the Women's Movement, made it possible and
now inevitable. What women are doing now is making the down-

fall or decline of the Movement clearly impossible. That awkward new presence in the world is here to stay.

This book is a record of my observations and cogitations on the process of birth and first growth of this new creature. Like millions of others, I have been a witness and participant; not "present at the creation," for the task is too large and will be too long for anyone to claim that, but fortunate to be one of the many who saw a little of the beginning. It has been, it is, an astonishing experience. I hesitate to put words to it, for words are limiting—but then a whisper in my ear hints that I may in fact be hesitating out of fear, out of the old female preference for privacy and seclusion, for not speaking out, not showing what one feels. That fear is a legacy of disvaluation, and of the old directive to please, for the woman who talks too much and gives herself away is mocked. She loses her attractiveness—gabby woman, can't keep a secret—and how can she operate in the world unless she can attract men? The pattern has bitten deep.

Which is not to say that women's fear of being mocked is ridiculous. Anything we say can be used against us. The process of consciousness-raising, for instance, has very properly been private because it is so exploratory and expressive. Half-formed emotions of fear, anger and frustration must be allowed to rip out unhindered if they are ever to be faced and controlled for use. Bringing them to the surface *at all* is a step toward accepting oneself through sharing, to making what was hidden known; but it is only a step. There is still a line between public and private, between what one only feels and what one has thought about and is willing to say and hold to. In a way, the old role, which made women private creatures, embodying emotional expressiveness, has taught us to be wary of making anything public on rather sound grounds; it is very difficult to express emotion fully and persuasively in words understandable to others. Even those of us who have been trained (self-trained) to do this as poets and writers of fiction find it hard to structure our own emotions, with the result that some of us exaggerate and some of us understate. Yet can women complain about misrepresentation if we ourselves do not try to report on what is happening to us?

Well then, what is happening to women involves a sudden enlargement of our world: the sky above us lifts, light pours in. Certainly that illumination reveals fear, anger and frustration, doubt and uncertainty. Confusion reigns. If we have an idea where we want to go (and we do) we are not at all sure how to get there. No maps exist for this enlarged world, we must make them as we explore, and we are not even sure we know how. We must muster our strengths, both old and new. We shall need patience and courage and endurance; stamina is the best word, I think. These are the familiar virtues of woman's place. But in addition we must learn some new ones, what I called (in *Man's World, Woman's Place*) "the prince's virtues of daring, honor and panache."

Add some unlearning of old assets. We need to be able to call on egotistic, stubborn persistence in the face of disagreement, to be right rather than pleasing. Since this trait will guarantee disapproval and actual dislike, we need a kind of selective insensitivity, the ability to strangle the indwelling "Sweet Alice," who used to tremble with fear at a frown. All this means a breaking away from the old role, and it isn't easy. Much of the internal distress recorded in recent books by women who are wakening to history and the world of events, and dwelt on obsessively by disconcerted men, is occasioned by the pull of these new needs against the tug of the old image assigned so long ago, in which we have striven so hard to shape ourselves, the image of the Good Woman, loving and giving and loved for her giving. Although she is a construct of others, although she demands submission and withdrawal and vicarious living, although we know her demands have become crippling, we have lived with her and tried to live *as* her for a long time. Giving her up is frightening, seems to leave the world barren. *Can* we replace her image? Can we trust this awkward, amorphous, unnamed creature who has invaded our consciousness and our lives to shape herself into a new ideal?

I believe we can, and one reason I do is that central to the experience of women coming together as friends and allies is *recognition*. We have been alone for a long time. Perhaps it has really made us a little mad. If the daily reality of life did not fit the old image, how could we admit that without admitting our failure?

So hide the failure, uphold the image, judge oneself abnormal; and what else is madness than this constant discrepancy between what one feels and what one accepts as being the right thing to feel? But now across this continuing maladjustment of mind and emotion streams a new knowing of each other, a knowing that authenticates the emotion one feels oneself. Recognition: one finds oneself in others. One feels a coming together, one talks with the confidence of being understood. But mark well that what we are finding is not simply common femininity. It is something much wider, infinitely extensive under that lifted sky above our heads. It is common *humanity*. It is the right to say, "I belong here. I am part of the whole, I understand." Distrust runs off the surface of the world like receding floodwater. Euphoric, intoxicating, transient—yes, even the uplifted heart knows that its joy must be reckoned as all those things, but neither should the experience be ignored or disvalued. Like the Ndembu women Victor Turner witnessed, we have found a way of singing together.

Considering that emotion and others like it experienced by other groups, Turner has adapted Martin Buber's *community* to the form *communitas*. "At certain life crises," he writes, "such as adolescence, the attainment of elderhood, and death, varying in significance from culture to culture, the passage from one structural status to another may be accomplished by a strong settlement of 'human-kindness,' a sense of the generic social bond between all members of society." In the life crisis of contemporary women, this bond supports us as we move to adult responsibility. If the euphoria dims, as it will, the mood has still left its mark in memory and something of the exhilaration remains within our grasp. To find oneself suddenly free to use one's full strength is intoxicating. The first burst of delight will pass, but the joy of using that strength, of facing the world and its facts and problems and dangers and difficulties in the knowledge that one can tackle it with a whole heart and undivided mind and comradeship with others, that remains. I wish that sense of joy in one's own useful energy and in one's connection with others to everyone in this world.

II

This book is as much a conversation as it is a monologue. Anyone writing or talking about women today, about their changing roles and position and aspirations, will find her (him) self responding to questions and prods, and profiting by insights and comments from audiences, editors and interlocutors as often as she (he) takes off on a singular flight. Not only is this conversation a great source of knowledge, it acts as a sort of gyroscope, keeping the exploring social mythologist homed in on reality. What are you worrying about? Tell me that, and I'll know where you are; and where I am too. If my responses are connected and focused, and I hope they are, it is because they stem from a continuing stream of thought and concern. These papers were written individually, but they connect and interact both in content and in development. The gambits offered me were taken as opportunities to discuss an ongoing investigation of the way in which man's world and woman's place have been growing together, flowing together—or how they have not been doing so. Themes cited in one place are reflected and enlarged on in another. My own thinking has progressed and deepened just because new questions have been raised and new insights given me. I owe a debt to my fellow conversationalists—my collaborators in the exact sense of the word.

It is through such communcation as well as by means of my own analysis that I have come more and more to see "the woman question" as germane to the whole structure of living and of power in our society. When, nearly five years ago, I began a review with the words "Half the human race is female," and went on to say that it was hard to remember that, sometimes, even for a female, I felt I was making a discovery. Today, it's a cliché; but truisms often wrap themselves round a kernel of truth, and if you reflect on this cliché before dismissing it for its banality, you can see it as pointing toward a less obvious meaning. "Half the human race" can be taken as separating the sexes; or it can be taken as emphasizing the connection and not the separation; which connection means, in the end, that the woman question can't be seriously discussed without considering its relationship to overall human problems of power, of politics and economics, of freedom and justice, of philosophy. It also means, reciprocally, that something new, women's experience, is being added to the old discussion mix.

The section which follows was written as an introduction to a collection of news items and comment about women culled from the pages of *The New York Times* over the years from the Civil War to the present. How we got to where we are seems a good place to begin. Just the same, let's not be simpleminded about history and its facts. No fact exists without its observer, and every observer brings a built-in frame of reference to every observation. Equally, every writer assumes the existence of such a framework in his readers' heads. History, especially cultural and social history, doesn't work in any straightline way, as if causality flowed from datum to datum. Lines of causation dip into human minds, get mixed up with emotions and blanked out by fatigue. They are modified sharply by little lessons from daily life, by what's possible and what isn't, by hope and despair. In my opinion, those who are looking for causes of human behavior had better augment their reading of history by fiction and poetry, which are sometimes more illuminating because they knowingly incorporate the emotional context of the times. Facts without that are a heap of pebbles.

The point of looking at *women's* history is that no one has heaped up these pebbles before and looked at them all together. Knowing about them and how they connect enlarges our field of vision and can force us to question theories that were constructed without regard for these pebbles.

Reflections on the History of Women

American women are not the only people in the world who manage to lose track of themselves, but we do seem to mislay the past in a singularly absentminded fashion. A century ago, observers as different as Mark Twain and Henry James noticed that our identities appeared to fit loosely and be readily subject to change. In part, this is because we are Americans, geographically and socially mobile, fellow countrymen of the Henry Ford who said, "History is bunk." In part, it is because we are women, people whose lives are recurrently jolted away from continuity. Look at our personal histories, and you will find old scars of passage from one state of being to another: tomboy to junior miss; drum majorette to sociology student; art historian to computer programmer; candidate for an M.A. to harried wife-and-mother; priestess of the Feminine Mystique to divorcée; housewife to financial analyst; and older woman who has suffered the feared and fracturing shift from busy middle life to lonely, widowed age.

Acquaintance with change has some positive advantages. These transitions should, and often do, keep alive our capacity to adjust to new circumstances and to learn new rules and roles. Women are less surprised than men when they find that they do not control their lives. They have less pride invested in setting up and maintaining a consistent image of themselves to front the outside world. They are, in fact, less apt to be engaged directly with the outside world. The dooms pronounced on them by Sigmund Freud and Erik Erikson still exert force: "Anatomy is destiny." "Women are concerned with inner space, with family and child-rearing." Challenged as these dicta have been, they remain at least partially true as current, demonstrable fact. It will take more time than we have yet lived to reduce them to the level of superstition toward which they are tending. Women can't help but know that they live in a changing world. The very fashions of dress, which even nuns are now allowed to follow, tell them so.

In the abstract, then, this ability to accept change can be seen as healthy, as a responsive adjustment which contributes to survival. But when we say this, we are at once raising the question of *who is it that survives;* of what core within us remains the same in a world of change. Certainly some of the energy of the current liberation movement derives from the urge among women to find more secure identities, the need to know who and what they have been in the past, in order to see themselves as participants with a stake in the present and a valid grasp on the future. Every emerging social group wants a history, rather as every aspirant nineteenth-century merchant wanted ancestors, roots and a coat of arms. Snobs can laugh but, in fact, a sense of one's own connection to the past, of one's continuity of being, is as much needed for healthy survival as one's ability to accept change. Particularly is this true for the sex which has been told for centuries by parents, prelates and philosophers that the traditional role of its members is to live for others and find their identities in personal relationships. To live in response to others is to live a life which is necessarily fragmented and ephemeral.

These reflections are called forth by the opportunity to take a long look at the social image of women in the last several generations, that period which hovers somewhere between hearsay and history. The first thing one discovers is that the scholarly historians who deride the idea of a special history of women are quite correct. Women have not been trend-setters, activists or protagonists in the drama of great events. If they turn up in the middle of some climactic scene, they are likely to have got there by the accident of marriage or, occasionally, of birth. Women monarchs have inherited power under laws made by men, not laid hands on it themselves, and rare indeed has been any influence their rule has had on the lives of other women *as* women. The history of women has not been made within their own ranks but has followed from external, male-initiated processes. Like their personal lives, women's history is fragmented, interrupted; a shadow history of human beings whose existence has been shaped by the efforts and the demands of others.

Even as subordinates, women have not formed a distinct group or class whose development can be treated coherently as, for example, black history can. Though women's activities have been circumscribed, the background of their lives has always been enormously diverse. They have been queens and slaves and prostitutes, ladies and laborers, poets and procurers. True, none has been president, few if any have been pornographers. They have rarely headed major industrial firms, conducted symphonies, functioned as trial lawyers or orthopedic surgeons. In top-level politics they are scarce on the ground. Once again, these limits are determined by external enforced conventions. Women's history must therefore deal less with what they have done than with what they have been allowed to do. Within the limits permitted, women have done everything, lived lives of variety and activity. They have simply behaved like human beings; and have, therefore, *no* special women's history. What is special is not their own plans and deeds but, rather, the roles, expectations and interpretations that have been projected onto them.

The paradoxical result is that any useful history of women has to be a history of what has been thought about them. It is the *image* of woman, originating in men's eyes, that alone gives her a special group identity. Which is not to say that women don't often accept such an identity—accept it whether they approve of it, resent it or (as today) see it as a unifying force, a challenge against which an attack can be mounted. The Women's Movement, indeed, is seizing on the old, demeaning image of women, the old submissive identity, in order to escape from it by overthrowing it. It is a kind of outsize palace revolution which is taking place; and those who are startled or put off by the anger the Movement activists voice might reflect on the frustration implicit in the situation of a group whose very identities have been forged by others, so that a woman's ego can hardly be trusted until it is reclaimed and made over. That will have happened on the day when women see themselves, and are seen, as human beings who happened to have been born with female sex; but it has not happened yet. The present and the recent past still bear out Simone de Beauvoir's admirable description: women are regarded as "object," misunderstood as "other" and dealt with as "the second sex."

Just the same, if we look at a compendium of popular attitudes toward women over the past century, we find much reason to hope that more realistic estimates of women's abilities are replacing the superstitions of the past. Like annals and archives, journalism can offer a pertinent and revealing selection of news items, essays, reports and advertising appeals having to do with women. Back in the 1860's for example, the drafting of men to fight opened new opportunities for women. True, a Victorian smog of condescension and contempt soon descended again; but from the 1890's on, we can trace a sort of social case history of woman-as-she-is-seen which does document a growing, if uneven, advance toward personal dignity, autonomy and freedom of choice. These are chronicles of change, source material for the historian of ideas—or, perhaps better, of myth.

For one can't really sort out these articles and items in terms of factual news stories on the one hand and opinion pieces on the other. Opinion and news are thoroughly mixed up together, and what turns out to be most illuminating is often the taken-for-granted background, or even the tone of voice. A news item reporting the successful elopement of young Miss Double and her fiancé, Mr. Wirth (pursued across Central Park by angry Mr. Double père), is a cheerful enough anecdote of young love. But it is also bread-and-butter evidence, worthy of Lévi-Strauss, that marriageable young girls were considered by their parents to be objects of barter just seventy years ago. Indeed, the patriarchal approach of men in general to women in general is a clear indication that women were habitually thought of then as being never quite grown-up. The authority of the father descended to the husband so that a kind of paternal sway was continued inside marriage; and the mode of address to women by such figures of authority as the writers of editorials apes the affectionate, rather waggish tone of the stage father. What we are witnessing in the background of what seem to be simply news developments (Carrie Nation arrested. Growing interest in athletics for women.) is the assumption and tacit assertion that women engaged in any activities outside the home are not to be taken seriously. We are being shown not only the limits of woman's place but also the means by which the limits were then enforced. That was seldom done by argument. Instead, it was continually suggested that *women weren't worth arguing with.* The effect was to devalue woman's experience, weakening her sense of identity and her ability to hold to her convictions.

In short, the fight for women's rights has always involved more than a struggle for tangible goals like equal pay, equal opportunity, the vote itself. It has been a fight for the very right to fight, to assert one's demands, to declare that one's ambitions and needs are as important as those of men. I emphasize this point because it illuminates the purpose of those consciousness-raising groups which puzzle many people, both men and women. Why, it is asked, do women need to come together and tell each other their troubles? Aren't they just indulging in self-pity and airing emotions which should really be private? But sharing experience is a declaration of the right to judge events and emotions by one's own lights instead of by received opinion. How distorting to women the received opinions of the recent past were is well documented in this collection. A good example is a turn-of-the-century discussion among several men of women's literary interests. Do they read books at all? Don't they simply parrot the judgments put forward in reviews? No, is the reply, they do read; for they think that they may pick up ideas and information which will make them more attractive to men. And, of course, some of them are lonely. One is reminded of the caricatures of Jews *Der Stürmer* printed in the 1930's and, chillingly, that both attitudes were eminently respectable.

To be fair, such views were in contention even at the time and not only by women. An editorial writer speculates that women may well turn away from the cultivation of higher values like literature, music and art because a concern for culture will "only unfit them for living with the dullards they marry." A few years later novelist Ellen Glasgow declares that "real women," human and articulate, are beginning to appear in fiction and drive out the stereotypes of the last century. But as late as 1913 we find that any serious discussion of women's work is apt to deal with—household management! Which turns out to mean the proper instructions to, and supervision of, a staff of servants, whose numbers may be twenty-five to forty in a "large establishment" or the "typical" six.

Part of the interest of such a chronicle, then, is that it introduces us to a vanished world and does so in contemporary terms. It is very hard not to look at the past through our own hang-ups and psychic scars. To many, the early years of the century seem a haven of comfort and certainty. To others they are surrounded by an aura of nostalgic glamour. To a few they are remembered as years of deprivation and strife. But they are seldom seen without some bias of emotion. Well, here they are as they were. We can see what we have lost, and that much of it is well lost; not only the rigidly defined sex roles but also the hierarchy of class. So important was "position" that many progressive causes are reported on simply as the activities of "leading clubwomen" who interested themselves in do-gooding.

At the same time, the stark facts of life appear, as in the report of an energetic young woman who spent a year moving from city to city to discover what jobs were open to inexperienced girls and what wages were offered. In Chicago a department store will pay beginners $5 a week, and mother's helpers are offered as little as $10 a month. In New York addressing envelopes brings $1 per thousand and a worker can soon manage to make $1.25 a day. Skill pays. Experienced stenographers ask for $15 to $18 a week in the ads placed at about this period. But what can we say to "Wanted: A little girl handy with the needle to learn fancy work. $2.50 to begin."? Or to the study of tuberculosis rates among textile workers, two and a quarter to five times those of women in other occupations? Such details underline the fact that pre-World War I America, like Disraeli's England, was made up of two nations, the "Haves" and the "Have-nots."

Intellectually, however, change was already under way in the pre-World War I years. Questions that have continued to engage the attention of women in their drive toward equality show up astonishingly early. In the two years 1905 and 1906 we find the brilliant theoretician of women's rights Charlotte Gilman noting (forty years before de Beauvoir) how women, seen as objects, take their standards and self-images from men; how social change has isolated

them from the world of work until their contribution to the
mainstream of life has dwindled to a point where the world could
practically run without them, except for their services as domestic
and industrial drudges. Susan B. Anthony discusses what women's
unpaid work within marriage entitles them to after divorce. An
Iowa couple (both, be it noted, veterans of earlier marriages)
agrees on a detailed marriage contract, defining their roles, limiting the number of children they will have, providing for a division
of money and setting a term at which they will review their life
together and decide whether to renew their agreement or not.
Elsie Clews Parson seriously sets forth the advantages of trial
marriage. Here is the philosophic background of the suffrage
movement.

Again, with the advent of World War I, we see how the need
for women as workers paralleled their advance toward getting the
vote. Unenthusiastic at first, President Wilson ended by presenting woman suffrage to Congress as a vital war measure. In 1918
women were being urged to go into war industry in order to free
men to fight; or, more accurately, to be drafted. Jobs were being
opened to women in order to force men out, for one aspect of the
War between the Sexes not often noted is its manipulative use by
the State and the Establishment.

With the 1920's we are in the era of the "emancipated" woman.
She had the vote, of course. She also had short hair and lipstick—
sermons were preached on this topic. But though we tend to
think of her as a Fitzgerald flapper, or as Zelda herself, the meaning of emancipation was wider than simple citizenship in the Jazz
Generation. Thus, young women with jobs didn't have to marry
the first man who asked them. Most of them were still in "women's
jobs," but there were not only women doctors and lawyers listed
in the 1920 census, but also women architects, engineers, dentists,
opticians and taxi drivers. There were also protests over inequities
of jobs and wages. And there was a hard-fought battle, paralleling
the current struggle for the right to abortion, over birth control.
In a very real way the 1920's forecast the 1970's in the range of
issues which questioned old ways and pointed up social change.

The Depression years of the 1930's produced contradictory tugs on women's status. Frances Perkins sat as Secretary of Labor in Franklin Roosevelt's cabinet, but massive male unemployment brought forth demands that married women be dismissed from jobs in order to spread work, and the National Recovery Administration put an official stamp on lower minimum wages for women workers. Another war changed this, drew women back into industry in the 1940's and for the first time in American history into the armed forces on a par with men. With the 1950's another swing of opinion persuaded many women that home was where they belonged. Young girls married earlier than ever and the baby boom began the population explosion. But, as we all remember, "Togetherness" of the 1950's began to come apart in the 1960's. This was not simply the effect of another change of mind. In spite of low wages and the restriction of women to subordinate, nonexecutive jobs, their participation in the labor force was steadily rising. Much of the affluence of the prosperous 1960's was due to the rising number of working wives and mothers. When the new Women's Movement got under way, millions of women knew from their own experience that "equal rights for women" was a phrase but not a fact.

In his memoir *Speak Memory*, Vladimir Nabokov recalls how reading Hegel on historical development via thesis, antithesis and synthesis brought home to him "the essential spirality of all things in time." History is not a linear process, in which syllogisms are posited, proven and left behind. It is a matter of human emotions, beliefs and behavior challenged by new demands, rising reluctantly (and only sometimes successfully) to meet them, falling back and then, if need be, returning to cope again with unappeased pressures. The Women's Movement began as an unfocused and almost inarticulate search for a more honorable and worthy life. It was shaped by external restrictions, some of them economic, some of them social, some psychological. It fell from time to time into absurdity, but seldom into absurdity approaching the majestic, pompous nonsense with which the status quo condemned it; take, for example, the 1909 interview with *Ladies' Home Journal* editor Edward W. Bok on the question of woman suffrage. Most women, he assured the *Times* interviewer, were *opposed* to receiving the vote, would not use it, were busy at home. Just so, psychology professor Joseph Adelson of the University of Michigan wrote in March 1972 that the Women's Liberation Movement was receiving support from only 3 percent of women interviewed and provoked in most "an attitude somewhere between irritation and indifference." So, though things have changed some, they have not changed all that much. The image of women still includes the belief that women are not capable of knowing what's good for them!

If every nation gets the government it deserves, every generation writes the history which corresponds with its view of the world. No one conceived that a record of the doings of women might be interesting or important until the old sex roles came into question. If, one day, sex roles blur so that women are fully integrated into mainstream activities, a history of women will cease to be significant. Historiography, that is, is nearly as transitory as historical events. Even so, the record of how women were thought of, what behavior was deemed proper to them, what doors were shut, and how sanctions were applied against the violation of assigned roles—these data will always be important. They explain the attitudes of the past, and the present is built on such attitudes. Their value is permanent, just because they supply a chronicle of what was thought and not an interpretation of it. Historians return to source material long after they have ceased to read earlier historians.

For all of us, historians and laymen, men and women, the reproduction of past certainties which have lost their plausibility and persuasiveness is always useful. "I beseech you, in the bowels of Christ," wrote Oliver Cromwell to the Elders of the Church of Scotland, "think it possible that you may be mistaken." Every cocksure ideologue needs to hear such an injunction once in a while. The men and women who lived out recent changes of role and relationship discovered for themselves how they were mistaken and sometimes, thank heaven, how they were right; right in their convictions and right also in their questioning. The most valuable thing we learn from the past (and I think sometimes the only thing) is that we may be mistaken. No certainty should be immune from questioning; and when the questioning springs from and is supported by experience, certainties will shift. There can be no better illustration of *this* certainty—that change occurs —than the annals of woman's changing role.

III

Some further thoughts about women's history and how it can enlighten us as to our present situation form the background of this paper which was presented to a seminar of women educators.

Woman's Place in a Changing World

The topic you've asked me to consider, "Woman's Place in a Changing World," has two parts to it—women, and the changing world. It's easy to understand why women themselves, hearing such a title, would tend to think first about the first factor—their own lot, status, role, position. We have been told for so long that we have a special role, in a special place, we have been told for so many years to stay there and fulfill ourselves at home, within our families and our inner space, that we have come to think in these terms even when we want to get out of our old place and change our old role. Nonetheless, it is worthwhile taking time to think beyond the woman part of this topic to the other element that is involved, and so I want to direct your attention to the changing world.

For the changing world is the primary factor. A great deal has happened to women in the last few years, continues to happen and will happen in the future. Nor have their own efforts failed to have considerable effect on what is happening. Women have looked hard at the new challenges which today's world sets them, many consciousnesses have been raised, political activist groups have been formed of all varieties of politics and all degrees of activity, books about women have been written and read and the field of Women's Studies is becoming a legitimate one for academic exploration and discussion. Women are not simply pawns of social and economic trends, being shoved about on the board of events. More and more, they are taking a hand in their destinies. But—and I want to emphasize this point because it is one we tend to overlook—*the changing world* is what triggers the push for change in women's thinking and women's behavior, it is what directs our efforts toward particular goals and, in the end, it is what limits the scope of our accomplishments.

True, these limits are very wide, wider than we have believed. We haven't begun to achieve all that we can. But until and unless we look at the world of reality about us, and relate our means and our aims to it, we will be living in fantasy land. In a way our traditional confinement in woman's special place has made this all too easy. Our lack of familiarity with man's world of action can lead us to confuse reality with fantasy. So a second powerful reason for looking at the changing world is to learn where dreams leave off and actions must begin.

Understanding the changing world demands that we talk a bit about history. We can't estimate where we are now, and we certainly can't begin to see where we are going, unless we know where we have been. And history isn't one great lump. The world has been changing for a very long time, and woman's place within it has changed too. Many life-styles have existed in the past. Many different ones exist today, in different places and cultures around the globe. Women have been told, over and over again, that they have a traditional role which they've always played, and that this means it's ordained by God—or at least by nature, or evolution, or biology or some other large and uncontrollable force. That is much too simplistic a statement, and a look at history will make this clear. Beyond that, history today is again different from what it was fifty or a hundred years ago, and this time the change is bigger than ever. There is absolutely no validity to the idea that women have only one role to play, that it has always been the same, that it was always played within the family, or that the family has meant the same thing from time immemorial. If liberating women from their traditional role is a revolutionary idea, it is because *the revolution has already happened,* out there in the changing world. What we have to do is try to catch up.

We have to try, that is, to free ourselves from the entangling myths which attach us to the past—a past that may never have existed outside our heads—and which prevent us from looking realistically at the present. Women, and particularly working, professional women, are caught in a very severe bind today. We have problems that are not of our making. They pertain to our own positions, beyond this to the status and the future of the family, and indeed to the whole social structure and the connection between the family and the community. We cannot possibly cope with all these problems by ourselves. But over and over again, conscientious, hardworking women are persuaded that, somehow, these aberrations of the social system are up to them to deal with. They feel personally responsible—worse, they feel guilty—if they can't manage to hold down an interesting and demanding job, run a household, manage a marriage and raise children who will be happy, adjusted and successful—and do this all by themselves.

Well, I have come here today to reveal a secret, and this is it. Nobody in the world has ever managed to do that all by herself, not since the beginning of time. And if we sit around and imagine that *not* doing it is our fault, and finding a solution is up to us and can be done by our single efforts, we are behaving like a lot of patsies, and it's time we stopped. The world has changed. Women had very little to do with the causes of these changes, but they have been profoundly affected by them. The rational thing for women to do, therefore, is to change the roles and the goals that they set for themselves. But—alas!—it is just here that myth gets in the way, by insisting that the old role is not just the right role, but the *only* right role. Too many smart women somehow find themselves agreeing that this must be so—and, consequently, trying to adjust their lives to a new reality while still fulfilling old obligations. The result is that they get stretched thin and nobody profits, not women, not husbands, not children, not society. Or else they resign themselves to playing only the old mythic role, and boredom and frustration breed resentment. Nobody profits from that situation either.

For the old role is pretty well played out. It's got so far away from reality that, in spite of lifelong training, it's become nearly as exhausting for a woman to act like a female all the time as it would be for her to act like a male all the time. There's less and less need for her to act like a female, too, because there's less and less of a purely female role that needs playing—and there's less and less room inside it for a whole, adult, human being.

I said earlier that we would have to do some talking and thinking about history, and I want to begin with a consideration of what the traditional female role entails, the one that's got out of whack with the world. We think of it today as being made up of three parts—wife, mother and housewife. But once we confine it to those terms, we've already got ourselves tangled up with myth and accepted a misrepresentation of reality. For this definition leaves out the whole of woman's public, outside-the-house role: her activity as a worker, as a participant in a community and special groups inside the community, as citizen of a society, member of a church, kin of an extended family, neighbor and friend, with her own stature and status. It's ridiculous to lop off all these connections and activities, and allow women only the work-role of housewife in our definition of the female role. It means that we see women, typically, in terms of other people, tied to one man and the children born to that man. We don't see them as individuals, interacting with other individuals, earning their livings, selling their skills or the products of their skills, joining in group activities and often undertaking responsibilities on their own. And yet we allow this absurd judgment to take root in our heads because we assume that woman's traditional role confines her to the inner space of a home and connects her only with her husband and children.

That happens to be very bad history, sociology and anthropology. In fact, women have undertaken all kinds of enterprises and taken on all kinds of jobs over the centuries and around the

world, often in innovative ways. They were professionals for many
centuries before the twentieth dawned. They can, for example, be
very clever traders. In many societies, they go to market to sell
what the family produces, not just to buy what it needs. How
much bread is won or bacon brought home depends on the
woman trader's judgment of the marketplace and her bargaining
skill.

In some parts of the world, farming is exclusively, or very
largely, a woman's job. For example, let's look at the Gusii
tribe of Kenya. The Gusii are patrilocal, patrilineal and
polygamous—but don't imagine that Gusii women therefore
live in harems attended by eunuchs. Each wife has her own
house where her children live with her, and is assigned part
of her husband's lands. She and her children, once they're
older than seven or so, do most of the work on the land,
breaking ground with hoes after the spring ploughing, taking care
of routine cultivation, and weeding and harvesting the crops.
When the herds are home, the women milk the cows. Part of the
time, the men take the herds off to graze, and then the women
do all the work at home. They make fairly tough mothers, by the
way, expecting obedience from all their children but especially
from their sons. It's interesting to see that this pattern of living
continues to hold the community together now that the modern
world has moved closer and the men may go away for months to
work in factories, mines or mills. Without the community formed
by the working women, there would be no Gusii tribe. Recent
reports indicate that the Gusii, unlike some African communities,
are growing in number.

Sometimes, as in this case, the women are conservators of an
old way of life. Sometimes they are quite the other thing. When a
backward state in Central India was transformed by big government irrigation projects from a feudal society to a cash economy,
women promptly set up as money lenders. In West Africa women
have long been known as skillful traders. Now they not only
dominate retail trade, but one of them, Miss Regina Addae, heads
the largest advertising agency in Ghana, and another Mrs. Addae
has established the first private medical laboratory there.

Back in our own Middle Ages, women managed manor houses

and oversaw farm work when their husbands went to war or had business at court. Wives of Renaissance merchants minded the store when their men went off on trading voyages. Established religions may be chary of women priests and preachers, but from Mother Ann of the Shakers to Mary Baker Eddy and Aimee Semple McPherson, they have figured as offbeat, charismatic evangelists. And most important, once we fight free of the mists of middle-class myth—which it is—and look at the whole world around us, we realize that poor women, peasant women, working-class women, have always worked—and worked hard. Thirty years ago, in the era of Rosie the Riveter, they were working in aircraft plants, munition factories and shipyards. Some of them still are. Now how do you fit all these women into a role stamped *wife, mother, housewife?*

Of course you don't. What history and anthropology tell us is that our usual stereotype of woman's role is too narrow—and *was* too narrow, even before we turn to present circumstances. The stereotype doesn't fit today, we know that, but we bow down to it because we imagine that it describes centuries and millennia and aeons of human life, and that if the myth and the role don't fit us, there must be something wrong with us. Not so. What we've got in our heads is a Victorian leftover from the nineteenth century, which could be applied even then to only a few women. Ladies of cities on the Eastern seaboard may have been dependent, subordinate, passive supports to the dominant male—but frontier women didn't play that role, hardworking farmwives didn't play it, for every fainting Southern belle there were ten Southern women who knew what it meant to chop cotton, milk a cow and tend a barnyard, or look after six looms in a textile plant. The women who poured into our ports out of Europe didn't sit down and fan themselves once they got here. They went to work—for unequal wages, and often under deplorable conditions. There was nothing dependent about them, and very little that was passive.

I guess the best adjective to describe their situation would be "exploited." Every time we think of that myth of the happy-wife-and-motherdom of the past, with its gentle, protected females and its staunch guardian males, see whether the word "exploited" shouldn't be factored in there somewhere. If it doesn't seem to apply to the upper- or middle-class wife, ask yourself about her unmarried sister, or the servant girls who worked for her, or the seamstress who came in to sew, or any of the other women that the myth forgets about, cut off from the world of activity, unable to operate on their own and mocked as graceless oddities if they broke away from a pattern that denied them real, autonomous lives. One could weep for these women, measuring out their lives in coffee spoons.

Now it's true that once upon a time there was considerable value to the old bargain between men and women, the arrangement summed up in the two tag lines that I used for the title of my book, "It's a man's world. Woman's place is in the home." Begin with physical facts. Women bear children and, traditionally, they rear these children—though be it noted, they have almost always had a great deal more assistance and support in this task than they do in America today, both from the community and from their families. Again, it's an incontrovertible fact that, in the past, when contraceptive methods were unknown, women spent a much larger proportion of a much shorter life pregnant, or nursing infants whom they had borne with little or no medical help. And don't believe that that's a natural, healthy thing for human beings to do, just because animals do it. It isn't. The myth of the sturdy peasant woman who lies down in a furrow, has a baby and gets up and finishes the ploughing is just that—a myth. We can judge how false it is by the lengthening of women's lives and the rise in the rate of live births in underdeveloped countries once medical care is available. Before that, pregnancy and breast-feeding (for which there wasn't any substitute except another woman's breast) added up to a real physical handicap for women. In those days, a protective male was a useful creature to have around. Not only did his physical strength provide a defense for his family, but it was also needed for some kinds of work that were beyond the average woman's strength—at least while she was carrying a child.

Again, telling women that their first job was at home with a family was less isolating and confining in the past because a good deal more went on then within the family than takes place there now. Families were bigger, not just because more children were born, but because older people stayed in touch, often living nearby if they didn't actually live in a three-generation home. Even more important than this diversity and variety of people, families used to function in ways that have been lost. Not only did children grow up there and receive physical care and learn the norms of social behavior, as they still do—at least, we hope so— but they learned actual skills, ways to make a living. Right up until modern times, most crafts and professions were taught by apprenticeship, within family enterprises, for family enterprises were the general rule. Many of these businesses were carried on right in the same place where the family of the master craftsman lived. The apprentices often lived there too, and part of the wife's job was to see that they were fed and looked after—and this included their morals.

Girls as well as boys were trained. They learned the skills they needed, and they were real, valuable skills, by the same kind of apprenticeship. Domestic service meant something quite different in the fifteenth and sixteenth century from what it does today, for the Big House functioned as a kind of academy for young women, teaching them how to provide food and clothing and manage a household. When this was going on, women were indeed subordinate to men, but they were also useful and active members of society, who were directly connected with the community around them. Not only were they teachers of the young, but they made a vital economic contribution to the well-being of the family. Peasant women often worked in the fields, hard work, but not lonely, for it was done in concert with men and other women. They had their own skills and were proud of them. They were spinners of yarn, weavers of cloth for clothes and hangings and bed linens, makers of butter and cheese; they knew the barnyard, looked after the animals, preserved the fruit harvest and, in the big houses, processed not only the food but also the drink—beer and ale and perry and cider and wines. Special goods were manufactured for market, for some of the big houses were part commercial establishments. Home remedies were often much more effective than those of the old barber-surgeons. Women, that is, not only had a place at home. They were sometimes skilled specialists working at valuable operations, and in touch with the world around them. Heaven knows, this was not a Utopian life. It included lots of drudgery, it could be very narrow and confining, it offered few new choices or chances to break away from traditional roles. You and I would not really want to spend our lives that way. *But,* allowing for this, we can still recognize that such a life did provide a kind of reciprocity, a giving and getting between men and women and a mutuality of effort, which sustained the old female role. Women were not cut off from life, and the work they did was respected.

One more point, a thing that is often overlooked. Women were subordinate and subservient to their husbands, but they lived in a strictly regulated, hierarchical society. They didn't represent the *only* subordinate class. Many men were subservient too. The peasant was subordinate to his lord, the lord to his king, and theoretically at least, the king to the Church—just as much as the woman to her husband or the maid to her mistress. Subordination, class and rank were an accepted way of life. Again, you and I would not have enjoyed that. But when it was a way of life, being subordinate wasn't an oddity, women were not the only creatures who were assigned a special place in the world. Every class, every rank had a place. It's summed up in the familiar old hymn:

> All things bright and beautiful,
> All creatures great and small,
> All things wise and wonderful,
> The Lord God made them all.
>
> The rich man in his castle,
> The poor man at his gate,
> God made them high or lowly,
> And ordered their estate.

And, in passing, he ordered the estate of women too. He did not give them control over their bodies by allowing them to decide whether or when to have children, but then, most of the rest of the world had little control over its own fate either. Childbirth was seen as part of the larger bargain, or the social contract, which religion explained in terms of the social mythology of the time.

Eve's sin condemned women to bring forth their children in pain, but Adam had sinned too and been condemned to labor in the sweat of his brow. If anatomy really was destiny for women, accidents of birth enforced destiny on men. The poor stayed poor, the serf remained a serf, the lord was born a lord. The baker's son thanked God for an honest trade to learn and inherit. In some ways, women might actually enjoy more power than some men did, for they were expected to exercise power over the children they bore until the children grew up. In addition, the use of the skills they knew must have given them a sense of satisfaction and of worth. If women lived a hard life, so did most men. But on the average, in terms of what was feasible, the division of humanity by sex roles, as well as by class and occupation roles, paid off sufficiently well for the whole structure to endure—as long as the old physical facts of life endured. As long, that is, as women were incapacitated for a good deal of the time by unsought pregnancy and the nurture of small children; as long as sheer physical strength had a meaningful premium attached to it; as long as families functioned as important subsystems of society, and not just as isolated cells in a residential ghetto.

Now we live in a world where these facts don't apply anymore, where they have ceased to be facts. Women *can* control their physical lives. They can choose when to have their children and how many to have, including none. Muscular strength is not a necessity, nor even an advantage, in the great majority of jobs. Put those two changes together, and they add up to a contradiction of the oft-quoted statement of Freud that anatomy is destiny. The world has changed, and because it has, the range of opportunities open to women has grown enormously.

Something else has changed too, because of this changing world, and that is the family itself. Let's take that old adage, "Woman's place is in the home," and ask, for once, not whether it's true or untrue, or even whether it's desirable or detrimental. Let's ask what we mean by it—what we mean, that is, by the simple word "home." As I've tried to indicate, "home" and even "family" are terms that don't mean now at all what they meant two hundred years ago. No longer are homes essential units of economic production and craft-learning as they used to be when the family

farm and cottage industry were significant ways of life and means
of earning. And that's because, beginning about two hundred
years ago, the Industrial Revolution got under way, and production moved out of the home and into the factory.

We're so used to this situation now that it doesn't occur to us
that it's anything remarkable. In fact, it has produced a way of
life that is absolutely unique. Let me take it at the simplest, nitty-
gritty level. If you need to earn money, you can't do it at home.
Nor can a family earn as a group, working a farm or at some
skilled trade, as they used to. What this means, for men, is that
their lives are divided into two parts—work life, and life at home;
and this has had very important repercussions on the family and
the function it serves. One very significant effect is that Father
drops out. He used to play a vital role in child-raising. Psychologists would point out that he operated as a masculine role-model
for his sons, and so he did. But he was also another adult around
the house, someone who had experience in the way the world
works, someone who could clue children into the life of action
and purpose and earning a living. Today, with Father gone for
many of the children's waking hours, the sort of family we think
of as being normal is actually a *less* than nuclear family. For a
lot of the time it consists of one tired young woman and a couple
of children.

Now suppose you're a woman who has to earn money. Again,
you can't do it at home, unless you're a rare bird like me who can
shut yourself up in a room and write for a living. But there aren't
many of us, and it's unusual, if we have children, that we can
operate without some help from another woman who will have
left *her* house in order to give us the quiet we need for our work.
Most women have to go out and get a job to earn money, and to
do that, they have to leave their children. That's something else
that we take for granted, but we shouldn't. Never before in history has a woman had to desert the very people—her children—
whom she's trying to help support. "Working wives are breaking
up the family!" cry voices of doom. "Send them home where they
belong!" This is just nonsense. Women have always worked.
Families, except for the rich, have never managed to get along
with just one member working. The only thing that has changed

is the locus of work, and it isn't working women who did that, it's the factory system: a change in this changing world that began two hundred years ago and that we haven't caught up with yet. Its effect has been to withdraw from the family the economic value which used to attach to it. Since that happened, the family has been subjected to a centrifugal tug from outside pulling its members away from each other.

Let me dwell on this difference for a moment. The function of the family, sociologists tell us, is to raise children; and if the family does it successfully, these children will become mature adults who are capable of dealing with the world of events adequately. In normal times—that is, when a society is not in a state of crisis or breakdown—young adults will have learned at home and through a community educational process how to fit into the world around them, how to make a living there, how to get on with other people—how to function, if not to succeed. They will have internalized the ideals of the society that they were born into—or most of them will.

Now, if the family is going to complete this process of education satisfactorily, the adult members will obviously have to have an adequate, ongoing connection with the outside world. If they don't, they won't know what to teach the children. Nor will they have processes of teaching available. Unless the family is an active part of the rest of the world, it can't function as a step into the world for the children born there. In my opinion (and not just mine) the family today suffers from *lack* of connection with the world of events and action. Kenneth Keniston, in his remarkably interesting book on the alienated young, *The Uncommitted: Alienated Youth in American Society* describes the locus of family living today as "a home haven." It is a retreat from a world of action which has come to be seen as "a rat race." Little pleasure and a good deal of boredom, mortification and frustration are to be expected from the world outside. One finishes work and flees from it, into the world of leisure, looking for emotional satisfaction. And the home is expected to provide much of this relief.

For adults, this splitting of life into unpleasant work-time and leisure in which one seeks to gratify oneself, often as a reward for putting up with boredom and frustration, is not really very

healthy—no fragmentation or splitting of life is. But even more
destructive—potentially—is the effect of this split on the children.
Homes, I repeat, used to be places where valuable economic work
went on. Children saw it and participated in it. Now all of this
has moved out to the factory, and children have no contact with
it. After the war, in the 1940's and 1950's—the era of family
togetherness, remember—a lot of people moved out to the suburbs
in a hazy dream of getting back to country life. But think how
different the small town or the farm of a century ago was from the
suburb of today. Children growing up in a nineteenth-century
rural community saw blacksmiths' shops, mills and farm work.
They milked cows, collected eggs, split logs, helped Pa and Ma
with all manner of activities—sugaring off, repairing farm equipment or, in the house, making clothes or quilts, cooking, preserving and so on. Nobody had to make an effort to show them
this; it took place under their eyes, and often they were part of
it.

Children today, at home or at school, are pretty much isolated
from this work of the world. Parents and grandparents mutter
that young people don't understand the value of work any more.
I don't find that in the least surprising. Perhaps they've been
lectured on it, but no one has been able to make it a natural,
normal part of life, showing, explaining and training them in
skills day after day as a commonplace, this-is-how-you-do-it sort
of thing. Neither home nor school has much connection with the
activities of adult life, and the adults the children spend most
of their time with aren't in a position to supply much information.

I have been wondering lately, in fact, whether the famous
generation gap and the existence of a counterculture in America
have not been due in part, and perhaps in large part, to the abyss
that exists between home and work, between the place where the
children and their mothers are kept and the world where political
and economic events and processes take place, far, far away, out
of sight and sound—except for what television transmits. Bread-
winners come home out of the world of work to a private world,
where they hope to find emotional comfort and allow themselves
expression of feelings. Of course, that's no doubt necessary. Any-

one who spends eight hours a day in what he thinks of as being the rat race needs relaxation and comfort. But—if all that the children hear about the world outside from the adults they know is that it is a rat race, they will get an odd idea about it.

There's a twist in here I'd like to call to your attention. It's perfectly natural for weary husbands to tell nonworking wives that it's great to be at home, and to concentrate on home and leisure when they are there. In fact, it's rather flattering. It's also perfectly natural for men to dump emotions, and gripe about their work to relieve their feelings. Any normal wife will sympathize. But if the man brings home his troubles and his grievances and nothing else, that's all the children will know. Their mother can't tell them anything different because she doesn't know either. Her life is at home, where her relationships are confined to intimate, personal and emotional connections. In addition, what she does is not continuous, it's dependent on other people's needs, it's measured by values which differ from the objective ones of the marketplace world outside. What is valued in her world is warmth, affection, the pleasure of being, not the pleasure of doing and accomplishment. Now these are real and needed values—but what happens if they are cut off from the world of action?

It seems to me that when we look at the youth movement and the counterculture we find that they are rich in just these emotional, expressive, traditionally female values. Absent are the attitudes and behavior norms patterned on the masculine role, such as purposive action over the long term, clear and reasoned decision-making, a sense of economic limits and possibilities, an awareness of political realities and how to deal with them. Certainly the world of events, man's world, if you will, can get too cold, too practical, too computerized. There's no doubt it needs to be irrigated by an inflow of warmth and emotion. Many of the moral goals of the youth movement and the counterculture are praiseworthy and should be taken seriously. But over and over again, the ways proposed to get to these goals succumb to fantasy, to absurd tactics and unrealistic gestures—methods which may make one feel better, but don't produce results in actuality. Is it not possible that these inappropriate techniques grow out of and reflect the intimate relations within the family, where they do fit much better? Children learn much more than they are ever taught, but they need to be exposed to experience to learn at all. If they are isolated from the male world of activity, work and process, they can't learn from it. If they are encapsulated in woman's place at home, they'll learn only what happens there.

At home these days they tend to learn a great deal about the expression of emotions and little about long-term work processes. That's no one's fault. The woman, isolated there with her children and expected to raise them on her own with only the emotional interaction between them as her instrument, is simply doing what she assumes she's supposed to do; or, what our world has persuaded her is the right thing for her to do. The barrier between home and world of work exists for her too. But the result is that this barrier is never penetrated, that children imagine the world of work as mysterious, alien, frightening, and that they are given no road maps at all to help them move into it.

Indeed it seems to me perfectly possible that the current explosion of drug use among young people is related to this same isolation from the ordinary world of events. In that world real rewards come as the products of a process of intention, planning, action, concentration, continuous attention, adjustment to change when it appears, decision-making—and knowing when to stop. But if you have never been part of this process of testing and then influencing reality, you will neither understand how it works nor be able to imagine yourself achieving real rewards. If you can't do that, you are apt to go looking for *unreal* rewards, for pleasure inside your own head, chemical experience. I suspect we really have no idea how many young people, including children, have tried one or another kind of drug. I wouldn't be at all surprised if the very risk associated with drug-taking is part of its attraction. Testing one's strength is part of growing up, and trying drugs is one kind of test, like playing chicken.

I was talking about this to a group of college alumnae in a Westchester County suburb of New York recently. Of course the whole subject of drugs is terribly upsetting for parents, not only because of the effects of drugs but because the mystery surrounding the reasons for drug use make that use seem uncontrollable.

Women are particularly vulnerable. Not only do they feel that they are failures if their children take drugs, but they feel that they will be blamed for it—isn't it their job to raise good, sucessful straight-arrow kids? Two women came up to me at the end of my talk and told me their solution—it's a simple one and, to me, perfectly appalling. "Always be home by four o'clock," they said. "They won't be able to take drugs if you're there when they get home from school." Act like prison guards, in short; don't trust your children or give them any privacy, tie them down more tightly into the home situation at a time when they need to form their own ties with the world outside—and your own fear of drugs will somehow, magically, keep the children safe and pure.

There isn't any safety, I tried to tell them, and the closest you can get to it is by giving your children a strong enough sense of confidence and value in themselves to cope with dangers on their own. It's probably impossible for a parent to keep a susceptible child from trying drugs and getting hooked. Your job is to try and keep your children from growing up susceptible—and that means offering them alternatives to fake drug pleasure, real alternatives, real pleasures, real rewards, and help and information on how to get them. Do that, and then trust them to be able to make their own choices and lead their own lives. But that takes some knowledge and connection with the real world on the mother's part, and it also takes self-esteem and confidence in one's approach to dealing with children, and the very confinement of women to the house and to the roles of wife and mother denies them self-confidence in dealing with the world and its problems.

In fact I think I could make a case, based partly on my own experience and on that of friends who are professionals, that working mothers stay in touch with their children more closely and for a longer time than do mothers who aren't familiar with the world outside. We aren't frightened of that world because we know something about it. We don't see the growing up of our children as a loss to us. We have more to talk about with them, and our judgment is regarded as having some authority. If we don't get uptight about woman's traditional role (which isn't all that traditional, as I've been saying) we are better able to offer help and advice to young people on all kinds of problems. Now, let's not

assume that they are always going to take it! That would be living
in a fool's paradise. But young people can tell the difference between affectionate but uninformed support and advice based on
the way things are. It is, I firmly believe, frightened parents who
don't try to see or understand the changes of the modern world
who fail their children worst.

So far I have been talking rather descriptively, if pessimistically,
about what woman's place in the old world used to be, and how
the outworn myths of the past have tangled us in trying to deal
with the present. What, then, can we do instead? In what way
should we try to adjust ourselves to the world as it is and then,
optimistically, try to shape the world to fit our hopes? Let me say
at once that I don't think women can do this alone; nor can they
bring their full force to bear if they think of themselves only as
women. And indeed, many, many women are ceasing to see themselves in the narrow terms of a second, or at least another sex.
More and more we are becoming whole human beings, thinking
in terms of full social responsibility, the equality of obligation
which will one day match the equality of rights we want.

This means that we must think about more than what happens
inside the family as being our business. Progress is more than
persuading husbands to share housework and child-care, for though
this is a perfectly sound way to change inadequate ways of living
and enlarge the narrow nuclear family, it isn't enough. It still
leaves families isolated from the large community, from society,
the economy and the political world of action. As things stand,
we're living in a kind of fragmented chaos. What we need is to
bring together anew, in a new pattern of living and working,
individual, family and community. We must reconnect the emotional, personal life with the larger experience, and do it not just
in communal retreats and emotional encounter groups, but as a
part of everyday experience, so that work is enriched by personal
involvement and the individual finds a significance in the activities by which he earns his living. For without such connections, all
these fragmented bits of life lose their meaning. Work, cut off
from personal relationships and pride in individual skill, turns
into repetitious drudgery that brings no reward in itself. The
working world seems arid and drained of emotion, and the per-

sonal world becomes frighteningly private and isolated. In action, people tend to judge themselves and their worth only in money terms.

I certainly don't want to sneer at money, because in our society it brings independence and control over the present, and it offers our elderly folk a chance to retain their dignity. But we need very much to supplement the cash economy by other ways of engaging people in work that needs to be done. Ecologists tell us, for instance, that the natural world is in terrible danger of collapsing unless our economic producers change their ways; and economists tell us that if they try to do so, we'll run into spending that will produce massive bankruptcies and awful unemployment. Well, that's a frightful dilemma. And, of course, a dilemma can never be solved by thinking in terms of the patterns and assumptions that got us into this bind in the first place. If we can't afford to pay money in order to save our natural world from disaster, we are going to have to find other motivations that will move men and women to work together to help themselves. Of course they can be found, but to do so demands new patterns of action, demands creative imagination and different ways of structuring approaches to the problem—an expansion of context, more input, more outreach.

And, at the same time, when we turn from the public to the private sphere we see, as I've outlined, that families, having lost their economic reason for being, are in danger of losing their social reason for being. They are growing too small and too isolated from the overall social system to do the job they ought to in raising the next generation. Parents and children alike sometimes seem ready to concede the necessity of a generation gap and give up on any chance of bridging it. Where once they fought over what was important, they now appear to agree that nothing very much is important at all. Well, that's a terrible way to live a life out, in the belief that nothing you do matters, can influence the future or even the present. Recently I clipped a story from *The Wall Street Journal* on the growing number of people in America who suffer from depression severe enough to demand psychiatric treatment. The writer suggested that this frightening increase might be due to urbanization. At face value that's nonsense—after all, people have lived in cities for thousands of years. But it isn't nonsense in terms of what urbanization has come to mean—which is isolation, fragmentation, disconnection of one part of a life from another, the loss of deep personal relationships which tie an individual into a functioning group held together by a common purpose. Somehow we have to do better than this.

And, again, I don't mean do better as women, just because we are women. Some of us flatter ourselves by imagining that, one way or another, we're better than men—that we are warm, loving, giving, nurturing creatures who are intended by God to bring human qualities into the mechanical, industrial, commercial side of life. That too is nonsense. Everyone, men and women both, needs to work to put our fragmented lives together. The only advantage women may have in this job is that because they start from outside the old stereotypes of male thinking, they can see better how ineffective the old myths are. We're a little less brainwashed, that is, about the Emperor's new clothes. But we still bear the scars of brainwashing—the idea that our first job is at home, and that home should mean an emotional haven, an escape from the rest of the world. It's this idea that needs rethinking.

Because the rat race is going to remain a rat race and the home is going to remain an isolated emotional ghetto, unless we begin to put things together and to feel that we are part of a like-minded group, that we can reach out for power without being burned by it. But such power will not reach its full potential if it limits itself to helping women. It can do more. It can begin putting all of society together again into an interconnected web of feeling and action where individuals can meet and mingle on many levels, and work together for many ends.

What we need to do is to begin to create a community in which we can all join. The glue for such a community is in the nitty-gritty details of everyday living, of getting on at social levels, working together in politics and for sensible economic goals. But in our thinking we need to do more, to reach out for goals which lie beyond the limits of these programs and processes, or else the means will overwhelm us and blind us to common aims.

What I'm saying is, think big! That doesn't mean think misty, or vague, or let fantasy take the place of practical reality. It means, put your practical thinking in its proper place. Understand that tactics are vital, but they can both win small goals and fail at large ones—unless they fit into strategic purposes. We can't change woman's role if all we think about is woman's role. We can't reshape the family if all we think about is the family. We can't get ourselves better jobs and equal pay and a fair share of elective offices if these ends aren't seen as being connected with other factors in society, other aspirations, hopes and fears. The last few years, as women have begun to face the changing world, have brought us the courage to dare to think about our place in working with change, and the power to deal with it. There's no doubt we'll do that. We will achieve most, I think, if we combine the efforts to reach immediate goals with a steady overview of how these goals are connected and how our efforts supplement each other.

IV

Sex discrimination in American business, the professions and the academic world has been taken for granted for so long that the first government orders to end it met with sheer consternation. "You mean that we've got to send women out to sell THE BOTTLERS!" cried the vice-president of an enormous soft-drink company at one management conference I attended. From his tone it was clear that an order to add a team of kangaroos to his sales staff would have been just about as welcome. Whether he's bitten the bullet and hired a woman yet I do not know, but some progress has been made under the stimulus of orders from the Equal Employment Opportunity Commission and class action suits brought by underpaid and underpromoted women. We've come a short way, Baby, and we have miles to go before we sleep; but women are moving up the escalator to management positions in business more regularly and in larger numbers than they ever have before.

If this seems like an elitist issue or a peripheral matter, considered in the whole range of women's activities, it isn't. Discrimination is discrimination at every level, and it is based on exactly the same misjudgments and myths: that women's nature is basically different from that of men and unfits them to participate in the world of action, especially at the level where decisions have to be made. Keep women out of management and you will keep wages down for women on the assembly line because you will be authenticating and perpetuating the theory of women's incapacity.

This effort to reconcile business management to the future was written for a newsletter circulated to executives across the country.

Women in Business

The chief barrier to the employment of women at decision-making levels of management lies today where it always has—inside people's heads. Some of these heads are male, some are female. Since most of those reading this discussion are male, let's start there.

Male assumptions about women are clouded by stereotypes of thought pertaining to "women as a group." Men see other men as individuals, each with distinguishable character traits. They see women as a set of people who share certain character traits which can be summed up under the label "feminine"; and before they can think about a woman as an individual, they have to fight their way through the stereotypes. Feminine human beings are expected to be passive, emotional, indecisive, devious and intuitive rather than rational. Some good traits are allowed to them, of course: warmth, sensitivity and concern for others. But these are felt to be good only in special situations—at home, within the family milieu of intimacy, and not in the business world.

There's some reason for such ideas. In the recent past, the private world of women has been more separated from the mainstream of activity than at many other times of history. Before the spread of the factory system in the nineteenth century, a lot of work was done at home, and women were part of it: farmers' wives, assistants to craftsmen-husbands, helpers in family shops, and so on. But in the last hundred years, big business has been eating up little business, and isolating homes, where people live, from enterprises, where they work. Women and children have been left at home alone together.

What we think of as "feminine traits" are an adaptation to such isolation and to a subordinate position. If you can't do things for yourself, naturally you sharpen your intuitive perceptions; and you're likely to learn to manipulate people by devious ways. Meanwhile, you cover "unfeminine traits," like ambition and personal drive, by appearances. You smile, look pretty and try to please people in order to get your way. If you're not called on to make decisions, you learn to be passive and wait. And so on.

Put men in subordinate positions with a ceiling on their ambitions, and the same thing happens to them. I imagine you can call some examples to mind from your own experience. But because of the way our society is set up, it's what *usually* happens to women; and so their adaptations to the situation have become "normal" and expected.

There's another wrinkle to this. When men do meet women as social equals, they do so in the world of leisure—at home, at parties, on holiday. Things are changing, but I would guess that not many of my readers have worked with women on an equal footing; and if they have, not very often. In the business world, the women men see are usually their subordinates. And so that's what they come to expect.

I've made this point at such length because it is central to the way men think about women as possible business executives. Because they have had so little experience of women as capable equals in the world of action, they find it difficult to imagine them there, and they tend to think of them as belonging in a different, more personal setting. The normal place for women, it's still felt, is in the home.

Well, that may be what men still feel, but it isn't what's happening. In the year 1970, half of the women of working age were counted statistically as being in the labor force. That comes to 31.5 million, at least 3 million of them heads of households. For the rest, America has become a two-income family—and the second income is almost always supplied by the wife today, not by an older child as would have been the case a generation ago. In 16 million families, the wife's income is what keeps them above the poverty line. Altogether, working women produce over 30 percent of family income.

Let's hope that continues for if it doesn't, if women go home as they did after World War II, we will run into a business slump that will curl your hair. The affluence of the 1960's was based on two dynamic phenomena: overtime pay for blue-collar men and the addition of women to the work force. The slump of the early 1970's cut overtime. Imagine what would have happened if it had driven women out of the economy!

So women in the work force are a fact of life. Once we accept that, we can move on to the next question: how can they be used best? Is it wise to keep them in subordinate positions, at women's jobs? Is it even possible to do this, with the Government pushing for an end to discrimination, for equal pay and equal opportunities for women? Moving them up will certainly make waves. Are there any positive advantages to doing that—aside from getting Washington off your neck by filing an affirmative action plan?

To be cheerful about it, I think there are distinct advantages. Number one is so obvious it hardly has to be stated. Employment for women increases the talent pool that can be drawn on. Companies that can face up to that quickly, by the way, are apt to be those which know how to use new talents and new ideas. So they'll not only get the cream of the crop by moving fast, but they'll also be better prepared to use these talents well.

The second advantage is more general. The employment of women, we've seen, has been a powerful expansive force. Promoting them and paying them more will continue this growth of income and, with it, growth of demand. Every now and then one still runs into the idea that working women take jobs away from men. It's not only untrue, it's foolish. Working women make jobs—for everyone. They spend money on everything from better food to medical care to college educations for their children to second cars and color television sets and vacation homes. America has grown by drawing people into the economy, not by shutting them out; women included.

How to do it? Besides the psychological problems, there are real social difficulties too, for woman's traditional role still assigns her certain jobs as priorities. Child-raising and homemaking are such priorities. How, I've been asked, does business deal with the problems of pregnancy, sick children, husband being shifted to the West Coast, the woman who only works from nine to five because she doesn't have a "wife" at home to enable her to put in executive hours? These are pertinent questions and we all know their existence hampers the rise of women in management.

The answer is that a change must be made in assigning responsibility for dealing with these problems. Most of them are now assigned to the woman and her husband, who are solely responsible for coming up with answers. To change this, business must enter the picture on its own; backed, I'm hopeful, by the larger society. And this is not really an outrageous suggestion. In the past, the community has played a much larger part in family care and child-training than it does today. The present isolation of the single, small family from community support is highly unusual. Moreover, I believe business would find that it gained by such interaction.

The most obvious example would be the establishment of model child-care centers by every enterprise above a certain size (smaller businesses could form groups or attach themselves to larger ones). Working mothers (or working fathers, for that matter) would have the right to bring children to these centers to be looked after during the workday of the parent. In fact, such centers should be much more than merely custodial. They could enlarge and enrich the experience of children, while still keeping them in proximity to the parents, who could visit their children during the day and spend the lunch hour with them. It's worth noting that a majority of parents who can afford to pay for nursery schools choose to do so. Trouble is, they're too few and too expensive.

In conversation with Government officials I've suggested that the cost of setting up such centers might be offset by partial Government support through tax credits, similar to those granted for capital investment, and have found the idea well received. Running these centers is, of course, a proper business expense. Some are now in existence, and material on them can be obtained through the Woman's Bureau at the Department of Labor. Expenses could be held down if a core of trained professionals were supplemented by volunteers, both male and female, ranging in age from adolescent to retiree. Churches, schools, unions, libraries are some of the groups that could be called on for joint sponsorship or special programs. With a modicum of imagination, one can envision a re-creation of the kind of small neighborhood community plus extended family in which most children used to grow up. Health services should be available, and after-hour and summer programs for school children could well be included.

Experiments in changing the length of the working day, which some companies have undertaken, emphasize the need for child care at the place of employment. While a three- or four-day work week offers a bonus of leisure time for family members to enjoy together, it burdens working mothers with enormous difficulties during the long-shift work week. Up till now, most companies setting up such short-week, long-hour programs have relied on individual families to cope with the demands made by the new schedule. This is uneconomic, for it sacrifices the efficiency of the woman worker.

Child-care centers would provide at least partial answers to other points raised. If they exist, women who choose to do so will be able to return to work after childbirth much earlier, so that maternity-leave costs would drop. Clearly, it's the committed and ambitious woman worker who will most often choose to return. Again, some of the household chores which extend the working day of the average woman would be avoided if at least one hot meal were provided for the entire family. The real gain to business, however, would be that capable women who saw their future careers with a company could stay on the escalator without dropping out for several years of child care.

It is this discontinuity of employment which has worked against the rise of many women to management rank. Stereotyped thinking says, "It's no use training young women, even bright ones, because they will only get married, have kids and leave." This becomes a self-fulfilling prophecy if young women have no choice but to leave employment in order to look after their children.

Equally, there will be less inducement to stay if they are denied a place in training programs that lead to better jobs and more interesting positions.

Even as it is, however, fewer and fewer women drop out of the labor force during child-bearing and child-rearing years. One-third of women with children under six are at work. The two peaks of female employment (at approximately age twenty-three and age forty-five) are now well above 50 percent of all women of that age level; even more interesting, the bottom of the dip between these two peaks doesn't go under 45 percent! But women with small children who must keep on working (and most women work because they need the money) are indeed less efficient and harder-pressed than those who are not doing two jobs at once. If business wants to use its working women well, it should consider helping them through these two-job years by offering support for social needs.

I hope it's clear that such support would be advantageous economically. The push by Washington for equal employment for women has produced a certain amount of stunned consternation in business. "Where are we going to get the women to promote to executive jobs?" is the immediate reaction. In my opinion, many of the promotable women are right there, working inside these companies and in possession of a good knowledge of their practices and problems. They simply have not been encouraged to think of themselves as potential executives.

And here we come to the barrier to the employment of women at management levels which exists inside *female* heads. Like men, they have bought the idea that woman's traditional role is subordinate and private, that competitive, aggressive women are unattractive, and that child care and homemaking are their primary responsibilities. If they have to work (and most of them, I repeat, work to earn), they tend to accept "women's jobs." Ambition and competitiveness make waves. Traditionally, it's part of woman's role to be pleasing; indeed, any subordinate had better learn to please the boss because she (or he) hasn't the power to act on her (his) own. Push too hard, women learn early, and you're in trouble. The pattern of male executive and female assistant shows up in high-school organizations.

For women, trying to get "a man's job" is not simply a personal effort, it means fighting the system. Not even an awful lot of men want to fight the system; and remember, please, that women have been trained from the word go to believe that fighting is un-feminine, unpleasing and actually "abnormal." Some of the anger expressed by the Women's Movement arises from recognition that this con game has worked so well, persuading women not just that they can't compete with men, but that they don't even want to. Well, some of them do want to—not out of hostility to the male sex, but because any talented, energetic human being natu-rally likes to use his or her talents and energies. But not many of these women are going to try until they are shown that the effort won't set them back from the place they've managed to reach already. The system, in short, has to make some signal to women to persuade them that moving up won't mean a fight at every step of the way.

How does the system do that? First, it has to want to. I think that quite a lot of business is ready to agree that talented women can be useful, but of course male executives continue to worry about what other men working for them will think when women show up in executive jobs. Again, this is a self-fulfilling prophecy. If the boss is nervous about having a woman vice-president, all the other vice-presidents are apt to be a bit shaky. Well, I'm afraid there's no way to reassure them in advance. There are some things, like making love and eating spicy meatballs, that you have to experience to appreciate. My own suggestion is summed up in those famous words, "Try it! You'll like it!" You may even end by finding that you ate the whole thing. At any rate, all the men I know who have worked for women, or on a level with them, are much calmer about the whole deal than those who haven't.

Practically speaking, I think the first task for management is to create a positive atmosphere for women moving up. That can't be done by preaching or threatening, but mightn't incentives work? Why not reward heads of departments who recommend women working under them for promotion, department heads who train them, and originators of schemes for finding capable, promotable women? I've seen talented women in small business move up fast and far because the size of the business promoted encounters between them and the boss. Twenty-five years ago my husband hired a young woman to run the switchboard in his office. She became his executive assistant and went on to head a Wall Street firm. The trick is to persuade men at lower management levels that they can profit personally from helping women whose abilities they get to know. Many companies already use incentive schemes and bonuses to strengthen motivation. Why not apply them to this problem? Make them long-term, too. The first man who starts a woman up the ladder ought to get a repeated bonus as she thrives and climbs.

There are other difficulties, of course, and they can't all be solved immediately. Top management wants to feel free to move its executives around, so what about that woman with a husband bound for the West Coast—and what about a woman who might be asked to move herself? Contingencies like this have got to be up to the individual. After all, if a woman is capable of making business decisions, she ought to be able to make them about her own life. And some contingencies hamper every executive move or promotion. The trick is really to think about women as human beings first, instead of labeling them female and getting hung up on the clichés that surround the word. Industries that have been using women for a while, like advertising and communications, seem to get on without too much commotion. At the moment, however, with women still figuring mostly as cheap labor, our society is not profiting fully from their employment, while it is already enduring the social burdens of hit-or-miss child care and workers who move in and out of the labor force. Equal opportunities for women will mean, at the very least, greater prosperity, and a broadening of the tax base that can help pay for these social needs and costs.

V

How a society raises its children is a very good measure of its goals and of its coherent ability to implement them. In our minds, children represent not just a future, but our future. What we can't have for ourselves, we want for them. First-generation Americans have always been willing to have less themselves if they could see evidence of a chance for their children to move up the ladder to a fuller life, whatever that might mean: status, money, education, opportunity or fulfillment. Of course such an investment of emotion in one's children as symbolic of one's own desires has its perils. Much of the hostility between minority groups that has exploded and rankled in recent years comes out of projected aspirations: I want the best for my children! I want what I didn't have! I won't let you spoil their chances! In such an emotional setting, racism seems to its perpetrators to be principled, even altruistic, concern. The fight over bussing has been so furious just because it can call for support on the common human desire to see one's own children get ahead.

A large question. I don't cite it here to offer a solution. In fact I don't think there will be any one solution but, rather, a multiplicity of solutions as education becomes more varied and flexible; which I think it is likely to do in an age of transition as profound as ours. No one sort of education is going to be adequate. I raise the problem as an example of how issues become battlegrounds because of the symbolic value attached to them, and then can't be settled in terms of rational discussion about their apparent meaning. The engine of myth has pumped them full of emotions.

Providing child care outside the home also raises anxiety, often compounded by guilt; and compounded, too, by the fact that the traditional female role has dwindled in its other areas, particularly the area of meaningful economic work done at home. In addition, sex before marriage and outside marriage has become more acceptable and acknowledged, so that the physical side of "wiving" has lost the value society gave it when it was the only respectable way to enjoy sexual pleasure. Such diminishment of other roles naturally emphasizes the importance of what remains: mothering. So does our very contemporary interest in the psychology of our children. Mothering was always the relationship in which subordinate women could exercise dominance over others; and the dominance has been justified ("purified") by the assurance that such power is only exerted for the child's own good. Today other aspects of housewifery have declined in value, as has the sheer time needed to complete these tasks. For many women, "being a good mother" is the one activity that sustains their self-esteem. If you tell them that other people can raise their children too, they are distressed.

But, in fact, other people can, and in the past other people have played an important role in child-rearing. The isolation of the small family today, reduced to two generations, both emphasizes the mother-child relationship and obscures the older pattern in which kin and community took a hand in the job of preparation for maturity. Meanwhile, the great increase in the number of mothers with jobs outside the home intensifies the need to find other sources of nurturance for children. We are beginning, finally, to see that this is a more-than-personal problem, calling for a larger-than-individual solution; but we are just beginning.

In raising the question of child care, and suggesting that businesses set up good, well-run centers at places of work, I was (naturally) coming at the problem from where the men I was talking to stood. But the creation of stimulating and enriching environments for children as a supplement to what the shrunken present-day family can offer its young is a much wider and more fundamental issue. It's as necessary for the reintegration of the family in society, and for the larger education of young people, as it is for the support of working women. The two short discussions that follow reflect some of the questions that seem to me involved, and some of the opportunities that this felt need—increasingly felt—offers.

The first was written for the Op Ed page of *The New York Times* as a response to statements by women who were caught in the difficult situation of trying to raise children in a single-parent family. Like so many other women, and like the men who face the same situation, they were contending with day-to-day difficulties, with their own ambivalent emotions and with a commitment to traditional views of what mothers ought to be able to manage to do and be; all of this complicated by their doubts about their success. The second article appeared in a *Saturday Review of Education* symposium on what we might expect of life in the year 2000.

I believe that child care outside the home will increase in the years ahead because the need for it is so great. Everyone will profit if this process can be seen as a supplement and addition to parental care, as support by society given to the family chore of child-raising and not as a threat to it, and as an adaptation of earlier methods of support to a new situation, not as a revolutionary innovation. Other caring adults extend children's knowledge of the world and stimulate their interest in it. Studies which predict that tragic maternal deprivation will follow the separation of mother from child are based on circumstances very different from those in which a working mother confides her child regularly, for part of the day, to a competent, steady, nurturing and learning environment but spends the rest of the day with the child at home. As. Dr. Mary Howell of the Harvard Medical School remarks in an exhaustive critique of the literature on the subject, most published writing about separation of mother and child deals with quite different, and extreme, situations: "These include the mother's total absence from the home, child-rearing in large formal institutions such as orphanages, mother-child separations in such distressing circumstances as serious illness of mother or child (even maternal death), and the separation of children from their families during wartime." These conditions, as Dr. Howell says, are hardly relevant to the ordinary job of parenting done by mothers who are employed. Her study (in *Pediatrics,* issues of August and September 1973) should be read by anyone interested in the topic.

Out in the middle-class Middle West of America, where I was recently talking on this topic, a question was urgently pressed: how can a family pass on its own values to its children if it doesn't control all their upbringing? Part of the answer is that parents should, of course, have a large voice in how any child-care center is run, wherever it is run. Centers located where one parent or the other works give them a good chance to observe the operation. But no matter what the method of raising children may be, no family controls all its children's upbringing. Presumably they look at television, go to the movies—and certainly they go to school. Even the Amish are having a time of it. But beyond that, what values are we talking about? If we mean the old sex-role stereotypes, then the answer is clear. A working mother quite definitely attenuates these stereotypes in the minds of her children, both male and female; usually (Dr. Howell notes) by making a wider range of behavior seem possible and normal for both sexes. Since 50 percent of mothers of school-age children are working right now, this weakening of stereotypes is already taking place (thank God), without much help from child care.

And other values? If we believe them we will live them, and children will know it. All children learn a thousand times as much as they are ever taught and one of the first things they learn is whether adults mean what they say. They will give our values weight if we do. But we don't own their minds. A chance to listen to speakers for other values will supply a depth and variety to education that it signally lacks today.

1. The Question Is, What Is a Family, Anyway?

Laments by Frances Kaufman and Shelley List—two women who struggle to cope alone with the social demands of the wife-mother role—call for some response from the reality principle.

I want to suggest that we widen the context in which we look at these problems. The family (as Talcott Parsons says), is a subsystem of society, not a complete-in-itself operating unit. It can't, therefore, resolve dilemmas that surrounding circumstances create. It's too small. And today, it's smaller than ever. Sociologists still talk about "the nuclear family," but Mrs. List's family includes only one adult, not two. There are twenty million other people living in families with one, female head. Those are less-than-nuclear families. Most families today can be described as less than nuclear—if you count how many working hours fathers and children are at home together, sharing each other's thoughts and company.

If a family runs into trouble, the reason may lie outside the family, in the surrounding circumstances. Trying to solve it inside the family won't work, and may make things worse because of the emotional strains that will result from effort and failure.

What *is* a family, anyway? What is it supposed to do? Its economic functions have changed over the centuries, the emotional satisfaction provided there is always a personal thing, but the one task it's always undertaken has been the rearing of children. Believe me, working women know this just as well as mothers who can afford to make the choice to stay home.

Now, to raise its children well, a family has to be clued in to the operations of the community in which it exists. Adults have to understand the goals of a society (that doesn't mean they have to approve of them), and show the children how to operate within the guidelines these goals set. Processes of living ought to be understandable and open to exploration and participation.

Families have become isolated from the world of action. In his book on the alienated young, *The Uncommitted,* Prof. Kenneth Keniston of Yale dubbed them "home havens," retreats from the rat race. No doubt that's a bitter and deserved comment on the rat race; but it raises a grave question. Can one really raise children successfully in a residential ghetto, cut off from the life of the world?

This is what women—mothers—are directed to do. They have very little help. Cross-cultural studies show American women have less support today from family and community than mothers in other contemporary cultures and much less than did their mothers and grandmothers. And when they fail, they blame themselves. To bear a load of guilt on top of the task of doing alone one of society's major jobs is a shocking, a crippling burden, which demands a conscious effort to set it right.

What the family needs is a re-creation, artificially, of the old community connections, the old extended family. Communal living is one way to do this and I expect it will spread in various forms. Another approach that can easily be undertaken and could have stunning effect is the establishment of childhood enrichment centers, or youth environments, or assemblies for educational opportunities. We call these places day-care centers now, and denigrate them in our own minds by doing so; for we appear to mean no more than places to dump children.

Giving them a new name won't ennoble them by itself, but adjusting our thinking and expectations to match the name can do so. I would like to see every plant, business, commercial establishment or gathering place above a minimum size establish such a center. Mothers (or fathers) could bring little children with them to the places where they work, could check on them during the day and be with them for meals. Older children could gather there after school. In so doing they would re-create something of the atmosphere of the old-fashioned big family which our attention to the population explosion has got to make less frequent. Retired men and women could come to talk and play with the children, and acquaint them with the grandparent generation, bringing a sense of the continuity of life to the everyday experience of growing up.

Government might well share the cost of these centers by granting a tax credit for establishing them, just as it does for other capital investment, and some Government officials I've talked with agree. In fact, I would guess that industry, faced with Government orders to cease discrimination against women, would find it profitable to have unworried mothers in the work force and to know that training given to young women would not be lost in the years when they might otherwise be dropouts.

Utopian? Nonsense. We're living with the alternative, and we know what it costs. Mothers of the World, Unite! What our children need from us isn't guilt, tears and frustration, but positive action to bring the community back home and open the home to the community.

2. Raising Children in the Year 2000

Some of the people who will be raising children in the year 2000 are already here with us. My grandson is four and my granddaughter is two. It's a little early to say what their future plans will be, but if their childhood influences them, they will remember growing up in a supportive network of relationships with adults who are not their parents. By some quirk they possess an actual, if dispersed, extended family on both sides and they stay, from time to time, with two sets of grandparents, while uncles, aunts and cousins turn up to visit, share vacations and baby-sit. Just as important is the "Mothers' Mafia" of the neighborhood which will take over an extra child when a parent is ill or away. The former circumstance may vanish, but the informal mothering (and fathering) by neighboring parents will, I suspect, grow stronger.

What our tiny nuclear, or less-than-nuclear (one-parent) families need today is just this kind of connection with a larger community. It used to exist in family compound, village or small-town neighborhood. In sociologist's language, it gave children a diversity of role-models. It also gave them a lot of experience in getting on with people, and a lot of people to try getting on with. It could supply comforters when they quarreled with their parents, much conflicting advice to test instead of just one set of "Do's" and "Don'ts"—and any single set of imperatives asks to be challenged —plus an instructive range of relationships. Television isn't the same thing for there's no feedback there, but in the fascination that it holds for the very young we can see how great is their curiosity and their urge to learn the wide world around them.

"The family," said Talcott Parsons, "is a sub-system of society." It is not, and never can be, a unit complete in itself. But it is harder today than it ever has been for children to move from family base to an adult place in society because the connecting links are so few. One reason is that the family has lost the vital economic role it used to have when much necessary work was done there. For the first time in history no one, male or female, can make an adequate living at home. (Or almost no one. Very few writers make an adequate living.) The factory system put an end to the economic function of the family group and children now grow up without a clue as to the ordinary process of earning their keep.

A recipe I would like to recommend is the establishment of enriching and exciting child-care facilities at industrial plants, commercial centers, educational establishments—everywhere that parents go to work; *model* care facilities cosponsored by unions and imaginative educators, with programs offered by libraries, museums, musical conservatories, theater and dance groups, the inheritors of ethnic and cultural traditions—you can think of many more, I'm sure. They should engage, use and entertain a coming-and-going population, directed by a professional core, of children of all ages, adults of both sexes and all the generations that could be called on, interacting, teaching each other, connecting. The separation of work life from actual living is taking a terrible toll from the workers of our nation; we have just seen this documented in the HEW study of satisfaction at work. God knows I don't propose the child care I'm talking about as a way to orient children to the drab, desperate, mechanized kind of work that is distressing us today. But I suspect that *reuniting* living and working is going to be necessary for all of us, and I think that children-where-you-work can be influential in humanizing work, just as work-where-you-grow-up can be informative and exciting for children.

Overall, my great hope for the year 2000 is the reintegration of the parts of our world that started to come apart when the machines moved in. We can't do without the machines, but we've been scared of them too long. Damn it, are we mice or are we men? Does it take a woman to ask that question? Then thank God the Women's Movement has arrived to stand up and shout for liberation for the human race—beginning with our children.

VI

"Depend upon it, Sir," said Dr. Johnson, "when a man knows he is to be hanged in a fortnight, it concentrates his mind wonderfully." No doubt. So does a commission to sum up the Women's Movement in ten thousand words, particularly when the summation is to appear in a textbook of psychiatry. Even the knowledge that the article was listed under the heading *Contemporary Social Problems* did not dampen my enthusiasm. If reckoned a problem, still I would be heard, and heard by an audience most of whose indoctrination would certainly have a distinctly patriarchal bias. The result of my concentration follows.

The Women's Movement

A study of the Women's Movement must begin with three descriptive statements. First, in its present phase, it is historically quite new. Second, it is diverse. Third, it has arisen in response to qualitative changes in the social and economic circumstances of women's lives. Since the Movement is controversial, an awareness of these facts is helpful as a means of avoiding false assessments and attributions. As with any social movement, a core area of agreement is surrounded by ongoing discussions and, indeed, disputes. These can best be understood as processes testing hypotheses explaining woman's role, position and potentiality against the reality of lived experience, and as actual efforts to adjust life-styles and behavior to new roles which women either feel themselves compelled to enter upon or are desirous of undertaking. But, though the Movement at present is still in a stage of experimentation and of rapid evolutionary development, it has already established itself as a substantial and influential entity. Moreover, since it stems from a reaction to long-term and continuing trends in our society, its interests and purposes reflect and illuminate the concerns of many women who are not conscious adherents of its tenets. Students of the Women's Movement should bear in mind that the experiences to which it is a response affect many times the number of women who think of themselves as being, or even as wanting to be, "Women's Libbers."

History of the Movement. Though the present phase of the Movement began only in the 1960's, its roots run far back in time. A convention of women held in 1848 in Seneca Falls, New York, under the leadership of Lucretia Mott and Elizabeth Cady Stanton, is often cited as the inception of feminist activity in this country. Early efforts concentrated on removing legal disabilities from women and obtaining for them such rights as that of married women to hold property in their own names, to sue for divorce, to gain educations on a par with those of men and, as a major and central goal, to vote. This last right of suffrage was achieved by the Nineteenth Amendment to the Constitution, ratified in 1920. After winning the vote the first wave of feminist activity died down, though women moved into professional careers during the next decades more freely than ever before. During World War II, their labor contributed greatly to the war effort and the work they did included many categories of heavy labor usually reserved for men. No organized movement protected their interests, however, or spoke for their rights. Unions were (and for the most part still are) uninterested in sponsoring demands for equal opportunity for women, and management has generally consigned them to areas of "women's work," where wages are low and jobs tend to be routine and dead-end.

When men returned to the civilian work force at the end of the war, many women left their jobs to return home and concentrate on traditional family interests. The atmosphere of the late 1940's and the 1950's was one of "togetherness," in which the large family was highly approved. The birth rate in fact rose significantly, though some of this was due to a catch-up in births delayed by the economic depression of the 1930's and the absence of males during the war years. A classic expression of proper female behavior of the time can be found in *Modern Woman: The Lost Sex,* by Ferdinand Lundberg and Marynia Farnham, which urged women to find fulfillment in the traditional nurturing role and assured them that neurotic unhappiness was the fate preparing itself for those who did not.

A convenient sign of the changing times which have witnessed the rise of the present Women's Movement is the publication, in 1963, of another book, *The Feminine Mystique,* by Betty Friedan. There had, of course, been other statements of feminist, and liberationist, feelings even during the years when the Women's Movement was hardly existent. Simone de Beauvoir's thoughtful, wideranging and (in the end) highly influential work, *The Second Sex,* first appeared in 1949 in France and was published here in 1953. But Friedan's book came at a time when an eager audience was ready to hear its message, and it spoke in a tone of passionate commitment which evoked a fervent response.

Originally the typical response was private discussion, of the sort that later came to be called "consciousness-raising." But in 1966, the oldest, largest and most structured organization of the Movement was founded, the National Organization for Women, or NOW. Three hundred educators, advertising copywriters, business women, editors and Government officials joined Ms. Friedan in setting up this organization which declared itself "dedicated to the proposition that women, first and foremost, are human beings, who, like all other people in our society, must have the chance to develop their fullest human potential." The board of NOW (which includes men) entered upon a course of intervention in public and political affairs in the cause of equal rights for women. NOW has become a nationwide organization, whose activities include backing legal actions to bring about equal employment opportunities for women, the passage of the Equal Rights Amendment and such social issues as the institution and spread of child-care centers. Although NOW has increasingly concerned itself with the problems of poor women, including those on welfare, it has been attacked by more radical groups as not only middle class, but overly pragmatic and basically reformist in policy. It continues, however, to occupy a central position, pressing for and supporting practical actions for women's rights though many other more specialized organizations pursue a number of political and professional goals as well.

Diversity of the Movement. Historically speaking, divisions within the Movement were soon apparent. The disputes can hardly be summarized in full here, for they are not only numerous, but many have been ephemeral. It should be emphasized, however, that this diversity of interest, giving rise to contests over priorities as well as over opinions, should not be taken as a sign of weakness, but rather of the range of appeal of the Movement and, equally, of its youth. The Women's Movement is challenging a formidable number of assumptions basic to our society, and challenging them not only at the public, institutional level, but at the private, psychological level. Some of these challenges will, in the course of time, prove to be more valid and of greater significance than others. Some issues will be discarded or left to one side. Some will be seen later as distractions. Some will be outmoded by continuing social change. A similar process can be noted in the previous history of the Women's Movement, during the nineteenth and early twentieth centuries, when (for example) an alliance was formed first with the Abolitionists and then with Temperance groups, while such private matters as "free love" (which might now be titled "open marriage") were shunted aside.

Nonetheless, certain questions have already proved themselves to be matters for continuing discussion among women, and will be noted here briefly. (Some will be examined later at greater length, and in a more structured manner, since they are of particular interest to psychiatrists, psychoanalysts and psychotherapists.) Issues involving *women's occupational role* are those on which most overt action has been centered. These are, of course, those most open to agreement and action. Demands for *equal wages* for women receive widest adherence. These are closely followed by demands for *equal opportunity,* which involves opening professional schools and job training programs at all levels to women, on a par with men. Government support for these demands is evidenced by legislative action and executive orders which instruct all educational institutions and Government contractors holding contracts above a minimum level to meet equal opportunity standards, or to file affirmative action plans which will enable the organization to meet such standards promptly.

Questions involving other segments of woman's role are felt as equally pressing, but they are a great deal less amenable to direct public action, or even to agreement on proper action. Much of woman's role has to do with her activities, obligations and behavior in what is thought of as the private sphere—within the family, as a wife and mother. In fact, the role of the family as a subsystem of society is not widely understood today, and part of the difficulty in grappling with women's new demands is that they seem to have to do only with private matters, although, in fact, they stem from social changes outside the family. A growing awareness of these public/private connections can be found throughout the Women's Movement, but it has not as yet been thoroughly ventilated nor coherently articulated. As so many general questions do, it is surfacing by way of particular issues. This diversity of issues and interests gives an air of confusion to the Movement, but in fact many of them are interrelated. The ways in which they relate to each other will be examined in more detail later for the illumination they throw on present attitudes and future goals, but here it need only be noted that the proper role of the woman at home, in her relationship to husband and children, is a major subject of consideration and reconsideration among women today.

In terms of her function as *wife,* some of the questions now being debated are: is the woman to think of herself mainly as support to her husband? Is his vocation to come first in every case? Is the relation of the family to the community to be maintained via the husband, while the wife's activities are confined to the home or to approved volunteer or leisure-time associations? If not, how are duties and obligations to be divided? Some couples have worked out detailed marriage contracts, touching on division of money earned by both partners, on home duties including housework and responsibility for child care, and providing for reconsideration of arrangements, including the marriage itself, at timed intervals.

Other obligations considered within marriage deal with sexual relationships. How valid are the traditional mores? Will sexual experience outside marriage enrich or disrupt the union, and can this be undertaken by the woman as freely as by the man? How useful and advisable are less formal relationships for living together? Can patterns of life which differ from the normal coupling be sustained, such as long-term three-way relationships, or group marriages among several adults, with children being raised by all members of the older generation? Should homosexual couples be deemed acceptable? Can children born to one member of such a couple be raised successfully by lesbian mothers? How is female sexuality conditioned by women's physiology, and does her physiology have a bearing on activities and behavior other than sexual?

Debate over woman's proper role as wife slips easily into the question of the *mother role*. Should children be raised primarily by the mother, or should the father be also engaged? If so, at what age, or from birth? Are child-care facilities outside the home helpful, baneful or neutral? Should the use of mother-substitutes be encouraged, and if so, is a plurality wise? What about single-parent families? If women, or couples, decide to have no children, will their lives be as fulfilled as those of parents or can psychological difficulties be expected? Should the family function as a democratic group, or are rules to be laid down by parents, and if so, in what areas? How rigid should such rules be and how are they to be enforced?

The position of women members of minority groups is another factor making for diversity in the Women's Movement. Black women in particular are concerned to define their priorities. Should they support the efforts of Black men to step forward to full equality before they insist on their own rights? Has oppression and deprivation produced a family structure differing significantly from the white home and, if so, what effect does this have on the larger social structure? The range of behavior among Black women is perhaps even wider than that among whites. At one end, we find that women are more numerous among Black professionals than among white professionals, while at the other, veiled Black women can be seen publicly in America, and some Black women actually argue for polygyny as a deliberate re-creation of the African background, and in order that they may "share the good men" (as expressed by a spokeswoman at a seminar held by the William Alanson White Institute, where the author was present).

These very different responses clearly indicate that Black women face choices and decisions even more complex than those of their white contemporaries. In addition, the disproportionate ratio of disadvantaged Blacks (as to educational opportunities, earnings, job openings and overall employment) puts a continuing strain on Blacks, and on none more than the women who are charged with the task of raising the next generation: what are their goals to be? It is not surprising that racial discrimination compounded with economic inequities seem to many more pressing than the demands raised by the Women's Movement. Yet, at the same time, Black women are aware of their position as workers receiving lowest wages, fewest training opportunities and least legal protection. The Women's Movement is committed to work for the eradication of these old injustices, but this very commitment means that debates over tactics and strategy occur.

Another factor making for confusion over priorities is that of age differences. Older women formed their life-style at a time when traditional roles were less questioned, and it was assumed that marriage and motherhood would set the pattern for their years of maturity. Though many are now employed, they usually see their work as secondary and peripheral to their husbands' careers and often, indeed, to their roles as housewife and homemaker. But young women appear more and more to be looking to a future which will include work and are, therefore, planning their lives differently. Their educational programs are changing, since the prospect of continuing employment makes the early acquisition of professional skills attractive. This means that women's education increasingly parallels that of men. In addition, the expectation of carrying on a vocation progressively invalidates the old concept that the choice of marriage partner is women's most significant life decision. No longer is a woman's status automatically dependent on that of her husband, for the work that she will very likely undertake serves as another determinant of her position.

Abstract and theoretical questions also occupy the attention of the Women's Movement, adding to its diversity of interest. Is polarization of the sexes healthy, or should the common humanity of both sexes be emphasized? Can sex-role stereotypes be avoided or changed, and how? To what extent are psychological differences between the sexes innate, and to what extent are they the product of social training? Beyond these philosophic matters are questions of methodology. If change is necessary, how is it to be brought about? Are the changes needed of a revolutionary scale?

The Movement as Response and Reaction. The diversity suggested by this sampling of issues is, in itself, evidence of the newness of the Movement but, perhaps more important, it indicates that widespread questioning of tradition is occurring in many fields. This questioning has arisen spontaneously wherever traditional patterns of behavior have proved themselves inadequate to new demands. Criticism of, or disappointment in, the Movement because it is not cohesive is thus a misjudgment of its origins. It is fundamentally a reaction to drastic social, economic and cultural changes which have taken, and are still taking, place. The very validity of the Movement derives from its responsiveness to these fundamental shifts in contemporary lives, both social and individual. Its adherents and spokeswomen are still in a stage of what might be called "primitive accumulation" of data, and efforts to arrive at a central ideology will be premature until the process of historic change is better apprehended. Role conflicts, however, can already be traced to social shifts. Thus, the changes in women's occupational role can only be understood in the context of long-term economic trends. Women have worked throughout history, but they have done so usually within a family group, which functioned as an economic unit: cottage industry and the family farm are familiar examples. Such work did not remove them in space from their children. Indeed, the children quite often participated in it, as part of the training which formed their education for adult life.

It was the introduction of the factory system, some two hundred years ago, which put an end to the ancient family work group. Few families have ever sustained themselves by the labor of the man alone, so the working wife-and-mother is nothing new. But the removal of the locus of work from the home has produced increasing strain and faces many women with a dilemma: their earnings are needed to support the family, but in order to win them they must leave the children whose support is sustained by these earnings. Over the last generation they have done so in a steady stream until, currently, 50 percent of women with children between the ages of six and eighteen hold jobs. Most of them do so because of objective economic need. Six million women are listed in the 1970 census as heads of families. Sixteen million women are cited in Labor Department statistics as contributing the wages which keep their families above the poverty line. Subjectively, the problem of these working mothers was summed up in a letter to *Time* magazine (issue of June 25, 1973):

> As long as we live in an inflated economy, the imperative for a working-class woman to be employed . . . will increase with each child. . . . Leaving the work-force was a luxury I could afford only before I became a mother.
>
> Carolyn Foust
> Memphis

This influx of women over thirty-five into the labor force shows no signs of abating. In fact, younger married women with preschool children have joined this trend increasingly since 1950. In 1970 one-third of married women, aged twenty to twenty-four with preschool children, in marriages with husbands present, were at work. This situation is supported not only by the need for married women to earn, but by objective demand for their labor. Dr. Valerie Kincaide Oppenheimer of UCLA reports ("Demographic Influence on Female Employment and the Status of Women" included in *Changing Women in a Changing Society*), that "the level of demand for women workers has risen to such an extent that no demographic changes that are at all likely to occur can return us to the situation that existed in 1940," the last year when the census reported that young women typically left their jobs either at marriage or at the birth of their first child.

It is clear that an economic situation which can offer women remunerative work only away from the home will strain family relationships predicated on the presence of the wife and mother in the home. Efforts of the Women's Movement both to redefine the mother's and housewife's obligations within the home and to support her by advocating an increase in child-care centers outside the home thus offer an example of response to a pressing existent situation. Again, since it is a situation involving many millions of women who are not in any way declared supporters of the Movement, the emphasis laid on it by the Movement indicates how useful a study of Movement concerns and programs can be for understanding overall social circumstances. To borrow a phrase from economics, the Women's Movement often operates as a system of leading indicators for growing social problems which in turn have psychological effects.

Questions Raised by the Women's Movement. Knowledge of present actuality is clearly of fundamental importance to physicians and therapists dealing with mental health and disability. The first question posed by the Women's Movement for practitioners of psychiatry is one of definition: *What is normal?* As the first edition of this work (*Comprehensive Textbook of Psychiatry*) remarked, "A definitive answer to the question 'What is mental health or normality?' . . . must evolve out of new research and new experience." Certainly the position of women, both in the exterior world and as reflected in their own self-images, has been changing with extreme rapidity. Though the Women's Movement is by no means the only source of data, its insistence on the need to broaden the "normal" limits of femininity and of the acceptable female role makes it a central resource.

The second question raised by the Movement is at least as philosophical: *How are norms to be established?* Are they to be drawn from innate biological factors, or is "normality" the product of social training and experiential learning? Is it manmade and thus subject to change, or is it immutable, and to be discovered within natural law? Most philosophers would doubtless declare that both elements play a part. The thrust of the Women's Movement here is to lay increased emphasis on the role of social training, or acculturation. This appears to be a judgment much in line with the development of analytic theory itself, which has steadily moved from the Freudian position, where innate drives and instincts are seen as primary, the infant's environment functioning causally only as a source of frustration or distortion, to such theories as that of Erik Erikson, by which the self is understood to grow throughout life in continuing interaction with its ambience. In this sense, the Women's Movement and analytic theory might be said to be moving on similar lines toward a shared goal: that of securing to the individual a greater degree of responsible and active control of her, or his, life, to be gained through such reasoned interaction with the environment.

Anterior to these questions is the basic postulate of the Women's Movement, for it explains the need to raise them at all. Whereas in the past, women have been held to have special capabilities and disabilities, special characteristics and special limitations, the Movement believes in a fundamental equality of talent, of mental capacity and character strength within men and women alike. This equality does not imply sameness. Rather, in its opposition to sex stereotyping, it posits individual diversity as great for women as for men. Most profoundly, it declares that women's lives, emotions and aims are equally as important and significant as those of men.

This point is worth dwelling on, for it is here that any dispute between the Women's Movement and traditional psychiatric theory is grounded. Both consciously and unconsciously, orthodox theory and orthodox therapy have approached women as members of "the second sex." The male role is seen as primary, and that of women as an adjunct. Perhaps by analogy with the supporting role assigned to the nurturing female, female psychology is seen as ancillary to male.

This tendency can be found in much analytic literature. Discussions of character formation, of psychological processes, of sexuality and of psychopathology begin with studies of what one would suppose to be human experience. But then follows an addendum on female character formation, or sexuality or development of the superego by way of the female castration complex. This is not to deny the historical reality of separate and different female experience. But an analysis of that experience is almost always undertaken as a study of a deviation from the norm, because the norm is arrived at by a study of male experience.

The corollary of this view of normal human psychology as based on male experience and behavior in a male context is perhaps even more disturbing to the Women's Movement. Not only will women's psychological difficulties be diagnosed in relation to male norms, which may or may not apply, but treatment will then be prescribed according to a definition of normality not primary to women but derived by men from male experience. Female norms are thus ascribed to and projected onto women from an external point of view; a point of view, moreover, arrived at on the basis of experience different from that of women. The Movement is speaking for many women outside its membership or supporters when it declares that the ascribed norms are no longer realistic. To take one example documented above, have theory and therapy fully accepted, and adjusted to, the *fact* that most women will now spend some years at work outside the home? Ninety percent of those alive today will hold, are holding or have held a job at some time in their lives. The return of married women to the work force post-1940 and, post-1950, at an earlier age, assures that women's occupation role now increasingly resembles that of men, and that holding a job is "normal." Do therapists fully agree to this? And if they do, are they aware of the strain sustained by working mothers who also feel themselves primarily responsible for the task of child-raising? And how do they counsel women on dealing with these strains, inevitable in the present situation? This is, admittedly, a rather *ad hominem* approach to the problem, but it is used here to illustrate the way in which outdated norms are felt by the Movement to diminish, or even to undermine, the value of therapy. The conflict felt by a working mother between her obligation to help support (or, in some cases where she is the only parent present, to support entirely) her children, and her obligation to be present and primarily active in their upbringing arises from social and economic pressures inherent in today's way of life. It cannot be resolved on a personal level.

Another sort of conflict between the directions to women of the traditional role and the realities of current lived experience affects women who are strongly motivated to work full time in fields where they are competent—that is, to be career women. They too almost always regard themselves as the marriage partner chiefly responsible for the maintenance of the home and the welfare of the family. Committing themselves to a career in a world where the "extended family" is a thing of the past and domestic help is approaching the vanishing point (two relatively new factors) raises a choice that is not an option but a dilemma: what comes first, family or career? Either solution sets up its own strains, as has been well documented by Dr. Eli Ginzberg in his *Educated American Women: Life-Styles and Self-Portraits.* Psychologically, the personal problem is compounded by lack of community support in the way of adequate child-care centers, or crèches, or of programs for training professional mothers' helpers. We are consequently witnessing a rise in the number of professional women who plan either not to marry, or to marry but not to bear children. Another reaction is that of women able to support a child by their own earnings, who have children without marrying. Here, apparently, it is the role of wife rather than of mother which these women find difficult to combine with a full-time work load. No doubt the incidence of working divorcées who support their children makes the out-of-wedlock baby seem a possible option for the working woman.

This brings us to another fact of change which deeply affects the present situation of women: the option to choose when, or whether, to bear children which has been so signally increased by new contraceptive methods. The decline in the birthrate, combined with the growing life-span of women, has now reduced the proportionate amount of time spent in actual mothering to an historical low. This has dramatically changed the pattern of women's lives in the last generation, as has been outlined above, drawing them back to work in their thirties and increasingly in their twenties. What effect this drastic shift in occupation, from work to home to work again, has on the ego identity of women is a question which would repay exploration. But leaving that aside, it clearly invalidates the old proposition that the chief and central role of any woman is that of motherhood. Certainly most women enjoy their years of motherhood, but they can no longer accept them as being the normative experience defining the value of their lives.

The diversity of reaction within the Women's Movement to these circumstances can be confusing and, in fact, makes it difficult to "sum up" any structured position on which positive solutions can be based. But, once more, this diversity should be seen as evidence of the large number of women affected by social change, who find the traditional definition of woman's proper role at best insufficient, while many feel it to be crippling and distorting. In this sense, the Women's Movement began, not so long ago, as protest, and many of its strongest statements are negative, because they arise from dissatisfaction with past standards which have become unrealistic today. To those who are still satisfied with the status quo, these statements seem to be attacks on the way things are, and the Women's Movement is consequently said to be turning women away from marriage and motherhood, and even from normal heterosexual relationships. Certainly, many statements are sharp, even bitter. Some examples from seminal works may be cited:

On marriage (Germaine Greer, *The Female Eunuch*):

> Every wife must live with the knowledge that she has nothing else but home and family, while her house is ideally a base which her tired warrior-hunter can withdraw to and express his worst manners, his least amusing conversation, while he licks his wounds and is prepared by laundry and toilet and lunch-box for another sortie. Obviously any woman who thinks in the simplest terms of liberating herself to enjoy life and create expression for her own potential cannot accept such a role.

On sex roles (Kate Millett, *Sexual Politics*):

> As the whole subject of sex is covered with shame, ridicule and silence, any failure to conform to stereotype reduces the individual . . . to an abysmal feeling of guilt, unworthiness

and confusion. Unalterably born into one group or another, every subject is forced, moment to moment, to *prove* he or she is, in fact, male or female by deference to the ascribed characteristics of masculine and feminine. There is no way out of such a dilemma but to rebel and be broken, stigmatized, and cured. Until the radical spirit revives to free us, we remain imprisoned in the vast gray stockades of the sexual reaction.

On the female sex stereotype (Shulamith Firestone, *The Dialectic of Sex*):

Sex privatization stereotypes women: it encourages men to see women as "dolls" differentiated only by superficial attributes—not as the same species as themselves—and it blinds women to their sexploitation as a class, keeping them from uniting against it, thus effectively segregating the two classes. A side-effect is the converse: if women are differentiated only by superficial physical attributes, men appear more individual and irreplaceable than they really are.

On child-raising (Juliet Mitchell, *Woman's Estate*):

The need for intensive care in the early years of a child's life does not mean that the present single sanctioned form of socialization—marriage and family—is inevitable. Nor that the mother is the only possible nurse. Far from it. The fundamental characteristic of the present system of marriage and family is in our society its *monolithism;* there is only one institutionalized form of inter-sexual or inter-generational relationship possible. It is that or nothing. This is why it is essentially a denial of life.

Many more statements by writers accepted as spokeswomen for the Movement on various aspects of dissatisfaction with traditional patterns of life can be found, but those cited are both typical and taken from widely read publications. It is worth noting that though they are negative in approach, this negativism is directed to special areas of irritation. Many of these writers go on to suggest alternative ways of dealing with these problems. In short, these may be revolutionary statements (and Firestone imagines a deliberately extreme Utopia as an antidote to negativism) but they are not intended to be destructive of emotional life, happiness and order, only of what seem to the writers to be restrictions, arising from outdated rules, on the free expression of emotional life necessary to happiness and order. The picture of the Movement as led and "womanned" by furious females out to attack and destroy men is not supported by any of the serious literature. The anger voiced therein is clearly related to specific past causes, and attempts are often made to suggest cures and alternatives. Many writers believe that too-rigid sex roles are inhibiting for men as well as women (see Millett, above) and that greater flexibility would promote the happiness of both sexes. The desire to reach *equality, but not supremacy,* is everywhere present in the literature, and the fear that the Women's Movement is working toward a reversal of roles, replacing male by female dominance, simply cannot be supported. Any statements to this effect should be regarded with suspicion, as attributions, made by outsiders, arising from ignorance, misunderstanding or outright hostility to the aims of the Movement. Movement statements may express anger and resentment against men, or "the system," but the desire for a dominant role over men is absent from them.

This section has sought to ground the Women's Movement in the realities of everyday life in America today, especially as they affect the interplay between women's place in the family and the labor force. In many ways, current experience has undermined the value and the usefulness of the orthodox feminine pattern of occupation, ideals and behavior. The part played by the Movement is largely to record, analyze and publicize this major social phenomenon, with its concomitant shifts in psychological norms. These should now be understood to include many years of work outside the home, quite often coinciding with the period of active mothering. The decision of married women to work is induced in a substantial majority of cases by economic pressures and is felt both to be a reality-oriented response to need and a proper supportive procedure for the family. In many cases, of course, a desire to work in order to use individual talents, to maintain a connection with the world outside the home or to hold on to one's independence is also present, but it is a mistake to assume that most working women see themselves as having a free option to work or to stay home.

It should be added that sociologists report that marriages which include a working wife may experience somewhat greater strains than those which do not, but that these marriages also produce greater happiness for both partners. (See Orden and Bradburn, *Working Wives and Marriage Happiness*.) Such strains as are felt, it is suggested here, should be seen by psychiatrists and analysts as arising from, or exacerbated by, *social* causes and not simply as resulting from the *personal* decision to work of a woman with a free option to do so or not to do so. In any case, the working wife and mother is now so common a figure that she must be counted as a normal variant within, not a deviate from, the accepted practice of the feminine role—even if this means enlarging the parameters of that role.

Effects of Shifts in Sexual Norms. The realities of everyday life have greatly changed not only the approved, and practiced, occupational role of women, but also the sexual activities now considered acceptable for them. Once again, the Women's Movement should be seen less as a spearhead of change than as an attempt to respond with some coherence to changes already set in motion by impersonal forces. These continuing historical forces are too numerous to be listed at length but some are certainly economic, connected with the increased ability of women to get and hold jobs which pay a living wage for individual work, and also with the disappearance of family groups working together (as on the subsistence farm or the peasant holding). By achieving the ability to support themselves, single women have gained immeasurably in independence and, therefore, in their freedom to choose a marriage partner, to abstain from marriage or to end a marriage which has become painful. Other forces for change in sex behavior are the products of medical technology, like the improved and more widely available methods of contraception, backed up most recently by access to abortion on demand. The cultural phenomenon denoted by "permissiveness" is far too vague to be analyzed here, but its effect can be seen in the more frequent involvement in sexual activities at an earlier age of both young men and women. These are also less confined to a traditional "normal" pattern. Various practices once considered perversions are now quite widely accepted.

The psychiatric profession has almost unanimously approved this spread of unashamed and open sexual activity. From Freud to Masters and Johnson, the crippling results of sexual repression have been noted and deplored. Dr. Alex Comfort, in *The Joy of Sex*, goes so far as to say that "sex is the one place where we today can learn to treat people as people." Moreover, while a century ago the pleasures of sex were almost exclusively a male prerogative, with eminent Victorian physicians like Dr. William Acton taking female frigidity for granted, women are now understood to be fully orgasmic. Indeed, the decline in female frigidity can be traced, decade by decade, through the figures given in the Kinsey Report on women (*Sexual Behavior in the Human Female*), while the data supplied by Masters and Johnson in *Human Sexual Response* appear to indicate that women are capable of longer, more sustained and more quickly repeated orgasm than are men.

But, like the profound changes in the occupational role of women, these changes in sexual attitudes and behavior have effects which are less clearly understood. The idea that "liberation for women" walks hand in hand with "the sexual revolution," though widely held, is a mistaken oversimplification. Once more, an example may illuminate the divergence. Neither liberation nor the sexual revolution has yet made it acceptable for women to appear as initiators in sexual encounters. Where they do, they are either declassed as a group (prostitutes) or, like the "groupies" who offer themselves to popular singing stars, they are acting an existential inferiority to the men they seek. The position of initiator is thus still reserved to men, unless the woman takes on the traditional role of inferior.

Even less obvious, but still strongly influential in the approach to sexual encounter, is a corollary to the male right of initiative. In the past, this right was balanced by a female right to refuse the man's request on general grounds of morality or propriety. Acceptance was seen as a personal sign of affection and favor, but refusal carried no stigma of personal rejection. This has now changed. The assumption that women enjoy sex as much as men, and that it is proper for them to do so, has been extended to the expectation they will respond to a request for sexual relations by agreeing. Consequently, a woman's refusal becomes as personally pejorative as it was personally rewarding in the older situation. The result is that, while a man retains full choice in a sexual encounter, since he can approach the woman or not as he chooses, the woman has not only not gained full choice, but her decision to take the disapproved choice (that is, to say No) involves her in an apparent personal disparagement of the man. This is not only unpleasant at the time, it shadows the future of the relationship in a way which refusal used not to.

Thus, the assumption that sex is enjoyable per se sometimes functions as a positive pressure on a woman to accept the advance of any man who approaches her, since a refusal will be seen as a personal rejection. She will be understood *not* as making some general statement ("I don't much like having sex with a stranger") or simply heeding her own physical desires or lack of them. Rather, a refusal will be interpreted as meaning "I don't like *you*." Thus, where it is perfectly possible for a woman to refuse an invitation (for example) to a concert on the grounds that the program is not to her taste, or to a movie on the grounds that she would rather do something active, refusal to take part in sexual activity can be invidious. The woman's awareness of this situation, plus her continuing sense of herself as a secondary person (who cannot, for instance, initiate a sexual encounter), means that the man's invitation now seems to contain an element of compulsion. Thus, while men assume that sexual freedom is as complete for women as it is for themselves, women do not find this to be the case.

It is important for interpreters of the psychology of women to be aware of complications of this sort. The idea is widespread that current acceptance of female pleasure in sex frees women fully from the disabilities that haunted them in the past, but this is not so. One might say that the content of the female sexual role has changed, but the format has not. A study of recent publications and current periodicals addressed to the mass market indicates beyond a doubt that, at this level of class and culture, initiative in sexual matters is still a male prerogative while the role of the female is traditionally submissive and pleasing. She is instructed to be seductive, sexually provocative, alert to her partner's desires rather than to her own, and always ready to accept his advances. This is as true in publications directed to women (*The Cosmopolitan Love Guide*) as it is in those directed to men (*Playboy* and *Penthouse*). Clearly there is a basic divergence between the ideals of increased independence for women upheld by the Women's Movement and the practices advocated by the sexual revolution as it is generally defined. This is not to judge between these positions, but simply to point out the conflict. Until sexual freedom allows women the right to initiate sexual encounters and to refuse them if they so choose (with equal rights of refusal allowed to men) it cannot be equated with liberation. Consequently, it is a mistake to imagine that the forces working for these two different ends are operating in tandem. They are not, and they must therefore be expected to set up cross-riffs.

Lesbianism. It may be advisable to touch briefly on another misapprehension of the attitude of the Women's Movement toward sexuality. A view occasionally advanced in the press attributes a large incidence of lesbianism to adherents of the Movement. The Movement does indeed include lesbians, fully approves their right to take part in the sexual activity which they prefer, and to advocate it for others, and supports their insistence on the social acceptability of such a preference. This should be understood as part of the diversity of the Movement, which refuses either to advocate or to condemn any particular form of sexual activity undertaken by consenting adults. A statement of the point of view which combines radical feminism with lesbianism can be found in *Lesbian Nation: The Feminist Solution,* by Jill Johnston. Other women have reported on lesbian experience and related it to dissatisfaction and personal unhappiness resulting from heterosexual relations, which appear to them to be based on male dominance. Outstanding among these personal testaments is *Combat in the Erogenous Zone,* by Ingrid Bengis.

Once again, however, it must be repeated that these statements represent individual responses to pressures which are seen as resulting from sex stereotyping. In desiring the end of one set of

stereotypes, the Movement should not be taken to wish the institution of another set. Enlarging "normal behavior" to include
homosexual relationships as a way of life for those who choose
them freely is simply a part of the general rewriting of norms to
match present circumstances which the Movement approves; and
approves, equally, for males.

Effects of Social Change on the Mother Role.   In discussing the
changes in occupational roles of women, the effect on the mother
role has already been touched on, evidence in itself of the complicated interplay of forces which the Women's Movement finds
itself attempting to deal with. The need for mothers to leave the
home in order to work, if their earnings are necessary to family
support, is not only a difficulty in itself but points to a wider problem, namely, the current isolation of the family from the wider
world of activity. The elimination of the breadwinning father
from an effective role in child-raising, both as present model and
active teacher and disciplinarian, is often overlooked, but this is
as great an historical anomaly as a partially absent mother. In
addition, other sorts of isolation now cut the family off from the
community. A study undertaken for the Massachusetts Advisory
Council on Education by the Massachusetts Early Education Project under the direction of Dr. Richard R. Rowe of Harvard lists
some as follows:

1. The isolation of wage-earners from spouses and children,
caused by their absorption into the world of work.
2. The complementary isolation of young children from the
occupational world of parents and other adults.
3. The general isolation of young children from persons of different ages, both adults and older children.
4. The residential isolation of families from persons of different
social or ethnic, religious or racial background.
5. The isolation of family members from kin and neighbors.

As a result, this study points out:

Parents are discouraged from becoming involved in major
aspects of their children's lives. Both young children and
youth are growing up without the benefit of a variety of

adult role models. Children are becoming increasingly ignorant about the world of paid work. Parents are increasingly replaced by three other socializing agents: the schools, the peer group, and the mass media.

The economic and social factors responsible for the contemporary isolation of families cannot be dealt with by the Women's Movement alone. But they are a fundamental reason for the desire felt by many responsible mothers to engage fathers more deeply in interaction with children, thus preventing dependence on the mother alone, a dependence easily productive of intense and binding intimacy. Efforts to overcome family isolation and to provide easy connections with other adults also play a part in the support for adequate child-care centers, which the Women's Movement joins. While the most pressing need for responsible child care outside the home arises from the requirement of working mothers, the social isolation of the family is also a factor acknowledged by many families. In fact, where family income is sufficient to pay for good out-of-home care in nursery schools, kindergartens and play groups, children's attendance rises sharply from an average of one-third or less for lower-income families to a full half for families making more than fifteen thousand dollars a year.

It is suggested, therefore, that the endeavor to engage adults other than the mother in active and continuing child care should be seen not as an attempt to replace the mother, but rather to support her socializing function. Much anthropological evidence can be cited, plus that from earlier periods of our own history, to indicate that the present American pattern of consigning small children to the sole care of the mother is unusual. A useful cross-cultural study of child-raising practices is *Mothers in Six Cultures*, edited by Leigh Minturn and William W. Lambert.

Much has been written recently, both for the general public and for more psychiatric-oriented readers, on the psychological difficulties which can be induced in the family relationship by isolation from the community and overintimacy within the family group. The work of Kenneth Keniston and R. D. Laing comes to mind, and the present author explored the question from the point of view of the wife and mother in *Man's World, Woman's Place*. Briefly, a consensus points to the danger of confining women to vicarious living through others by binding them to a narrow and isolated home situation. The inability of a woman to gain public reward and acknowledgement of success for individual activity and the injunction to find her reward in the success of husband and children tends to produce a manipulative and devious personality, which will seek covert power since independent open endeavor is denied it. The influence of such a woman on children in her care has sometimes been found to be alienating or even schizophrenogenic. Far from downgrading or belittling the mother role, the Women's Movement emphasizes the importance of child-raising and socialization to the community at large by seeking the participation of others in this process. Such participation provides the positive result of variety in role models and avoids the negative effect of binding the child too tightly within the maternal relationship.

Theoretical Considerations.   In outlining the most important activities and most generally agreed upon positions of the Women's Movement, this discussion has sought to place it in context with the forces that evoked it and, also, to correct some frequent misunderstandings of its aims. Students of psychiatry may also find it useful to become aware of instances where the Movement is in fundamental disagreement with orthodox psychoanalytic theory. Much of this can be surmised from statements made above, but examples can often be especially helpful.

The work of Freud and his disciples has borne the brunt of attacks by feminists, no doubt because it is the most influential, but also because the analytic psychology of C. C. Jung, and especially Jung's conception of *animus* and *anima*—that is, the presence in each sex of an undeveloped and significant aspect of the other—has seemed to run counter to the masculine dominance found in Freudian theory. This is not to suggest that Freud's theories are totally and blindly denied. Juliet Mitchell, Shulamith Firestone and the present author (to name but three) have all publicly noted the influence of Freud's powerful concepts and brilliant analysis on their own thinking. But aspects of Freud's theory are challenged, first, by the primary postulate of the Women's Movement, namely, the equal significance of women's lives and experience with men's and, second, by the evidence of experiential divergence from theory arising from the changes in social circumstances since Freud wrote.

Thus, where Freud grounded the inferiority of women in their physiological difference from men and saw their recognition of this as a necessary, and necessarily limiting, part of their progress toward maturity (the female castration complex and penis envy), the Women's Movement sees female inferiority as attributed to women by dominant men in the social circumstances of a particular time and place. Freudian theory declares the primacy of the male as innate, based on biology. Possession of a penis is the cause of this primacy. The Women's Movement holds that male primacy is a social construct, fabricated (whether consciously or not) as a means of upholding male dominance in power relationships. Penis envy is not denied, but it is understood as envy of the male position of dominance in society and in the family, of which possession of a penis is not *cause* but *symbol*.

Now in fact Freud himself, by consistently using the concept of "female castration" (which is symbolic, since no female has ever been castrated), appears to accept a symbolic interpretation of the psychological difference between male and female. The whole question of male superiority, indeed, is taken as axiomatic by Freud and never explored. The child is assumed to recognize that possession of a penis signifies the right to dominance, but no attempt is made to explain why this recognition should occur. The problem is seen only in reverse: if the girl child rebels against the meaning of right-to-dominance assigned to possession-of-a-penis, this is a sign of immaturity which must be overcome. But to assume that male superiority is validated by possession-of-a-penis implies awareness of this superiority in the child at the time he or she learns of the physiological difference between the sexes; else why should the connection be made at all? "Penis means dominance" is a syllogism which could be formed only in a context of already understood male dominance, which is to say that the concept is a justification of a preexisting belief, and not a logical cause of the belief.

It is possible, as suggested here, that Freud was aware of the symbology of penis envy in a submerged way, just as references

can be found throughout his work to the character structure of
women as the product not simply of biological forces but of social
forces as well. Nonetheless, he was largely content to derive theories of female development from the biological base of penis envy,
with the maternal urge seen as a transfer of desire for a penis to
desire for a child. Some of his followers, however, notably two
well-known female analysts—Marie Bonaparte and Helene Deutsch
—took up a brief suggestion of Freud to the effect that femininity
may have "some secret relationship with masochism." The idea
that women are by nature masochistic clearly grounds their inferiority even more securely in physiology. As an explanation, it
appeared to account both for the high incidence of frigidity noted
among women two generations ago and for the concurrent assumption of a self-sacrificial or even martyr role of many mothers. In
addition, the idea that it is natural for women to wish to suffer
justified the existing inferiority of the sex, both to men and to
those women who questioned their place. It should also be noted
that the insistence on a passive role for women in sexual activity,
tied up with the theory of vaginal orgasm as the only norm, follows from the premise of female masochism.

Challenges to these ideas have arisen over the years. Alfred Adler did not deny to women the common drive toward superiority
which he perceived as basic to humanity, though he assumed that
the social situation of his time would usually prevent this "masculine protest" from achieving any real success. A generation ago,
Karen Horney declared, in *New Ways in Psychoanalysis,* that when
considering the etiology of feminine masochism "one has to look
not for biological reasons but for cultural ones." The effect of
social pressures on women is well analyzed here, especially "the
cultural situation which has led women to regard love as the only
value that counts in life." Horney notes that neurotic fear of aging, which will decrease a woman's attractiveness, follows from
this, as does a general sense of insecurity and self-devaluation;
and, indeed, that "the all-embracing expectations that are joined
to love account to some extent for that discontentment with the
female role that Freud ascribes to penis envy," since these expectations are, in the nature of things, rarely achieved in full.

These theoretical difficulties have been reinforced both by the actual experience of many women whose lives no longer conform to the traditional pattern, and also by scientific advances. Direct research into sexual practice and sexual response, undertaken by Masters and Johnson, has overthrown forever the assumption of female passivity, of less frequent and lower female response, and of a necessary evolution during maturation in women from clitoral to vaginal orgasm. Some women indeed appeared capable of multiorgasmic response to stimulation far beyond the capacity of men, but overall, Masters and Johnson found "parallels in reaction to effective stimulation [to] emphasize the physiological similarities in male and female responses rather than the differences." It is clear that these physical findings call into dispute any theories based on lowered sexual drive in women being innate to their biological makeup, or to a passive, nonorgasmic reaction being normal, as put forward by Deutsch and Bonaparte.

Another scientific discovery challenging old theories was announced in 1953 by the French endocrinologist A. Jost, and developed by the work of M. L. Barr, R. H. Burns, J. J. Van Wyk and E. Witschi. This is reported and commented on most accessibly by Dr. Mary Jane Sherfey in *The Nature and Evolution of Female Sexuality:*

> Genetic sex is established at fertilization; but the influence of the sex genes is not brought to bear until the fifth to the sixth week of fetal life [in humans]. During these first weeks, all embryos are morphologically females. If the fetal gonads are removed before differentiation occurs the embryo will develop into a normal female, lacking only ovaries, regardless of the genetic sex.

Burns (Sherfey reports) suggests that the femaleness of the mammalian embryo is directly related to viviparity, since in reptiles and birds all embryos are innately male, with the female hormone acting as the inductor of sex difference. In mammals, however, intrauterine life would expose a basically male embryo to feminization even without the intervention of female hormone. The hypothesis thus is that in the evolution of mammals the inducing hormones became the androgens and the innate embryo female through an early adaptation. However that may be, it is now

apparent that analytic theories which see women as immature, or
partially developed, males have lost any genetic grounding. Obviously, no more should be assumed from the original femaleness
of the embryo in mammals than from the maleness of the embryo
in oviparous vertebrates. Both appear to be adaptations to changing evolutionary circumstances. But the discovery does emphasize
the danger of arguing from physiology to psychology in too simpli-
fied a way.

Conclusions.   The appearance of a new Women's Movement in
the 1960's is, in itself, a challenge to many psychological assumptions about women. The very suddenness of its advent contributes
to this effect of challenge, but, in another way, raises the question
of the seriousness and extent of the Movement. In addition, the
time frame of its appearance made it, originally at least, seem to
be a mere addendum to other rebellions of the period: that of
Blacks demanding civil rights, and that of the young of both
sexes which culminated in the unrest on campus so widespread
during that decade.

This study puts forward the thesis that, on the contrary, the
Women's Movement is deep-rooted and promises to be long-lasting. No doubt the climate of the 1960's promoted—or provoked—
movements for social change, but this merely suggests that the old
orthodoxies were proving themselves inadequate in many fields
at once. Just so, over a century before in the 1840's, movements
of economic and political protest had surfaced together throughout Western society. Already attitudes toward women and women-
oriented demands for social justice and a wider role in active life
can be seen to have changed, in areas ranging from employment
standards to the literature addressed to women (as in popular magazines), to an extent that cannot be appreciated without examining the period of the early 1960's, before these reactions began.
Much reexamination of basic thinking about women and their
proper behavior is taking place, among both women and men.

Specifically, the traditional role of women has changed, and is
now seen to have changed, in all its aspects. The occupational role
of women has been reviewed here, and the steady rise in the employment of married women and mothers, even mothers of young

children, has been discussed. This shift, as has been noted, has increased the similarity of experience for men and women. What this may mean for future relations between the sexes cannot be predicted, but it is certainly simplistic to imagine that similarity of experience will reduce sexual attraction. Erich Fromm has expressed concern that a lessened polarization of sex roles will produce such an effect, and this may of course be so; but, equally, extreme polarization has been accompanied by a high degree of homosexuality in the past, notably in Periclean Greece and Victorian England. We cannot, consequently, predict the direct effect of women's new occupational role on their sexual activities, beyond the unmistakable evidence that an increase in independence will make for a greater degree of freedom of choice in love object for both sexes and, thus, for greater diversity.

The effect of changes in women's occupational role on the mother-child relationship is also apparent. Again, predictions of how these changes will affect child-raising in the future can be no more than guesses. The most that can be said is that it seems probable that the narrowing down of the family to one parent present in the home, with almost no other adults regularly available for child care, has reached its peak. It seems likely that involvement of the father, interaction with other parents or adults, as in communal living, and out-of-the-home child care will become increasingly common. This can be expected to reduce the intensity of the mother-child bond which has recently characterized American life, a bond which has been exalted as the central and most significant relationship for the mother while, at the same time, it has been vilified by critics so disparate as Philip Wylie and Philip Roth as a crippling "silver cord" for the child. Perhaps a loosening of this ambiguous tie will produce a healthy reduction of tension within the family.

Turning to women's estimate of themselves, it would appear that we are experiencing a "revolution of rising expectations." Today's college generation of women is planning to undertake demanding careers to a greater extent than ever before; and it is, of course, a generation much more numerous than that of the earlier ambitious feminists of the 'teens and Twenties of this century. The trend toward later motherhood and a lower birth rate, combined with a lengthened life expectancy, means that women will necessarily have more time and energy to spend outside the home. This generation, however, is not content merely to see itself as replicating male experience and acting out male roles. Women are increasingly seeking a new self-image for themselves. The Women's Studies programs to be found on so many campuses today are a response to these desires; but older women as well are reconsidering the form and content of their lives. This does not mean that they will, or should, downgrade their special experience as wives and mothers, but rather that they may find new substance in evaluating it, and new bases for extending their experience into activity in other fields as this becomes possible for them.

Once again, the Women's Movement is best understood as a response to deep environmental changes in our society. We must expect these changes to continue and, thus, the Movement to change in its practical emphasis and immediate interests. Already, we have seen, these interests are very diverse, representing the areas of response of women of all kinds and classes, all races and regions, of diverse backgrounds and individual characters. Fundamentally, however, the premise that women's lives are of equal importance with men's, to women themselves and to society, will endure and grow stronger. In a time of rapid change such as the present, not only should women's talents and energies be tapped, but the application to them of standards extrapolated from the past will necessarily be distorting to the psyche. The teaching and the practice of psychiatry can only profit from using the rich experience of women in seeking to understand the effects of social change.

VII

Another challenge-plus-opportunity was an invitation to comment on the famous last discussion by Freud of women's sexual situation. *Female Sexuality* was first published in October 1931 and appeared in English translation in 1932. In his biography, *The Life and Work of Sigmund Freud,* Ernest Jones summarizes the paper as follows:

> *Female Sexuality* . . . was written in great part as a response to the special interest that several analysts in England and Germany had recently been taking in this subject. Although, according to Freud, it contained no ideas that had not already been expressed in the psychoanalytical literature, he summarized his experience and conclusions in his own clear and characteristic fashion. Perhaps the main novelty was the stress he laid here on the duration and intensity of the girl's early attachment to her mother, which he thought had been previously underestimated. This plays a part in psychopathology, e.g., in female paranoia, as well as in normal psychology. An example of the latter in married life is its transference to the husband, who may thus inherit both the special demands the girl had made on her mother (being "mothered") and the hostility of this early phase.
>
> Freud maintained that in this phase of attachment to her mother the girl's attitude is predominantly active. Even her fondness for playing with dolls later on shows traces derived from it in the active behavior toward the doll, who may represent not only a child but the mother itself. The later change of love object from mother to father, one which the boy does not have to make, betokens, therefore, more than a simple

exchange; it signifies also a change of attitude, from active to passive.

The idea of castration, i.e., the discovery of the anatomical differences between the sexes, may lead to three characteristic lines of development. The shock and accompanying sense of inferiority may lead to an extensive renunciation of all sexuality, with fatal consequences for adult life. On the other hand the belief in the possession of a penis, or the wish for it, may be obstinately retained, leading to a permanent "masculinity complex" or even homosexuality; this is usually accompanied by a defiant masturbation. The third path open is the normal one of turning to the father and developing an Oedipus complex.

Freud then discussed the many sources of hostility toward the mother in this early phase. It is invariable and is only strengthened by the subsequent rivalry during the true Oedipus phase, which is far from being the only cause of this hostility. There are the unavoidable frustrations of infantile life, and also the ambivalence which seems to be a normal accompaniment of that stage of development. Most important appears to be the girl's resentment that her mother brought her into the world less well equipped than the boy. When another child is born the girl may have the phantasy that she had created it with the mother before her discovery of the part played by the father.

In responding to, and commenting on, this last integrated commentary by Freud on women's fate, I have tried to bear in mind both the continuity of his work and the immediate situation in which it was undertaken. Freud was seventy-five in 1931, and the cancer of the jaw and palate which had been tormenting him since 1923 necessitated a series of treatments by radium therapy and surgery. This was particularly distressing because the original, radical operation was now proved unsuccessful: a further malignancy was found. Freud's future, it was clear, would be plagued by painful recurrences and equally painful efforts to contain them. These he bore with heroism and overcame, so far as might be possible, by stoic dedication to his work. *Female Sexuality*, then, was written during months in which Freud endured much physical distress. In addition, the worldwide economic depression was deepening and the growing menace of Hitlerism to the north had already sent some of Freud's colleagues overseas.

What effect did such circumstances produce on Freud's thinking? Certainly he felt himself touched by shadows. In a letter to Romain Rolland he speaks of himself as "approaching life's inevitable end"; and in another, to an emigrating medical man, he qualifies his thanks for good wishes by adding, "I am afraid I am so old that wishes are rather wasted on me." Nonetheless his curiosity and involvement with life remained strong. So did his dedication to scientific objectivity, an objectivity which, defined in nineteenth-century terms, aimed at quantifying qualities and dealing with psychic events with the rigor of the physical scientist. It is a rigor which may seem naive to us today, when relativity and probability theory have invaded the physical sciences themselves, but in Freud's time it represented a necessary struggle to demythicize the interior world. Another element of Freud's commitment to scientific objectivity might also be noted: he worked from clinical data and it was here that his theories took root. We know now and, as I suggest, he was aware to some extent, that his data were culture-conditioned; but I wonder whether the very creativity he brought to his consideration of this material may not have invested it with more symbolic importance than we could possibly allow it, in part because we live in an age oriented to cross-cultural values but also because—under Freud's own direction—we have looked at such data longer, and looked at more of it.

My far-from-unique effort to place Freud's thinking about women in a social and historical frame is not to be taken as a venture in debunkery, but as an attempt to build on the foundation his work laid for human understanding, of ourselves and others.

Freud's View of Female Sexuality

Freud's ambivalence toward female sexuality has often (too often) been cited simplistically as evidence of male chauvinism. This conclusion is not only unfair to the powerful and analytic mind of Freud but, more important, it short-circuits our understanding of his work and deters us from mining it for perceptions that can be very useful in any examination of the position of women today. In my discussion of his 1931 paper, *Female Sexuality*, I shall call attention to some ambiguities and, indeed, some outright inaccuracies of speech; but it is for a positive purpose. I believe that these faults can reveal, as geological "faults" do for the earth, positions of strain in Freud's structure of concepts which tell us a great deal about the society in which he lived and to which we are the heirs, as we are the heirs to his thought. In raising questions of motivation and of emotive personal relationships I am not seeking to discredit Freud's enormous achievements but rather to put these in perspective, so that we can more readily call on their dynamic energy.

Let me begin by calling attention to the remarkable repetition of Freud's inaccurate reference to "the fact of castration" in the female. Little girls have not "in fact" been castrated. Not only are their bodies intact, but not one of them has even suffered the penile trauma of circumcision. What, then, can Freud's consistent use of this term signify? It would be faithless to our respect for Freud's own work to pass over such a striking example of the psychopathology of everyday life. We must assume that this slip is meaningful; and indeed I believe that it leads us to the heart of Freud's dilemma about the female sex. "What do they want?" he asked and, when forced to reply, he declared that they wanted a penis.

I wish to suggest that Freud meant this symbolically, but that he did not ever (for reasons which I believe can be discerned, at least in part) find it possible to undertake an investigation of what it is that the penis symbolizes. The curious misstatement implicit in the words "the fact of castration" seems to point this way. Was not Freud, in repeating this false phrase, calling attention (unconsciously) to a latent meaning in his theory of the castration complex which differs from its surface presentation? Indeed this meaning is so close to the surface that, time and again, it all but breaks through. No woman has been deprived of a penis—she never had one to begin with. But she *has* been deprived of something else that men enjoy: namely, autonomy, freedom and the power to control her destiny. By insisting, falsely, on female deprivation of the male organ, Freud is pointing to an actual deprivation, and one of which he was clearly aware. In Freud's time the advantages enjoyed by the male sex over the inferior female were, of course, even greater than at present, and they were also accepted, to a much larger extent, as being inevitable; inescapable. Women were evident *social* castrates, and the mutilation of their potentiality as achieving human creatures was quite analogous to the physical wound, reference to which recurs in both Freud's 1925 and 1931 papers.

The difficulties of adjusting to the feminine role are succinctly described in *Female Sexuality* in contrast to the little boy's development, which follows a straightforward path. In him, the first attachment to the mother runs head on into the fear of castration by an angry father, but the two drives then operate together in a progressive process. As the boy relinquishes his early incestuous attachment to his mother he builds, out of respectful fear for his father, his own superego, which will guide him toward normal maturity. What he loses is unreal—his dream of incest. What he gains is progress on the road to the time when he will occupy his father's place in a new family, with a woman of his own.

With the girl child things go differently. "She acknowledges the fact of castration," writes Freud, "and with it, too, the superiority of the male and her own inferiority." She does not, however, accept this in good part, but rather "rebels against this unwelcome state of affairs." Consequent on this rebellion are three possible developments; and while the normal male progression to maturity issues in a satisfactory solution, it is interesting to note that *none* of the three developments open to the girl child is really satisfactory. (As I have called attention to the significance of Freud's misstatement, "the fact of castration," I would like here to remark on the general feeling tone of *all* Freud's writing about women: there is always a note of sadness in it, a sense that women's condition sentences them to an unfulfilled life. This is true not only of the later papers written at a time when Freud's natural tendency toward pessimism must have been emphasized by his physical condition. As early as 1905, in *The Case of Dora,* and 1908, in *"Civilized" Sexual Morality and Modern Nervousness,* Freud describes the lives led by women as actually precarious and threatened and as abstractly painful.)

In *Female Sexuality,* the first possible reaction of the girl child to her knowledge of her inferiority is given as a "general revulsion from sexuality. The little girl, frightened by the comparison with boys, grows dissatisfied with her clitoris, and gives up her phallic activity and with it her sexuality in general as well as a good part of her masculinity in other fields." The renunciation of the pleasure of clitoral masturbation, the lapse into passivity—these accompany the knowledge that one is inferior.

In *The Case of Dora,* reporting an analysis which took place in 1900, we find these three elements occurring at the start of the girl's first neurotic illness. Freud notes "her declaration that she had been able to keep abreast with her brother up to the time of her illness, but that after that she had fallen behind him in her studies. It is as though she had been a boy up till that moment, and had then become girlish for the first time. She had in truth been a wild creature, but after the 'asthma' she became quiet and well-behaved." The "hysterical symptom" of asthma was, in Freud's view, a substitute for the masturbation which Dora gave up. (I am uncertain whether Freud himself, at the time he wrote *Female Sexuality,* would have admitted Dora's experience as evidence of the onset of the positive, i.e., father-directed, Oedipus complex, for she was seven and this is rather old. However, he speaks throughout *Female Sexuality* of how late the pre-Oedipal mother-attachment can linger in girls, allowing five years as a possible "normal" age for the shift to father as love object. In any case, it is Freud and no other who associates in both works the three elements of passivity, knowledge of inferiority and cessation of clitoral masturbation.)

The second development which may overtake the girl child who discovers the physical difference which symbolizes her social difference from boys "leads her to cling with defiant self-assertiveness to her threatened masculinity. . . . The phantasy of being a man in spite of everything often persists as a formative factor over long periods." It can go so far as to result in "a manifest homosexual choice of object." I need hardly point out that to Freud and his followers such an "abnormal" choice of love object connotes a failure to reach the goal of normal maturity. The road to such maturity takes a third tack, by way of the feminine form of the Oedipus complex, in which the small girl fastens her affections on her father. It is, says Freud, a "very circuitous path." But even when this goal is reached, the ending is not entirely happy. For, with the turning from early love for the mother to the father as object, "there is to be observed a marked lowering of the active sexual impulses and a rise of the passive ones. [And though] the active trends have been affected by frustration more strongly . . . the passive trends have not escaped disappointment either . . . and often enough when the small girl represses her previous masculinity a considerable portion of her sexual trends in general is permanently injured too." One is left with the depressing conclusion that the normal development to maturity in women demands not only the sacrifice of the "wrong" (active) sort of sexual impulses, but of the "right" (passive) sort as well.

There is no reason whatsoever to doubt that Freud's assessment of the disadvantages of the feminine role was entirely accurate for his time. It has been said often enough that he formed his theories, necessarily, on the basis of the clinical data that came to him, but as a general observation, this is less enlightening than it seems. What, in fact, *was* the clinical data that came to him? How did it direct his theory formation? What did Freud take for granted as brutal and unchangeable facts of life, the ground of existence to which the Reality Principle had to adjust the overweening desires and drives of the Pleasure Principle? In *Female*

Sexuality, Freud is discussing the effect on the little girl of her discovery that she is not a little boy; and, in particular, how this contributes to her passage from the pre-Oedipal phase of attachment to the mother to the more adult, more realistic, positive Oedipal attachment to the father. Her realization that she and her mother are alike has two effects. It convinces her that she is inferior, and it causes her to reject her formerly adored mother. Freud assumes that his readers will accept this twin assertion unquestioningly. What I am questioning is *not* Freud's assumption, for it has clearly been justified. But why did he assume it, so immediately and unreflectively?

A very simple way to reply is to look at some of the clinical data that came to Freud. Let us take the well-known case of Dora which I cited a moment ago. I choose it for several reasons. First, it *is* well known. Second, it was an early analysis. Though not published until 1905, it was undertaken in 1900 at a time when Freud's theories had not grown toward rigidity. And third, it was of short duration, is easily followed and turns for its problems and its solutions on just the issues under discussion: the position of women as understood by Freud in their time and context. The story of Dora is profoundly affected by the anonymity and impotence of women, beginning with her mother, and it therefore illuminates one of the axioms on which Freud founds *Female Sexuality:* the catastrophic effect on the child who discovers that she is a girl.

Dora was eighteen when her father brought her to Freud and he brought her there, it appears, because Freud had earlier been able to put him on the course of a cure for a venereal disease. Dora had been suffering from depression and a series of psychosomatic illnesses, but it was the discovery of a suicide letter in her desk (though she did not in fact attempt suicide) which really alarmed her parents. She suffered a loss of consciousness after a quarrel with her father and was then induced to accept treatment. Her analysis lasted only three months, but in that time Freud uncovered much material about the girl's background. What he sets down as relevant includes not only her psychological history but a great deal of material on her social position. It is of the latter that I wish to speak, not simply because it places Dora for us, but because it placed her for Freud. It is what he took account of.

Dora was on bad terms with her mother, whom Freud never met. Nonetheless, he writes, "from the accounts given me by the girl and her father I was led to imagine her as an uncultivated woman and above all as a foolish one, who had concentrated all her interests upon domestic affairs, especially since her husband's illness and the estrangement to which it led. She presented the picture, in fact, of what might be called the 'housewife's psychosis.' She had no understanding for her children's more active interests, and was occupied all day long in cleaning the house. . . . [It is, Freud comments, a] condition, traces of which are to be found often enough in normal housewives. . . . The daughter looked down on her mother and used to criticize her mercilessly, and she had withdrawn completely from her influence."

So much for the mother's possible therapeutic influence. Dora's older brother had served as a model when she was younger, but she had now realized that she could not follow this male pattern and her relations with him had grown distant. He tried to keep out of family disputes but, if drawn in, supported his mother. Before we come to Dora's relationship with her father, we should also note that a governess had, at one time, looked after the girl. Dora had been greatly attached to her—"until she discovered that she was being admired and fondly treated not for her own sake but for her father's [with whom the governess had fallen in love]; whereupon she obliged the governess to leave."

We see, then, a young girl who has had no trustworthy love and support in her family except for and from her father. Her mother has betrayed her by her incapacity for real life; her beloved brother has withdrawn into the male world; the mother-substitute, the governess, has demonstrated her disloyalty. It is now her father's turn to do the same.

Dora's father was carrying on an affair with a certain Frau K. and Dora knew it. Not only did this affair disrupt her sustained Oedipal attachment to her father, but she had in earlier days been deeply fond of Frau K., serving as her confidante and sharing her bedroom when she and her father stayed with the Ks. Suddenly she finds herself caught in a repetition of the relationship with the loved and betraying governess. Frau K. does not really care about her, only about her father.

We can surmise the effect of this psychic shock. But there is another element in the situation, and that is Herr K. He has presented himself to Dora as a possible lover. She had felt affection for him at one time, but under this strain she rejected him with disgust. It seems a little odd that Freud should find this reaction so unexpected for, after all, it was what a respectable young virgin should have done, and Freud understood the need for outward respectability very well. Indeed, he congratulates himself in this very study on the fact that patients have told him of how "respectable" they find his treatment. Freud's attitude becomes even odder when we realize (and he writes himself) that Dora was being offered to Herr K. as part of a bargain, *by her own father:* "He had handed her over to this strange man in the interests of his own love affair."

We need not deal in detail with Freud's treatment of Dora, except perhaps to note the girl's attempt to rescue herself by appealing to the conventions of the time. She demanded that her father break off his affair, and she refused to meet the Ks. I wish simply to present the situation in which a comfortably off, marriageable girl could find herself in Freud's Vienna. Dora had indeed been attracted to Herr K., so his attentions were tempting. The one parent for whom she had had any respect and affection was tacitly urging her to yield herself to the tempter. And, of course, all her social education had informed her that if she did so, she would lose the "jewel-box" (she expressed it thus in a dream) of her virginity, the one possession of value which was hers. She had no adult protector to whom to turn. Woman after woman betrayed her, the men she loved attempted to seduce her. Under the circumstances, Dora's inner strength appears to me the most remarkable thing about her case.

This, then, is part of the clinical data on which Freud's theories were based. We can't, of course, know whether or not Dora's situation was typical, but fortunately we don't have to. Freud's theories are grounded not in what may or may not have existed in reality, but on what data came to his attention out of reality and appeared to him plausible and relevant. Clearly he did not find Dora's plight unusual. In fact, at one point he told her that her reactions were exaggerated, and he also took pains to point out her own complicitous contribution to her involvement in the K. affair as, for example, her early collaboration with her father in his efforts to visit and meet with Frau K. Before we condemn this approach as hard or cruel, we might note its realism. If Dora did in fact want to save her virtue from Herr K., she would have to do it by means of her own determination, for there was no one else to whom she could appeal. The last thing she needed was sentimental ignorance, or ambivalence, about her own purposes.

If we now come back to the 1931 paper, *Female Sexuality,* with Dora's case in mind, we find that the two cast much light on each other. In 1931 Freud was emphasizing his new appreciation of the importance of the pre-Oedipal phase for the little girl, its long duration and its possible later effects, even in the choice of a husband. A passionate father-fixation (and Dora had that; it was her father's betrayal of it which brought on her hysterical symptoms) was, Freud declared, evidence of an earlier phase of "exclusive attachment to the mother which had been equally intense and passionate." In addition, he remarks that the pre-Oedipal phase, and especially its long duration (and we suspect that Dora had also experienced that), were intimately related to the etiology of hysteria; and this was his diagnosis of Dora's complaint.

More significant, however, is what Dora's story has to tell us about Freud's general theory. As we have seen, the "normal" (if necessarily unhappy) development of the girl child involves the renunciation of her exclusive love for her mother when she understands that she is of the same sex as the mother. Freud offers a number of possible reasons for this reaction, including such physical ones as that she is bodily unfitted to play the male, complementary role with another female. But, he adds, "the strongest motive for turning away from her [is] the reproach that her mother did not give her a proper penis—that is to say, brought her into the world as a female."

Now if Freud were to leave it there, if the girl child's revulsion from the mother were to be based only on her physical incapacity for sexual connection with another female, we could not argue; as long, that is, as we accept the idea that lesbianism is an unnatural, or at least an only marginally satisfying, mode of sexual pleasure. But Freud does not leave it there. He speaks of this knowledge as convincing the girl child of her *inferiority*. And here we must ask a variant of our earlier question. Why, if the mother has been so greatly loved, should the discovery that she and the girl share the same sex convince the child of being inferior? And Freud does not answer, does not tell us in so many words what his analysis of Dora makes certain he knew perfectly well: that the adored mother was, in truth, inferior all along. Instead, he puts the cart before the horse and brings forward again the old "fact of castration." "The little girl discovers her own deficiency," he writes. "When she comes to understand the general nature of this characteristic it follows that femaleness— and with it, of course, her mother—suffers a great depreciation in her eyes." And certainly this happens; but it could not take place unless the girl child had already absorbed a bitter knowledge that femaleness equals inferiority. Why else should she regard the physical difference between one body and another as "a deficiency"? If she is *like* her mother, and her mother is the object of passionate attachment, how can their likeness convince the child that "this characteristic" denotes inferiority?

What I am saying is that the difference between male and female, active and passive, which Freud notes, is social as well as physical; and that the social difference, the inferiority of the female, her lack of power and freedom, slides into Freud's theorizing by the back door. The lack of a penis implies, denotes, inferiority; and when we ask why this must be, we are fobbed off with the false statement that women are castrates. That statement cannot be taken seriously *unless it is taken symbolically*. I take Freud's discoveries and illuminations very seriously indeed; and so I believe that we must admit the symbology. We must allow that women's inferiority, in Freud's mind, was somewhere understood to be the result of her lack of power; and that her lack of a penis did not simply *denote* this, but *stood* for it.

This is a statement that is either all but self-evident, or else extremely daring. Orthodox Freudians will no doubt reject it out of hand as shortsighted and reductive. They will recall Freud's rejection of the views of Alfred Adler, in whose theories the drive for superiority as an attempt to compensate for feelings of inferiority is prominent, and who was an early exponent of what Kate Millett has taught us to think of as "sexual politics." Well, like the orthodox Freudians, I find Adler too simpleminded for belief; but I think that in rejecting his overt awareness of social context and of political urgencies (both in the psychic drama and in the world at large) Freud cut himself off from a mode of thinking that could have added a dimension to his theories. Without it (it seems to me) some of Freud's more labyrinthine formulations— and I would specifically include some of these ruminations of the female Oedipus complex—take on a pre-Copernican, epicyclical air. In addition, one must surmise that the whole post-Freudian development of analytic thought by the ego analysts (like Erikson) is due to Freud's hesitance to admit the reality and depth of the ego drives toward individual and sexual power, and their use as an instrument of investigation.

One can see why he hesitated. A Jew in Hapsburg Vienna who wanted to make a psychological revolution surely had his hands full. Freud was attacking an interlinking network of shibboleths as it was. To question woman's role and her natural and proper subordination to the male, to give the weight to it which Adler did to the idea of "masculine protest" (although Adler agreed that successful protest by women was hopelessly unrealistic), would have added fuel to the fire. And, indeed, we know from Freud himself that he regarded woman's proper role as that of happy wife and mother, subordinate to the male, for he told his fiancée so in no uncertain terms. And yet—

And yet Freud notes, time and again, the difficulties which the traditional role laid on women's shoulders. I have spoken of the tone of sadness that pervades his writing on women. Specifically, in *"Civilized" Sexual Morality and Modern Nervousness*, he describes the female marriage role in terms which make one's blood run cold. Here are a few excerpts:

> The "double" code of morality conceded to the male in our society is the plainest possible admission that society itself does not believe in the possibility of adherence to those precepts [of abstinence] which it has enjoined on its members. But experience also shows that women, as the true

guardians of the sexual interests of the race, are endowed
with the power of sublimation only in a limited degree [this
tenet of Freud's is connected with his belief that the less
powerful Oedipus complex which he posits for the girl child
necessarily provides an inadequate foundation for the development of her superego]; as a substitute for the sexual object
the suckling child may suffice, but not the growing child, and
under the disappointments of matrimony women succumb
to severe, lifelong neurosis affecting the whole course of their
lives. Marriage under the present cultural standard has long
ceased to be a panacea for the nervous sufferings of women;
even if we physicians in such cases still advise matrimony, we
are nevertheless aware that a girl must be very healthy to
"stand" marriage. . . . Marital unfaithfulness would . . .
be a much more probable cure for the neurosis resulting
from marriage; the more strictly a wife has been brought up,
the more earnestly she has submitted to the demands of civilization, the more does she fear this way of escape, and in
conflict between her desires and her sense of duty she again
will seek refuge in a neurosis. Nothing protects her virtue so
securely as illness.

Freud then goes on to discuss the effects of abstinence on men:
not good. "On the whole I have not gained the impression that
sexual abstinence helps to shape energetic, self-reliant men of
action, nor original thinkers, bold pioneers and reformers; far
more often it produces 'good weaklings.' " As for women, he continues, "The injurious results which the strict demand for abstinence before marriage produces are quite particularly apparent."
The young girl has been educated to set a high premium on her
chastity and kept in ignorance of what her part in marriage is to
be. "The result is that when the girl is suddenly allowed by
parental authority to fall in love, she cannot accomplish this mental operation. . . . Psychically she is still attached to her parents
. . . and physically she shows herself frigid, which prevents her
husband finding any great enjoyment in relations with her . . .
so that the training that precedes marriage directly frustrates the
very aim of marriage." For once, in these remarks, Freud shows
himself thoroughly aware of the effect of the social context, for he
declares, "I do not know whether the anaesthetic type of woman

is also found outside the range of civilized education, but I consider it improbable."

Now this is nothing less than a description of how a particular social milieu tends to produce neurosis in those most deprived, by its social ordinances, of libidinal reward. It certainly implies a recognition that woman's inferiority is socially conditioned, and not simply directed by her anatomy. Indeed, it would be well to point out here that when (in his 1912 *Contribution to the Psychology of Love: The Most Prevalent Form of Degradation in Erotic Life*) Freud made his famous statement "Anatomy is destiny" he was not referring to the fact that women lacked a penis or possessed a womb. Rather, he was commenting on the universal human situation that "excremental things are all too intimately and inseparably bound up with sexual things; the position of the genital organs—*inter urinas et faeces*—remains the decisive and unchangeable factor. . . . The genitals themselves have not undergone the development of the rest of the human form in the direction of beauty; they have retained their animal cast; and so even today love, too, is in essence as animal as it ever was." This conflict between "animality" and the demands of civilization is of course a recurrent theme in Freud's writing, and the destiny which denies us complete instinctual gratification is not confined to women. In *The Case of Dora* Freud applies it specifically to the male.

Is it possible, then, that the ambivalence of Freud's theories about female sexuality is (in part, at least) the result of an effort to justify a real historical situation that existed and could not (it appeared at the time) be challenged in any useful way? It would be spurious to suggest how Freud's experience of being an inferior in his society—a Jew—related to his awareness of women's experience of being inferior in the same society. We cannot know. We do know, however, that Freud's attempts to better his position and satisfy his ambitions were never public or political. They were not ideological or collaborative, but were instead contained within his professional life. In this sense they were personal and they involved his acceptance—in action, in behavior, that is, and not, of course, in principle—of the restrictions placed on him. This was his cast of mind and it seems to me perfectly reasonable to find the same cast of mind at work in his behavioral acceptance of woman's traditional place. If he did not rebel against the social structure, how could he counsel them to?

His differences with Adler, I believe, reveal the same cast of mind. Freud abjured politics and direct action. Adler was a radical Socialist, his wife was a friend of Trotsky's. In his theories he emphasized the influence of aggressive drives within the psyche. Freud, on the other hand, turned his ambitions from the political to the private, professional area. He saw, and used, the respectability of bourgeois life as a defense behind which he could conduct and extend his own astonishing creations of thought. And yet, Ernest Jones tells us in his biography, Freud took Adler's ideas very seriously. The break with Adler was bitter. It had the effect, says Jones, of convincing Freud that he must explain and expound his technique more thoroughly. In so doing, he emphasized his differences with Adler. I shall not labor the point, but simply indicate the obvious: the break with Adler and Adler's theories of aggression and practice of politics could only reinforce Freud's disposition to ignore the existence both of aggressive drives and of political methods.

In addition, underlying this determination was Freud's sensitivity to his own formulation of "the reality principle" both in his own situation and in his theories of female sexuality. Freud's enormous achievements could not have been won by wish fulfillment or infantile surrender to the omnipotence of thought. And then, as a physician, his goal was therapy; and his cures had to take place in the world as it was. In that world the idea of the inevitable inferiority of women was unchallengeable.

I hope I have not developed this thesis simply as speculation. It seems clear that Freud believed that women were peculiarly disposed to neurosis. He attributes this, in *Female Sexuality,* to the complicated course that their emotional attachments must follow if they are to achieve the goal of normal maturity. (For Freud, normality was not something that happened, but something that was achieved, which seems to mark his idea of the starting place as one of inferiority.) The very best road to maturity for a woman leaves her with diminished sexual drives and less resistance to the episodes of life which can evoke neurotic response. But I believe that we can use the earlier material I have cited to go further than this and insist on Freud's awareness of a social element molding women's lives. Certainly in his outline of Dora's position Freud was not surprised by her isolation within her own family; by her mother's incapacity to support her, or even acknowledge her daughter's danger; by Dora's expectation, based on experience, of betrayal by other women who claimed her affections—in short, by the impotence of women and the way they saw themselves, and were seen by men, as property which could be bartered about.

Not to accept this impotence (this fact of *social* castration) would have demanded a challenge to the whole social structure. Freud's appreciation of reality suggested that this was wasted effort. Even Adler, the Socialist, did not imagine that the "masculine protest" felt by his female patients could change their ordained lot. "If we are to help [a girl]," he wrote (in *What Life Should Mean to You*, published here in 1931), "we must find the way to reconcile her to her feminine role. . . . Girls must be educated for motherhood and educated in such a way that they like the prospect of being a mother, consider it a creative activity, and are not disappointed by their role when they face it in later life." Freud at least did not share Adler's optimistic view that "we" were going to accomplish this just because "we must." Rather, his sense of the world told him that "we" were not going to accomplish this very often, and that marriage-as-it-was-practiced in the world he knew was a neurosis-genetic relationship, especially for women.

Much has changed since Freud wrote. The inferiority of women, while still widely enforced, has been challenged successfully. The relationships of parents to children have also changed. For example, automatic punishment for masturbation occurs less often and less angrily; and in Freud's theories such punishment was a fundamental contribution to the child's fear of castration, and thus to the onset of the Oedipus complex. In both instances we see that the distribution of power has shifted, weakening the male figure both as husband and as father. Would not Freud have seen it too? Would he, with his strong orientation to the evidence of reality, not have assessed the changed clinical data coming to him in a different way and developed, perhaps, rather different formulations? In *Female Sexuality*, Freud is telling us that a girl child's relationship to her mother is more important than he had previously thought; that the father-attachment itself is shaped on the earlier love for the mother. If, then, the mother's actual position in the world has changed—and it has—may we not suppose that the nature of her relationship with her daughter, longer-lasting than with her son, would also change? And with it, its effect on the daughter's later life? I think we are justified in doing so, and I believe that the underlying, if not quite admitted, symbology of Freud's thought, which I have attempted to investigate, actually directs us to this view.

VIII

The relationship between women's liberation and the accelerating movement toward greater sexual freedom is not a simple one, as I noted in the account of the Women's Movement I contributed to the textbook on psychiatry. Liberation for women certainly implies the removal of restrictions on their right to enjoy the pleasures of sex. But the idea that removing these restrictions is going to produce either instant Eden or instant promiscuity is misguided. Our reactions to sexuality are profoundly influenced, below the level of consciousness, by past patterns of living. At the same time, our conscious knowledge of history and the weight we're willing to admit we give to tradition have become minimal. How many of us remember that less than a century ago the pleasure of sexual intercourse had to be tied, in women's minds, to the pain of childbirth (with no anesthesia) that was expected to follow it? Or that the first method of contraception practiced by loving husbands, to spare their wives, was withdrawal before climax, not only his climax but very likely hers? Sexual pleasure for women was infinitely more difficult in such circumstances, and when it did occur, the aftermath, the pain of childbirth, must have reinforced the ever-present puritanical idea that it was sinful.

All right, that's over; but we are still reacting to the behavior and the standards that this sort of sexual practice produced, and reaction isn't action—that is, it isn't truly creative. We are just beginning to feel our way toward really new patterns of feeling about sex and its practices. In spite of all the contemporary brouhaha on the subject, this generation is not able easily to reach the roots of its own feelings. Our behavior and our emotions are far removed from the abstract notions we usually advance as counters in discussions of sex. Result: a lot of inchoate, turbulent feeling at the personal level, and very few agreed upon, easy ways to behave when in its grip. I keep being reminded of the situation described so vividly by the White Queen in *Alice Through the Looking Glass:*

"It was such a thunderstorm you can't think!" ("She *never* could, you know," said the Red Queen.) "And part of the roof came off, and ever so much thunder got in—and it went rolling around the floor in great lumps—and knocking over the tables and things—till I was so frightened I couldn't remember my own name!"

If you substitute sex for thunder, it seems to me a remarkably apt description of current circumstances.

No doubt we need such a shaking up. If we are going to remake the way men and women look at each other and think about each other and approach each other, we have to get rid of the deadwood. In the paper that follows I have tried to explore some of the unspoken assumptions and unconsidered overtones of current attitudes toward sex, and how these link with the Women's Movement both positively and negatively.

What Do You Mean by Liberation?

When Dr. William H. Masters and his research associate, Virginia E. Johnson, published their book *Human Sexual Response* in 1966, they described it as "a faltering step . . . but at least a first step toward an open-door policy." It would, they hoped, help to end the fear which crippled scientific discussion of sexual activities: "fear of public opinion, fear of social consequences, fear of religious intolerance, fear of political pressure, and, above all, fear of bigotry and prejudice." How misguidedly tentative those words sound today, less than a decade later, when open discussion of human sexuality has become central in almost all forms of expression and communication! The briefest glance at the theater, at films, books and periodicals, whether popular, highbrow or underground, reveals revolutionary changes in what can be said, shown and read. Can it really all have happened so fast?

Not entirely, for customs and attitudes are slow to change. What we are witnessing today is largely the culmination of a long series of small shifts in human attitudes. There *is* a new element, however, and that is the confirmation, by accepted public display, that behavior which was long held to be illicit and unorthodox is normal. Even those who don't like the revolution admit that it has taken place. On the newsstands, *Penthouse* sets out to prove that *Playboy* is a lovable old fuddy-duddy, and *Viva* tries the same game on Helen Gurley Brown's *Cosmopolitan* girl. Sex manuals are as common as those dealing with auto repair used to be in the days of the Model T. News magazines run cover stories on the sex therapy which Masters and Johnson originated, now spread nationwide by disciples and imitators. Even *The New York Review of Books* offers its readers an opportunity to communicate to each other a need for more than scholarly discussion; though its personal columns indicate that those using them must be better at such discussion (on pain of unemployment) than at conveying poignant emotion. Masters and Johnson, declaring their devotion to science, found a popular mainstream audience waiting for them in 1966, and since then supply has been rising to meet demand.

But demand for what? At first blush (appropriate phrase) the sexual revolution appears to be almost totally random, concerned primarily with substituting individual ways of behaving for those sanctioned by social rules. The designation of "permissiveness" bestowed on our contemporary practices reinforces this idea. And the overt message which the sex manuals deliver is an emphasis on sex as private fun and games, sex as pleasure of the body with no moral overtones. In the past, the assumption is, rules about sex had to be public because there was, inescapably, a social issue involved: in the absence of effective contraceptive measures, sex meant babies and babies raised questions. If they were legitimate, they had a claim to inherit rank or property. If they were not, their upkeep and status fell to society to provide and determine. Today, in theory at least, this is no longer so, and sex can be enjoyed as a simple physical pleasure.

Oddly enough, however, there seems to be little disposition to follow through on this supposedly attractive proposition. Perhaps it is just a hangover from the past, but even those writers who declare that the importance of sex is its sheer pleasure do so with an evangelical zeal that is directive rather than permissive. Some of the more popular manuals go off on another tangent, and suggest that sex activity is both a method of manipulating others and an arena for competition toward some goal of maximum pleasure which will both ring a gong inside, and gain the sexual athlete a reputation in the world. Serious writers turn in a different direction. They are exploring the data on sexual attitudes as the basis of a new morality. Meanwhile, women are demanding that their hitherto overlooked experience of sex be included in any view of normal sexuality, and lesbians and male homosexuals are declaring that their ways of loving must also be incorporated in the mainstream.

Clearly these are not simply personal reactions, individual breakouts brought on by an atmosphere of permissiveness. Yet, at the same time, they insist on the value of personal, felt experience. We have to see, I think, that questioning the value of old rules is different from simply breaking them, and that what is going on is much more related to the first activity than to the second. In a profound shift of emphasis, the private, personal world of feeling is being called on to suggest more valid patterns of conduct than the old rules held up to us. In order to do that, a private—indeed, a secret—world of feeling must be opened to the light of day. Yes, the rules governing sex practices had been public, but the emotions that sex aroused and the intimate human behavior which climbed the framework of rules like a rose up a trellis had been set apart from the rest of lived experience. Now this separation can no longer be sustained, and so sex is becoming a kind of testing ground for the validation of experience which reaches far beyond the physical. It is a symbolic area where a search for sincerity, authenticity and the sense of one's full and responsible identity is taking place.

Which is to say that just because sex *is* private as it is felt, as private as poetry or pain, it can illuminate the rest of the world by serving as a touchstone of feeling, both physical and moral; a place where body and soul join. It is surely obvious, then, that any testing of sexual values reaches deep into the unconscious mind. Such testing will not be undertaken lightly, for changes at this level are profoundly disturbing. That it *is* being undertaken, therefore, indicates how badly our traditional rules for living are working. Once upon a time they served us well, for they told us what was happening to us when sex touched our lives, and how to behave in response. They placed the private storms of passion and sensuality within a frame of ordinary day-to-day living and ritualized them by ceremonies, ceremonies which not only legitimized these overwhelming emotions but operated as celebrations of agreements on what to do about them in a public way. For the individual, the rules provided time-and-emotion-saving instructions about how to behave in stressful situations.

But our belief in the old rules has faded. Take the question of adultery. Western moral tradition long ago declared itself on the subject. It defined a double standard which condemned women more sharply than men and thus justified the different behavior it recommended to the sexes. Wives were held to be wise when they condoned the offense, since a wandering husband would often return and a bird in the hand was worth two in the bush. Indeed, wives who insisted on separation were warned of future loneliness. Husbands who condoned the transgression of a wife, however, were judged more harshly. In Latin lands murder of the wife's lover was held to be quite proper, and in others divorce was recommended as a substitute for a *crime passionel*. Forgiveness was possible, but the male who accepted his wife's adultery either lost status by assuming the position of cuckold, or lost the image of normality by tending toward uncomfortable sainthood. The situation might be painful, but at least one knew what was right, for procedures to deal with the difficulty had been laid down.

Certainly these procedures still have force in some circles, but not in all. Marriage (or alternative-to-marriage) counselor Carl

Rogers describes a current confrontation with adultery in his recent book *Becoming Partners*. A couple married some years each met the infidelity of the other with an effort not simply to accept it, but to welcome the third party into their marriage. "I tried to incorporate the idea of having a three-way relationship here," says the wife (in a tape-recorded conversation), "and I went as far as I could in saying yes to this." She did not succeed, nor did her husband avoid jealous reactions to her several affairs. But each sees this reaction as something of a personal failure based on individual character and the particular nature of the tie between them, and each comments that the crises they have been through have helped them to know themselves and improve their relationship. To them, the proper behavior when confronted with adultery follows no general rules. It is, rather, to search oneself for one's honest response and act upon it. The effort to turn a pair into a triad was seen by both members as open and generous, and thus as ethically admirable.

Here we see how a personal effort to feel truly and deeply is at work to substitute new patterns of behavior for old ones. The new ones, of course, may be unworkable in the long run, and one may ask whether this couple was not being naively optimistic to imagine that three-way love could survive its own problems. But though we may do that, we must not dismiss the serious striving that went into the attempt to establish a larger, more generous kind of relationship, for whether misguided or not, it was a committed effort; nor should we overlook the fact that this insistence on personal search for new ways of living is in process of becoming a norm itself. This kind of insistence on thinking things through for oneself and testing behavior against one's own feelings, instead of taking a prescribed road, is no longer idiosyncratic. It is increasingly typical of the way people feel and act. And the fact that such a decision can be made privately has a significant public aspect.

Something has happened, in the public sphere, that is, which has caused our society to resign its sway over proper sexual behavior. When dealing with adultery becomes a matter of private choice instead of public rules, middle-class morality, that bastion of social stability, has ceased to function. The sexual revolution has swept over us so rapidly, it is clear, because we had already lost our faith in the old rules. But—why did we do that? Why have centuries of morality gone by the board with so little upset to anything else? The sanctity of the marriage bond! The purity of the home! The chastity of women! The honor of men! Weren't we told over and over, and our parents and grandparents before us, that these were the fundamentals which alone preserved our social order? How the devil has it come about that they have vanished, with so little ado?

Several reasons come to mind. The first is the sheer complexity of our universe and the rapidity of social shocks which are buffeting it. We are being tugged, or shoved, in different directions, and the effect is to break the relationships that were once felt between this part of life and that. Then, there is the possibility that "The Power Structure" which used to police our lives in so many ways has succumbed to these changes, and is no longer sufficiently powerful to keep an eye on everything. Perhaps the Big Brotherhood of the elite has only enough strength left to maintain its grip on a part of society. And this, I think, is true as far as it goes, for the demands of the sexual revolution for new patterns of living are certainly not the only ones being put forward. The embattled Establishment might well wink at *this* revolution because it seems to center on private activities, on "sexual politics" which, to the mighty, may appear to involve no more than power relationships between individuals. Any power elite will ignore the desanctification of the home in order to deal first with overtly political difficulties, if these are pressing. The crises of the three "E's," economics, ecology and energy, confront us. Minority demands, the need to rebuild the cities, the problems of population control, must somehow be coped with. Confronted with the possibility of public catastrophe every tyrant will opt to let permissiveness rule in private.

Besides, will not such permissiveness turn the attention of the people away from public problems to private pleasures? One can imagine a modern Machiavelli suggesting to his prince that sex would make a very good opiate for the people. Political revolutionaries, at any rate, often tend to be puritans, and one need only cast one's mind back to the high old days of Roman bread and circuses to remember that contemporary imperial morality was lax indeed. Not that history is really this simple, but difficult times may well tend to concentrate rule at a single, dictatorial center, while also leaving the central hierarchy with little time or energy to spend on supervising the morality of its citizens.

Nevertheless, if the old rules of morality had been working well, they would have continued persuasive, Establishment or no, for they would not have required support or reinforcement. Though human beings tend to argue about morality in abstract terms of right and wrong, a moral order succumbs to change for quite another reason: *it becomes inappropriate,* which means that it ceases to work. Abiding by the rules doesn't pay off. This is what is happening today. The copybook maxims don't live up to their promises. The pragmatic dissatisfaction this produces arouses a sense that they are unrealistic, inauthentic, out of touch with the actual lived experience of this generation.

Obviously the very young will be most ready to lay tradition aside, if only because they have least invested in it. In a surprisingly little noticed study, published in 1973, Dr. Robert C. Sorenson examines the mores of our young between the ages of thirteen and nineteen. *Adolescent Sexuality in Contemporary America* reports on an investigation in which depth interviews with two hundred young people were correlated with responses to lengthy questionnaires by some four hundred more. The sample was nationwide and selected to be representative, the study undertaken by experienced professionals, the adolescents approached only with parental consent. Both in its scope and its content, it can fairly be compared with the Kinsey reports.

Most of these young people (80 percent of the boys and 75 percent of the girls) are experienced, though not all of them in full sexual intercourse; the degree of their experience depends, naturally enough, on age. It does not vary greatly by geographic region, nor by urban versus rural living. They tend to regard themselves as a new and separate generation, strongly bonded together, to the extent that even Blacks identify with their age group in preference to race, and all identify by age over religion or sex. "For them," writes Sorenson, "sexual activities have no relevance to morality, *except in the way they are used.*" (My italics.) To these young people, no behavior, no sexual practice, is good or bad in itself, but only in relation to the individuals involved. One might or might not be willing to do something oneself, one might even regard it as "abnormal," but if it gives pleasure to others and hurts no one, it will not be judged wrong.

Once more we see, as we did with the couple Carl Rogers reported on, that sexual activity is not to be banned or prescribed by rule, but judged by personal values. The young condemn the adult world because its rules (they feel) ignore personal feeling and thus invite hypocrisy to taint human relations. Their attitude toward marriage falls in with this. It is respect, not disrespect, for marriage which makes them avoid it. They want, sometime, to contract solid, long-lasting marriages in which to bear and rear children, and they know they are not ready to undertake them. The traditional connection between sex and marriage which (they think) forced their parents into wedlock is rejected out of hand by the great majority. It produced unhappiness, mismatches and dishonesty.

Meanwhile, they enjoy sex but enjoyment, they say, is not what they want most. At any rate, 69 percent disagreed with the statement, "The most important thing in a sexual relationship is just the sheer physical pleasure of having sex." It is more important to them as a way of exploring themselves and testing their emotions, of communicating with others and, to some extent, of escaping from loneliness, pressures and problems. One sixteen-year-old boy said, touchingly, "It's nice to have sex with a friend." Running through the whole lengthy analysis is the insistence on personal choice and feeling as a touchstone. Yes, we are defying the rules of society, say the young people, but not simply out of defiance. We are looking for guidelines we can trust because we have tried them out ourselves.

Their mistrust of the old rules, then, does not imply a lack of trust in the world. Indeed it may indicate a naive overestimate of their ability to remake the old rules and find satisfying new ways of living together. Young or old, skepticism about conventional wisdom can give way all too early to a relapse into credulity before the allurements of new certainties. But we are mistaken if we assume that the refusal of young people to live by old rules is an irresponsible, self-indulgent vote for permissive promiscuity. Rather, the acceptance of a ready-made way of life that cannot justify its tenets seems irresponsible to them. Which doesn't mean that they can't often be very irresponsible for themselves, toward themselves. They fail to use contraceptives or to take precautions against venereal disease even when both could be done without too much difficulty. They are romantic and confused and sometimes silly. But their overall view of the importance of personal freedom, as long as it does not infringe on the freedom of others, is not ignoble. Nor is the insistence that honesty about personal relationships has got to be part of the pattern that directs what those relationships should be. In general, one feels that Dr. Sorenson's study reveals a world that is less compelled, more open and more tolerant than that of the past. In a time of change, that's good news.

But if it is good news, it's hardly conclusive. What is the bad news? Can we really let sex loose in the world, unfenced by rules and prescribed behavior? If the children think they can cope with it, isn't that just because they are children? Certainly, tolerance isn't enough. To some, freedom can be chaos. There are those who need commitment in order to find themselves. Happy, friendly sex may be shallow sex too, and reading the manuals reinforces this view. None of them confronts the depths of emotion that sex may arouse, either frightening or joyful, which means that they treat it in a way that is more superficial than most of their readers actually feel about it. Perhaps an Earthly Paradise of casual, cheerful, nonjealous promiscuity would be an excellent solution to our problems; but it doesn't exist, and when the manuals pretend that it does, they are falsifying experience as much as did the old puritan regulations. Have fun! they cry. Look at the pretty pictures. Watch Dick and Jane make love! You too can make love like Dick and Jane.

But the manuals don't, in fact, manage to treat their readers as if they were simple extroverts happily pursuing pleasure and looking only for tips on new subtleties. The impulse to write as if you were selling something is strong in those who address the American mass audience, presumably because what that audience is most accustomed to read is advertisements. So sex manuals tend to "sell" sex, surely an odd treatment of an activity which has always been held to be a primary instinctual drive; a treatment which may, moreover, rouse in the reader's thoughts the question of why the author is so keen to have him undertake something he wanted to do anyway—what's up? The sales pitch is, of course, the simple but universal contention that sex is good for you. So we find these popular guides to antipuritanism approaching their readers in a tone that is curiously reminiscent of the Protestant Ethic: "Put yourself together, work hard, enjoy yourself, damn it!"

"Well, Seventies girl," says the *Cosmopolitan Love Guide,* "it's time to clean your mental closets, shake out the dust and rummage of years of accumulated subconscious inhibitions. Your love affairs should be the most zesty fun you'll ever have—not one miserable crying jag after another. Can you rouse yourself sexually now?" it goes on to ask. "We think that's a *must.*" *Cosmo* supplies the italics, and they are almost enough to make me opt for the crying jag.

Dr. Reuben, the guru who told us what everybody had always wanted to know about sex, is equally free with his "musts." Take an example from his recent compendium, *Any Woman Can.* Convinced that a man is happiest if he manages to marry his "ideal mother," he directs his ready-to-wed feminine readers to supply the classic food of infancy to any candidates for spousehood. "On every occasion they are together, she must provide him with milk (or the symbolic equivalent) in some form," he advises. And, though substitutes are permitted (milk chocolate, pudding, ice cream or even beer), "the closer a girl comes to supplying the original beverage, the more control she is bound to exert."

Even the more sophisticated *Joy of Sex,* presenting itself as a gourmet cookbook for lovers, tends at times to become more effortful than joyful. "The aim of this book," say the anonymous couple who speak for its author, Dr. Alex Comfort, "is pleasure, not psychiatry, but we expect that the two coincide." Perhaps they do for Dr. Comfort, but one wonders whether the real aim of going to bed together is to straighten out one's head. Later, we are given a definition of "nakedness" which brings in the Protestant Ethic with a clear trumpet tone: "the normal state for lovers who take their work at all seriously." One feels that Dr. Comfort's couple do indeed take their work seriously, in the conviction that sex, like psychiatry, is good for you, and that pleasure can be prescribed.

They are not the only ones. When, in November 1972, *Newsweek* ran a cover story on sex therapy, they quoted Dr. Wardell Pomeroy, a former Kinsey collaborator, to this most specific effect. Said Dr. Pomeroy, "I'll say, 'Take your clothes off, take a shower together. Make notes and tell me what happens. Think that I'm giving you a prescription at the drugstore that you have to go and fill.' " "Sexual intercourse is assigned for homework" by other therapists, this article goes on; and it includes an estimate, undocumented but supported to some degree by the waiting lists for treatment by sex therapists, that "Sexual problems of one kind or another afflict at least half the married couples in the U.S. today." Against this background the sexual revolution seems to involve a confrontation with anguish at least as often as it does a plunge into bounteous sensual pleasure.

It's tempting to decide on the basis of this publicized distress that the revolutionary changes of our time have moved too fast and been too sweeping; that a return to the old rules is in order. I don't agree It seems to me that, on the contrary, much of our discomfort is due to the fact that we have not sufficiently redrawn our picture of the world. Though the barriers to sensual pleasure have gone down, though open and experimental partnerships are (rather grudgingly) allowed, these exterior behavioral shifts have not yet received enough interior, psychological support. Perhaps, indeed, such support can only come through lived experience.

Though public behavior can be prescribed, sexual relations cannot be dealt with abstractly. They are private and they take place between individuals. But just because this is so, the images each sex holds of its opposite and of itself get into the private encounter. They act as directives toward proper behavior, and so they can confuse any encounter badly if the images are too disparate. In the world we have left behind and to which we cannot return, male and female roles were not only clearly defined, but agreed on by both sexes. Accepted views of the "natural" character of each sex, its capabilities and duties, existed and were supported by a groundwork of what I have called "social mythology." Men were held to be active, aggressive and imaginative, women to be passive and subordinate, though happily fulfilled by taking care of those they loved. Myths divided the world into proper spheres of activity for men and women and also instructed both sexes how to behave, including how to behave with each other. One of these myths emphasized the weakness of the timid, affectionate female but another, older and more frightening, underlined the *power* of women.

The idea of female power, and the sway it enjoys in the male mind, is perfectly understandable when one once realizes its source. It is a cast-back to the earliest days of life, when a powerful female figure controlled, satisfied and sometimes denied the desires of the infant. To the baby, his mother is truly a mother goddess, and many a sensitive writer, whether he or she approves the aims of the Women's Movement or not, is aware of the effect of these early memories. I quoted two such writers in *Man's World, Woman's Place* to this effect, both of whom happen to be highly opposed to women's liberation—Norman Mailer and Phyllis McGinley. More recently, in *Sexual Suicide,* George Gilder, another enemy of feminism, hails women's control of "the economy of eros" as "the life force in our society and our lives," declaring, "What happens in the inner realm of women finally shapes what happens on our social surfaces, determining the level of happiness, energy, creativity and solidarity in the nation." A magical power, it is, and quite unreal; but it still haunts the mind, and that raises problems.

Today the myth of female weakness is losing its credibility, as women demonstrate again and again that they are capable of functioning above the level of the private or the subordinate. Unfortunately, such demonstrations don't do much to defuse the other myth. Increasingly, women are able to keep themselves by their own work, they can choose when, or whether, to have children and they can—if the sexual revolution is to be believed—choose their lovers as freely as men have been accustomed to do. So to many men, this new sexual freedom poses a troublesome question. With the old rules for masculine superiority fading in the public sphere, how can men face the feminine superiority they

have posited in the private world? Gilder raises this point with
some anguish. If women are able to earn as much as men, men will
lose their only claim to superiority in the modern world; and
since (in his view) women are endowed with magical power in
personal relations, men are thereby condemned to soul-destroying
inferiority. Poor engineer, hoist with his own petard! And
strangely unable to imagine that men and women might ever
stand equal and level, that inferior/superior might not be a necessary part of male/female relationships.

Not only has the comfortable agreement on proper definitions
of sex roles vanished, leaving a confusing muddle behind, the
sexual revolution is clouded also, from the masculine point of
view, by an uneasy feeling that changing the rules may mean
more than simply getting rid of old restrictions and repressions.
The old restrictions may have been frustrating, but they did tell
you what to expect. A woman might say No when you hoped for
a Yes, but you could at least be sure she would wait to be asked.
If the revolution simply banished frustration, if the freedom
granted women were merely the freedom to say "Yes!" when a
man asked for their favors—well, that would be fine. And indeed
that is the image of the revolution which is widely promoted. But
the masculine fears we find surrounding this image indicate that
it is seen to be superficial even by those who would appear to
profit most from it.

Certainly women are edgy about this kind of freedom. To them,
the freedom to say Yes, when asked, is hardly freedom at all.
Moreover, the selling of sex as good for you, as "zesty" physical
therapy, plays down its significance, and especially its relational
significance. If it's good for you, it doesn't much matter who your
partner is. But this means that any emotions you may have about
sex can't be important either. Human beings, however, do have
emotions about sex: even *Cosmopolitan* found it necessary to
mention those crying jags. And the adolescents in Dr. Sorenson's
study felt that their sexual connections with others were a vital
means of getting to know each other, and communicating with
each other; of understanding life and the people who live it. A
sexual revolution which declares that sex is great fun but doesn't

mean much is a pretty funny kind of revolution. It invites its participants to belittle their own feelings.

If, as Midge Decter suggested in her critique of women's liberation, *The New Chastity*, feminists are antagonistic to sexual freedom, the reason lies here. The kind of sexual freedom which this revolution is offering is not very attractive to women who are learning to value themselves more highly as individuals than they did, and who feel that exercising control over their own destinies is an important and highly desirable aim. As yet, no sexual revolution has got far enough to give them the same freedom to initiate sexual overtures as has been traditional for men. They are still the second term in the equation. In the past, women were controlled by their husbands or fathers, or, if they were prostitutes, by their pimps. The degree to which they were counted as people or the degree to which they remained property, this varied from culture to culture and age to age. But control over one's body has always been central to the issue, and it has never been granted in full. It is not granted today—and will not be, until the sexual revolution is understood to mean that freedom is freedom for both sexes not just to enjoy sensual pleasure, but to initiate, direct and end these pleasures, and to enter into them with whomever they choose. It may well be, I think, that one reason why lesbian relations are taken so seriously in the Women's Movement, even by those who feel no sexual attraction to other women, is that they do offer women equality of choice. Love between women is seen as a paradigm of love between equals, and that is perhaps its greatest attraction.

If we look back for one last time at our sex manuals, we see that they raise this question of equality of the sexes—and don't resolve it. When they urge active participation in sex for men and women alike, they seem to be telling women—as well as men—to take control of their sex lives in their own hands for the sake of the pleasure it will give them. But read on, and one will find that the authors don't seem to understand what this means. Dr. Reuben's *Any Woman Can* is intentionally ambiguous about what it is that a woman can do; have an orgasm, that is, or catch a man. But it assumes that the man-catching job is really the fundamental

one, and that "any woman" will maneuver her way to this goal
by using sex as a means along with every other ploy that comes
to mind, including those drinks of milk. *The Cosmopolitan Love
Guide,* directed toward a young and swinging female audience,
curtseys every now and then to the importance of female gratification, but devotes much more space to Do's and Don'ts which will
"turn on your man": sexy things to say in bed, ways to chase him
without letting him know it; and it concludes with "Your Zodiac
Seduction Handbook," where you can "look up your man under
his sign to find out everything you have to do to make him yours."
Sexual freedom? Nonsense! These are directions for the greedy use
of freedom in old, manipulative ways in order to gain the traditional feminine "catch-a-man" goal. Crude as they are, they offer
excellent examples of the mystique of the myth of female power;
and equally good examples of why women on their way to personal liberation shy away from this aspect of sexual liberation.

Even the more adult *Joy of Sex* is unconsciously revealing a
split view of freedom when it advertises itself as "A modern Kama
Sutra," for the Kama Sutra assumes the most basic and profound
inequity between the sexes. It posits a world in which the male
must be pleased and the female must labor with desperate skill to
please; and, incidentally, a world in which her purpose is expected to be exactly that expected by Dr. Reuben: to get herself
married to the man. "All the ancient sages agree on one point,"
says the Kama Sutra firmly. "No matter how much a woman loves
a man she should never offer herself to him or make the initial
overtures to sexual intercourse, because a woman who behaves
in this way exposes herself to ridicule, scorn and refusal. Only
when a man expresses a desire for her, should she show her affection for him and allow him to embrace her . . . and only when
she is completely sure of her lover's passion, his sincerity and fi-
delity, should she ultimately allow him to take her, making sure
that he will marry her promptly." How to do that the sages don't
say. We are left with Dr. Reuben's milk diet.

Now *The Joy of Sex* itself manages pretty well to concentrate
on pleasure for pleasure's sake. Indeed, it concentrates on it so
thoroughly that it warns its readers they may have to choose between this sort of sex and having children, for children are ter-

ribly apt to get in the way; which is another instance of how an emphasis on physical sex pushes personal relationships and emotions to one side. There is, however, some evidence that the old view of the world still surrounds the bedroom, and that it is a world in which men are to be pleased and women to strive to please them; a world in which female anxiety about her success at pleasing is expected. "Any woman," it tells its readers, "who herself is ready to enjoy and understand sex, and meet her partner's needs as fully as a professional but with love, can outclass anyone hired." In addition, its view of rape is the male-oriented idea that it's something that happens to women who deliberately excite men. Put those glimpses of the underlying set of mind together, and you get a sense of joyful sex taking place in a male-dominated setting. Which is not to deny that it may be joyful, but only that it is free.

So perhaps the conflict is not really between women's liberation and the sexual revolution; perhaps it is inherent in the latter. If sexual freedom means freedom for men, but the old manipulative, cheating role for women; if partners are equal in name only; if there still remains the old pattern of the one who pleases and the one who is pleased—well, there's trouble there already. The adolescent children seem wiser than that. They insist on personal values in their meetings and matings; and so, really, does anyone who is seriously seeing the sexual revolution as meaning what it says: as a revolution that will bring freedom of full sexual choice and full enjoyment to all, male and female—both.

In fact, the sexual revolution involves a great deal more than sex. One is reminded of the remark attributed apocryphally to Jung: "After all, what is the penis but a phallic symbol?" Whether or not the good doctor actually said it, the point is well taken. Sex cannot be contained within a definition of physical pleasure, it cannot be understood as merely itself for it has stood for too long as a symbol of profound connection between human beings. Around the storm center of actual sexual practice swirls a great weather system of emotion and behavior affecting a much wider arc of relations between men and women. The efforts of women today to reach a new place and to work out new roles for themselves do indeed complicate the pleasant idea of sex for pleasure

—but if we ever get close to the latter, we'll have done so by making progress in the former attempt as well.

The mysteries and terrors of old-fashioned sexual attitudes deserve to die. They were the product of mysteries and terrors that haunted all the relations between the sexes, however, and they can't be got rid of except as those overall relations shift. The honest effort of women to understand their needs as people and evaluate their emotional responses to others is, it seems to me, an essential part of a true sexual revolution. Such a revolution will go beyond the simple sensual pleasure promised by sexual freedom, and will build upon it strengthened relationships between lovers which would accord with personal values; which would be ways of demonstrating, and working out, personal values. Certainly, if the old roles are played out and the old rules no longer appropriate, we can't return to the directives and the mythology of the past. We will have to feel our way forward through complications and problems, learning as we go. We won't tame sex—who ever has?—or turn it into a draft horse, or a pussy cat. We will do best to realize that its wild power can help us reach the depths of being. That is where the profound transfigurations of personality take place and where our new experience of life can be tested and validated.

IX

Women who are moving out of their old place into man's world are taking on new responsibilities, and new kinds of responsibilities. We know that but I'm not sure we say it often enough. The women educators who asked me to speak to their annual meeting clearly had such responsibilities in mind when they chose the topic "Realizing Human Potential" for discussion. Thinking about this subject demanded a look at the affirmative values that the existence of the Women's Movement brings to American society today.

Realizing Human Potential

I like the theme of your meeting, "Realizing Human Potential: Focus on Women." But as I sat at my typewriter communing with the keys, and thinking of all the art and the wisdom that was potential in them, that is, in the Latin alphabet, and wondering how to reach it—as I sat there, it came to me that this title reminded me of an old story, a story about Calvin Coolidge. Maybe it's such an old story that it's new. Anyway, it seems to me pertinent, and so I shall repeat it here for those who have forgotten

Silent Cal, the man who never used two words where one would
do. It was told of him, nearly fifty years ago, that he went one day
to church while Mrs. Coolidge stayed home with some indisposi-
tion, and when he returned to Sunday dinner, his wife asked him
the topic of the sermon. What had the minister preached on? "On
sin," said Mr. Coolidge, and stopped. "Oh," said Mrs. Coolidge.
"And what did he say?" "He was against it," replied the President.

Now, realizing human potential is sort of the other side of the
coin. Who could—consciously—be against it? I can think of few
people since Hitler who have openly advocated suppressing human potential, and so I worry that it may be a little too easy to
say, Yes, yes, let us realize human potential, go right ahead, why
don't you take yours around the corner or out in the backyard
and get busy realizing it—where you aren't going to bother anyone
else. In fact, I am beginning to suspect that one of the problems
women have today (and I don't confine this to women in my mind,
but I am focusing there, as I have agreed to do) is an excess of
agreement at a superficial level, an excess—if you will—of lip
service.

I think, for example, of the directives issued by the Department
of Health, Education and Welfare on affirmative action programs
for educational institutions, all designed to realize human potential, and all pretty much negated by the recent revelation of Mr.
Secretary Weinberger that, while human potential is dandy, quota
strikes him as a dirty word. I think of the firm, straight-from-the-
shoulder declarations of business executives and presidents of
banks and chairmen of committees and school boards and—well,
you name them—who assert their belief in equal wages for women
and then find it beneath their dignity to wonder why these equal
wages somehow average out at a median income for women only
60 percent that of men.

And so, instead of talking positively about realizing human
potential, it occurs to me that it might be worthwhile to talk—or
at least to begin by talking—about *not* realizing human potential.
To concentrate, that is, on what gets in the way, and why this
aim, so widely subscribed to, must still be fought for. Because,
quite clearly, it must. Universal agreement that it's a fine thing
has not resulted in every capable human finding a spot to utilize

her or his capabilities. Something intervenes; or, more probably, some things intervene, some enemies must be fought.

Who can they be? They have not declared themselves openly. Even Mrs. Phyllis Schlafley appears to be opposing the Women's Movement on the grounds, articulated a quarter-century ago by Marynia Farnham, that women can best fulfill themselves by embracing the traditional female role of service to and exaltation of the male, and that thus will we best realize our potential. But they exist, these enemies, engaging like the White House plumbers in covert operations which, I'm afraid, succeed far better than those of the notable bunglers Liddy, Hunt and Ulasewicz. Who are they?

I think they are a lot of people but in the first instance, focusing on women, I think they are us. I think they are the creatures present in our minds who say, Why fight? Who say, Why go after that job? It will mean a hassle. Who say, Well, maybe I could have got it if I'd tried harder, but I really did not want it anyway. That's the woman in us—the old-fashioned, programmed-to-please woman—and we all contain some of her. I think she's fine, where she belongs—but she belongs at home. She belongs in personal relationships with people who are equally eager to please *us*. She does not belong in public, telling us that if we get tough about what we want, somebody isn't going to like it.

Let me talk about her a little, because while she inhabits and inhibits women, she isn't confined to our sex. Her male, Black, counterpart is called Uncle Tom. Uncle Tom says, Be a good nigger, smile and bow and scrape in public, in front of The Man, and then go off in private and choke on your hatred and rage—rage against the whites, and rage against yourself too. Black men have had trouble with him for centuries. And not only Black men, either. There's a famous letter that Anton Chekhov wrote, when he had got himself finally to Moscow and set out on his career as, really, the first of the great Russian writers who came from any class below the nobility, gentry or upper professions. (Dostoevski was at least the son of a physician, but Chekhov, whose grandfather had been born a serf, made himself first a physician and then a writer, and dragged his family along with him.) "Bit by bit," wrote Chekhov, "I am squeezing out of my veins the blood of a serf." And he didn't mean by that any snobbish distaste for his background—you have only to read his magnificent and understanding stories on the life of the poor, both urban and rural, to know that. What he meant was the acquiescence in degradation, the acceptance of it, the choice of a shameful humility that distorted the true human being, which had been forced on his ancestors. Uncle Tom, the blood of the serf, the pleasing, compliant woman—they are all related, all aspects of the same image.

What is that image? It is the image of a secondary person, an adjunct to the owners and rulers of the world, by whose leave only we live and move and have our being. Such a secondary person at best is assigned the role of helpmeet to others, and at worst, is seen not as human at all, but a living machine, a robot. A robot is programmed by others. It cannot direct its energies toward its own ends. In fact, it's not supposed to have ends—except the end of serving its masters. It is dehumanized, depersonalized. The very picture it has of itself is imposed from outside, and thus its sense of itself is divided and falsified. It is cut off from its own talents and their use, from a grasp on the world and a connection to the world of its own, from the pleasure of direct action, of stretching the muscles of body and brain and enjoying the confrontation of thought and reality. It means denying oneself—on order, yes—but an order that is taken in, accepted, factored through oneself. It means saying, I am labeled inferior, and the label is correct.

How many of us are really free from that image? How many have truly squeezed out of our veins the blood of the serfs we used to be? It is not an easy exercise and, let me remind you, while serfs in Russia and slaves in America were freed in the 1860's, the image and the self-image of woman had hardly begun to change in that decade. It's true that the New York State Legislature, in its wisdom, had already in 1860 granted married women the pitiful right to keep their own earnings, and to function, equally with their husbands, as the guardians of their children—rights they had not before possessed. It's true also that the demand for labor, and especially for nurses, during the years of the Civil War affected the fortunes of women, but these were not advances that were retained, nor were they even very great.

Writes William O'Neill in his study of the rise and fall of feminism in America, *Everyone Was Brave,* "In reality, women gained little of permanent use from their large contribution to the war. . . . The war only slightly increased the demand for women teachers . . . and when coeducation came into being, it was largely because there were not enough male students left to keep the colleges open. A few women became government clerks, and after the war some hung on to their ill-paying jobs, but government service did not become an attractive or important occupation for women until the next century."

There are many reports of what life was like for an active woman in those years. A famous one dates from the summer of 1873. In June of that year Susan B. Anthony was arraigned in a federal court in Canandaigua, New York, for violating the voting law. What she had done, in the election of 1872, was get fifty women to register and a dozen or so to vote. Within two weeks, she and they were arrested and charged with voting illegally, under a statute that provided for a three-year jail sentence. When the trial began, "the judge would not allow Anthony to testify on her own behalf. Her attorney and the district attorney presented five hours of argument, after which—without leaving the bench—the judge drew a previously prepared written opinion from his pocket and read it. He ruled that the Fourteenth Amendment—which guarantees the vote to all citizens—was inapplicable and directed the all-male jury to bring in a verdict of guilty."

He then made the mistake of asking Miss Anthony whether she had anything to say. There followed a duet, in which the Judge's remarks were confined to telling the prisoner to sit down and be quiet, while Miss Anthony, in whose veins no serf's blood ran, spoke of the denial of her right of consent as one of the governed, the denial of her right to a trial by jury of her peers, the denial of her sacred right to life, liberty and property, and enjoined the Court to remember that since the day of her arrest the previous November, this was the first time that either she or any person of her disenfranchised class had been allowed a word of defense before judge or jury. Unmoved except by exasperation, the judge fined her a hundred dollars and costs, to which Miss Anthony responded that the only thing she possessed was a debt of ten thousand dollars—which she intended to labor to repay but she would not pay one cent of the fine levied against her. "And," she concluded, "I shall earnestly and persistently continue to urge all women to the practical recognition of the old Revolutionary maxim, 'Resistance to tyranny is obedience to God.'"

It was a wonderful speech but it produced few immediate results. The serf status of women continued unchanged. It took another war for their demands for the vote to bear any fruit, and it took still a second one for their labor to be seen to be so necessary that the work they undertook was actually welcomed, praised and paid for at going rates. They had, of course, been working for generations—but it was women's work: work in the textile mills, where the tuberculosis rate ran three times normal; work on the hard-scrabble farms of the poor backcountry; dead-end office jobs; dull work, routine work and, above all, work with low pay. Call it serf's work and you won't be far wrong.

For the Victorian Age, the nineteenth century, which freed slaves and serfs, did quite the reverse for women. It attacked any independence and self-confidence they possessed, until so firm and determined a character as Florence Nightingale declared, in fury, that women didn't consider themselves as human beings at all. Over and over again, the Victorian Miss was praised for her child-like innocence and infantine simplicity—yes, really. When she married, she was told to merge her being in that of her husband, for only there lay a woman's true relation to the world and, even more astonishingly, to God. "He for God only," ran the lines of John Milton which Victorians loved so to quote, "she for God in him." Not only was the good wife instructed to give her whole life and being, body, time, property, thought and care to her husband, her *soul* was to be his too. The whole force of society, it would seem, was brought into play to prevent the ordinary process of growing up to adult and responsible maturity from taking place within the female mind and the female breast.

Of course it couldn't work, and it couldn't last, but this campaign for female fatuousness has left its mark. We are not rid of it yet. It lives on in our minds still, persuading us that second place is really very good, and probably all we deserve. We've come a long way, Baby, haven't we, so why should we complain if we haven't yet got to the top? If we can realize more of our potential than our mothers and grandmothers could—isn't that good enough?

Well—is it? You know, I think that really is the biggest question that women face today. Have we got far enough? Had we better stop here? It's a question that implies another—a sort of philosophical parallel to the first, and one that is perhaps even harder to answer. How seriously do we take ourselves? Do we consider ourselves, in Florence Nightingale's century-old formulation, as human beings? If we don't, human potential can't mean very much to us—not for ourselves, at any rate, though we can, of course, dedicate ourselves to helping other people realize theirs, which is what the Victorian canon recommended. But if we take ourselves seriously, we have to press on, until we can say that we are really responding—that is, being fully responsible—to the human demands made on us and, thus, bringing into play the potential talents and energies we command.

It sounds easy, in generalizations. It isn't, and you and I both know it. Even for professional women, the pattern of male activist and female adjunct or assistant is so deeply ingrained in us that we simply don't question it. Variants are odd, the old pattern is normal. Hannah Papanek talks about the effect of this kind of thinking in her very interesting contribution to the earlier mentioned collection of essays, *Changing Women in a Changing Society*. Dr. Papanek is writing about the two-person career. Basically, in our society, this means the husband-wife team which works to sustain the husband's professional vocation. Executive wives and, preeminently, political wives are prime examples.

But, as Dr. Papanek points out:

> These pairs [can also] include doctor and nurse, executive and secretary, principal and teacher, editor and research assistant, among many others. In each, the division of labor stresses the indispensability of the woman along with the man's higher status and higher salary. In each of these pairs, there are also obvious incongruities between expected and recognized areas of responsibility, as the woman's potential responsibility in her complementary job is tacitly recognized by all concerned to be very large, while neither her status

nor her salary recognizes this potential in formal terms. For
instance, nurses are tacitly expected to take over several important medical functions in cases of emergency, as is also
the case in the roles of many secretaries, assistants and
teachers. There is usually very little reciprocity, however.

That's an understatement!

I am sure that some of you recognize friends, at least, in this
description, if not yourselves. I was especially amused by seeing
not only women friends but wives of men friends explored in
another area which Dr. Papanek aptly names "helpmeet activities." These, she remarks, "include typing and editing manuscripts, collaborating in the laboratory, taking notes in classes
and meetings, and participating in fieldwork. Judging from the
frequency of authors' acknowledgements to their wives—'without
whom I would not have been able to work with the women in
X community'—there exists a large group of paraprofessional
sociologists and anthropologists in the United States." I was reminded vividly, reading this passage, of a Christmas card which
I received last year from a professor at an Ivy League university.
It greeted my husband and me and proceeded to report on the
activities of this good man and his wife. "We are hard at work,"
he wrote, "on *my* new book." By a preposterous coincidence, it
arrived on the morning I was scheduled to join a panel discussing
"Women in Literature: Has Anything Changed?" Has anything
changed indeed! I thought. Dear Countess Tolstoy, laboring over
Leo's manuscripts a century ago, I am sorry to say it has not.

The trouble with this situation is not really in the idea of a
two-person career. We live in a very complicated world, and
there are undoubtedly many areas of work which cannot be
handled well by one individual, without support from others. The
trouble is that when the two are of different sex, the roles in
the career are assigned in advance. The man is the lead figure, and
the woman is the chief of staff, along with being, quite often, the
chief cook and bottle-washer too. There's nothing wrong with
dividing the work, but why is it always divided this way? The
only variants occur in a very small area—an area in which we find
that the old Freudian tag "Anatomy is destiny" really happens to
be true; that is, when a woman has such a supreme talent—and it

is almost always a physically related talent: a singing voice, or an acting ability—that she and her manager form a two-person career unity. And there, we might note, it makes us very nervous if the manager, chief-of-staff type, is married to the star. Every good macho male, who might like to take the lady to bed himself, wonders how the husband can put up with the relationship. In short even a woman who is so superior that she can't be put down is considered out of place if her superiority extends to marriage. Perhaps she is only Galatea to his Pygmalion, but our minds still bristle at the idea that he stands, in any way, in her shadow.

How are we going to get rid of this pattern? We are all hesitant to assert our value, we women. We are all afraid of being called abrasive and tough. How many of us have not said, of radical liberationists, "Oh, I agree with a lot of things they stand for, but I certainly don't like their methods." Well, before you say that again, I wish you would stop and ask yourself just *why* you dislike their methods. Is it because they are not being womanly? Is it because they are likely, by these aggressive tactics, to alienate men? Well, maybe they are. Now take a deep breath, and repeat with me—So what?

Because it seems to me highly improbable that women are going to realize their human potential without alienating men—some men, anyway. Social change upsets people, there is just no doubt about it. Even so seemingly innocuous and aesthetic a measure as the trend for young men to grow their hair and their beards produced an enormous amount of alienation among their elders a few years ago. It was taken to be a very aggressive tactic. High-school boys were banned from classes, young men were bundled out of their cars on the highways and subjected to having their heads shaved, all because they had done nothing more than assert, by their appearance, that they did not share their parents' views on the relationship of cleanliness and godliness. We women are going to have to go a lot further than that. We actually want to be treated as equals by men, we want to compete openly for their jobs, if we can do them as well, we want our opinions to be listened to and our applications to medical school to be processed as if we were our brothers. Do you really imagine we aren't going to run into resentment? Of course we are. So what?

That doesn't mean, obviously—or I hope obviously—that it is sensible to go about using Kung Fu methods and kicking people in the crotch, or insulting the man who can give you a raise or a promotion. It certainly doesn't mean attacking the man you live with because he's a man. It is important for women to distinguish between behavior proper to the world outside and behavior proper to personal relationships, just because we have been for so long confined to the world of personal relationships. One of the chief things holding women back in the business world is that men who have not often worked with women assume that they are going to behave in public as the myth maintains they do in private —going to burst into tears if they are thwarted, gossip cattily, react emotionally to run-of-the-mill events and activities. Any woman with a job knows that, and most of us are quite capable of restraining our emotions when restraint seems proper—at least as capable as most men. But we clearly do have to bear in mind that what we do, in public, will often be interpreted according to the ideas in men's head. The important thing is not to get hung up over that. And that includes not getting hung up over being persevering, and even stubborn, if the situation warrants, out of fear that we will be called aggressive. It takes a while to change people's minds, but it can be done.

It can be done, that is, when we get clear in our own heads that going along with someone you love is one thing, and going along with someone you work for—or with—is quite another. Be prepared to know best; quite often you do. And be prepared to stick to it if you're sure you're right.

Look at it this way. The pattern of submissive woman supporting active male is one that both sexes have learned from the word go. Such patterns are oppressive to women and they are, increasingly, unrealistic and irrelevant to life today. But who is most aware of this? Who is most affected by the changes in the world which have drained these old ways of life of their validity? Women, of course. For the first time in history, I think, and it's a solemn thought, the massive changes in social and economic conditions, the long-term trends of technological advance, the results of medical research, have had an effect on women's lives which is greater than their effect on the lives of men. Suddenly, and really for the first time, it is women who are in the forefront of change—or, realistically, who are bearing the brunt of it. Future shock has knocked on our door first. We know more about it than men because we have been coping with it longer—coping with it without much help from the rest of society.

A good deal of my book *Man's World, Woman's Place* was devoted to a study of how changing reality has made out-of-date the old myths summed up in the two familiar phrases "It's a man's world" and "Woman's place is in the home." It's quite a long book, and it took me six years to write, so I shan't try to sum it up here, but let me touch on a high point or two. Once upon a time, a great deal of economically valuable work was done at home, by women who lived there, as men did, and by the children born to both. And during those long centuries, almost every human being had some kind of place, assigned by class or inherited vocation. To have a place, to work at home, was the fate of humankind, and the real meaning of home was very different from what we think of it as being today. The rich and the great lived in manor houses or castles, with some of the lesser kind clustering there—about 20 percent of the population. The rest of the folk lived around the big house, in slum dwellings, or else they scratched out their livings from the earth, or from under it in mining villages, or on the coast, from the sea. As the cities arose and grew, the great merchant houses also maintained their service population and the satellite slums around them. Only with the rise of the middle classes, beginning toward the end of the Middle Ages and spreading widely just three centuries or so ago, did we begin to get the sort of patterns of living that we think of when we use the word "home"—the house where one family lived with its children and a few relatives and servants, a place which was more residence than workshop. For in the old days, the great houses were factories and academies and trading centers as well as places to eat and sleep.

Those middle-class homes are what we still have in mind when we use the word—but another change has overtaken them now. They too have vanished, replaced by the four-room high-rise perch, or the suburban split-level or, increasingly, the jacked-up mobile home. The old folks have moved out, and if they haven't moved away, to Leisure Village, Southern California, the young marrieds have crossed the country and settled temporarily a thousand miles away. Social mobility has destroyed the remnant of the extended family. And that is one of the most important factors resulting from social change.

Even more important, perhaps, than the departure of kinfolk or domestic help from the family hearth is the departure of economically valuable work. Even when I was a girl, a lot of sewing was done at home; so was the laundry and the mending, and food was prepared pretty much from scratch. That was in the city. On the farms, where a much greater proportion of our population lived, the family worked as a group to make its collective living. A generation or two before that, it wasn't uncommon for even more of the necessities of living to be manufactured at home. Today we find them delightful artifacts, but women didn't make quilts as artistic endeavors—though the making did allow them to use their creative abilities in a satisfying way—they made them to keep their families warm. They stuffed pillows with down from the geese or feathers from the chickens, they slept on cornhusk mattresses, and slaughtering and preserving in the autumn provided food for the winter. I'm sure I don't have to labor the point. Some of you perhaps grew up in the middle of that sort of life, on the busy farm, and many chronicles exist of the chores and the joys of that existence. But it is an existence that has vanished.

Vanished not because anyone intended it so, but because of a long-term, profound, economic shift. Work moved away. We don't make clothes, we buy them. We don't make soup out of a veal knuckle and the carcass of Sunday's turkey and a soup bunch culled from the kitchen garden at a cost of nothing at all or a penny or two a serving—we buy it in a can. And because we buy it in a can, the cash economy has replaced the old do-it-yourself work of the home, and the things we used to make have to be paid for. Which lays upon the adults in the family the obligation to exchange their labor for dollars. Which means that women have to go to work—outside the home, because you can't earn much inside it.

Now the old-fashioned pattern of thinking which directs the structure of the outside world and of the minds of the men who run it stumbles right here. Why, it asks, do women have to work for money? That's man's job, isn't it? Aren't we men supposed to look after women, win the bread and bring home the bacon? And, fairly often, these good kind men get upset at the thought that we women don't think they can do it. They find it a reflection on them, a criticism of them. And that's too bad—because they *can't* do it, by any means, and they never have. Women have always worked, and worked hard. The family that can be sustained by the work of one pair of hands has been the exception rather than the rule throughout history.

So today the fact that 50 percent of women of working age hold jobs is not remarkable. The real change is that they do their work outside the home, and away from the place where their children are raised. They followed the work, in the normal course of economic events, just as men have, not because some "monstrous regiment" of liberationists told them to, but because if you need money, you go where it's at. And roughly two hundred years ago the textile tycoons of northern England discovered that it was cheaper to put power looms in a large building called a factory, and hire hands to weave the cloth there, than it was to contract out the work to handloom weavers at home, in the old-fashioned way. The social changes we are trying to cope with do not arise from some fiendish plot of bra-burning females, but from our old, old friend—the Industrial Revolution. It has remade work, remade society, and now it is remaking the family. I submit to you that coping with its demands is a larger task than can be undertaken by women alone—especially by one woman, desperately trying to keep her head above water, and thinking her family's problems are unique and personal. They are not. They are social, and they demand a social response. The great importance I assign to today's liberation movement is that it *is* a response to these public, social demands.

So when we talk about realizing human potential, we are talking about a desire and an urge that will reward us with personal satisfaction, but that cannot be achieved individually. As we change the ideas in our own heads, as we begin to think of ourselves as human beings whose opinions and values and judgments are as weighty as those of other people who share this earth—that is, men

—we will get nowhere if we try to act alone. True, we must begin at home, in our own minds and hearts. We must cast off the crippling image of the past, of woman the second sex, the eternal helpmeet, the nurturer who wins her reward through others and by their favors. This, I repeat, is not to say that the affection and regard of those we love is not a great reward. But why is it a reward that is sex-linked? The ability to take pleasure in the achievements of those who are dear to us is surely a quality that we can allow to the male sex as well as the female. What has held women back and down is not affection for others—we need more true affection and always will. What has limited women is the enforced behavior exacted from us *as if* we stood in a relationship to all men that demanded the loving help which can only be given sincerely to a few. It is the insistence that what we want to give to some should be given to all whether we like it or no, automatically, because we are women.

That first step is vital. Denying that one is by nature assistant and helpmeet is not self-assertion, but simply the affirmation of self-confidence. With it comes the ability to plan and think ahead, to hold to convictions and intentions and to steer a course through life to a desired end. Confidence in oneself and one's judgment is the basis on which we conceive the future. It is a proud thing for older women to see how our younger sisters are beginning to do this today in terms of their own lives, how their conceptions of the future are no longer bounded by the day on which they marry and live happily ever after. More and more, they are projecting lives for themselves in which their own self-determined activities will play a continuing part. Careers and vocations are being factored in and taking their place beside the day when one weds and goes ahead to make a happy life thereafter, but no longer simply expects one as ordained by a fairy tale. This is a recognition of reality, for happiness is a process that must be made and remade, not a state of eternal beatitude which can be won once and for all.

But when we have changed our own self-images, there follows the task of seeing that those images become visible and operant to others. We all know that female stereotypes still haunt the minds of most men. We are the *other* sex as well as the *second* sex, and the very idea of that otherness stamps a great similarity upon us.

For in one primary way we are all alike to men—that is, we are different from them! When men think about each other, they think of individuals with various capabilities or defects. But when they think of women, it's a rare male who doesn't begin with a stereotype—women are emotional, women can't plan ahead, women vote for a candidate because he's got sex appeal, there's no sense in giving them job training, they'll quit to have a baby, they can't make hardheaded, tough decisions and stick to them. I daresay you can supply other bits of ancient wisdom to fit in here. Now, with a little help from their female friends and colleagues, men can get over these hang-ups, which stem from their inadequate educations, and realize that women are actually as various in their interests and potential capacities as men—but they need that help, and it is up to us to give it to them. So I think the second step toward realizing our human potentialities lies here. First, let's believe in them ourselves. Second, let's be willing to talk, and act, on our beliefs. That means joining together with other like-minded humans—at the moment that mostly means women, but it won't always—to take political action; to support the Equal Rights Amendment; to prevent the reintroduction of crippling abortion laws; to see that adequate affirmative action programs are put into effect. Beyond these, there is an infinitude of neighborhood, local issues that touch our lives as women and as human beings.

Group action at political levels can be very effective, if it is patient, persevering and longheaded. And what's more, it carries a bonus, for the more you do it, the more you know how to do it. Professional politicians have been under attack lately for cynicism and corruption. Well, let me suggest to you that the solution to these malpractices is not leaving politics to the politicians, nor is it wandering out into the arena as amateurs in the belief that purity of heart will win battles by itself. The solution lies in accepting the fact that politics is a lengthy, complicated process and not a one-time thing, and learning the ropes. Women have done that before. Some of the first wave of feminists, like Carrie Chapman Catt, were very able politicians. The defense against corruption lies inside. It consists in knowing what you're aiming at, getting your priorities straight. Political action, in short, is a very good school for learning how to deal with the world at large and with all complicated structures and processes.

It's also an area in which able women can help men to learn something about how effective women can be in dealing with public affairs, and in coping with large-scale human problems. Over and over again I've found that men who have worked on a level with women, in politics or in business, have a quite different attitude toward women from men who have not. The stereotype has faded. They listen when we talk. I'm sure you've noticed this too. Give men a little time, demonstrate enough female talent, and the reality principle will go to work to prove that all capabilities don't belong on the male side of the fence.

For reality is on our side. We are working with history and not against it. If women are bearing the brunt of social change, if we have more than a nodding acquaintance with future shock, that's tough, but it also gives us a head start in knowing how to cope with change. What's more, we may be more flexible and imaginative in dealing with it than men are because we have fewer old rules prescribing traditional actions to tie our hands. I note, for instance, the attempts of worried business managements to deal with the problems of worker alienation that are plaguing industry today. These managements are discovering, to their intense surprise and dismay, that assembly-line workers are bored and frustrated by the repetitious, machinelike quality of their work, by their lack of control over it, by its inhuman, machine-made tempo, by the fact that they never finish anything but only do a little piece of a whole job. It's pretty astonishing to me that they're astonished, but they are, and the reaction of the labor unions isn't much more relevant. Some of them, like the UAW, are asking for early retirement and voluntary overtime, which at least signifies a recognition of the terrible pressure of this kind of work (which of course isn't confined to men. There are plenty of women on the line, tending machines). But the usual reaction is, pay them more money and they'll put up with these life-denying jobs.

However, where attempts are being made to change the jobs themselves and remedy the evil, it's fascinating to note that making work more bearable simply means reintroducing old human patterns—patterns with which women are familiar, even if men have forgotten them and pushed them aside. Instead of work norms and tempos dictated from on high, set up work teams, let them decide how they want to tackle a job, all of them together. Let them shift jobs around instead of sticking to just one. Invite input and ideas from the men and women on the job instead of taking it all from the efficiency expert with the stop watch. Retraining for those who want to change their jobs in middle life is recommended; so is continuing education that can help not only wage workers but management men get over the hump of a dead-end job. It's all documented in the HEW report *Work in America,* prepared under the direction of Elliot Richardson. I read it with great interest, and as I did, I kept thinking—but we *know* this! It's what women have been doing for themselves more and more; it's nothing but ordinary common sense, to try and get human dimensions and satisfactions into work—how funny that it's such a big deal!

But then I began to think—good God! Maybe the blindness that squeezed human qualities out of jobs and work life in the first place is the price we have paid for dividing the world in two by sexes and excluding women from public activities. Society has been assigning emotional rewards and personal involvement to the private sphere and making them women's business, out of place in the world of work. And now we find that the world of work has been so drained of emotion and reward that it's become almost unlivable. It isn't man's world now, it's the rat race. And the only ones who can realize their potential in a rat race—are rats.

In closing, then, let me suggest that realizing human potential can only be done by calling on all the human race for its achievement. If we begin with ourselves and move on to group action as women, we are not going to stop there. Just by moving out of our secluded place we are bringing a much needed refreshment to the world of action, the world of men, if only by insisting that its values need rethinking. If our assigned sphere has got too narrow, that other world has suffered too, grown superficial and nonsupportive, maybe even a little lunatic, for madness is often characterized by the absence of appropriate emotion; and surely a world which assumes that a day's work is bound to be made up of frustrating, burdensome boredom seems a little too madly calm about that judgment to me. So we have much to do. Let us remember that what we do for ourselves, in sober responsibility, in taking seriously the needs we feel and the ideas we generate, is not done for ourselves alone. It will profit others too. Perhaps in the end, if man's world and woman's place can flow together, they will join to make a human universe out of the rat race.

X

This short piece was conceived of as something jolly to do, and so it was; but it turned out to be something else as well, a perfect example of what the article itself was saying. Since both editors involved in its history have departed from the magazine that commissioned it, I think I can tell the story without embarrassing anyone. And it's certainly a parable.

Very well. A couple of years ago, *Esquire* decided to put out an issue on women, edited by women. One of the women in charge asked me to contribute a piece responding to the familiar query, "Why Does the Women's Movement Have No Sense of Humor?" I did so. The woman editor called me to say it was fine. Two weeks passed. One morning the mail brought the article back, with a letter explaining that while the women doing the job enjoyed it, masculine top brass didn't feel that it was the thing at all—distinctly not funny.

"Well," as I remarked to the woman editor at our next meeting, "now you know why the Women's Movement has no sense of humor."

Happy ending—well, sort of. The article was bought and published (though cut) by a woman's magazine; which was nice for me. But I still wish it had run where the male eye would have fallen on it more easily.

Why Does the Women's Movement Have No Sense of Humor?

What a good question! I'm glad you asked me that since I believe (perhaps too optimistically) that inside every Male Chau-
vinist Pig there's a human being struggling to get out. Maybe a
candid reply will inspire those striving humans to struggle harder.

In the first place, why *should* the Women's Movement have a
sense of humor? Do you burst into peals of laughter reading
Malcolm X or *The Thoughts of Chairman Mao?* Who played that
smash week in Moscow in 1917—Smith and Dale, or Lenin and
Trotsky? The Women's Movement is *serious*. Some of it, not all
of it, is revolutionary. I think myself that a revolution in technology, economics and the underpinnings of social relations has
already happened, and that we all would do well to face up to it
and adjust our minds and our myths to the data of existence. But
revolutionary or no, and the Movement is anything but mono-
lithic, it is serious about its aims; especially so because one of the
severest limitations on women's ambitions and activities has been
the male view that their work and their goals are secondary if not
actually frivolous. A good way to support this view and hold down
rising feminine confidence is to describe Movement actions as
jokes. Thus, the drive for equal opportunity and access to male
prerogatives is often presented as those pickets around McSorley's
Bar. What's serious, men ask, about *them?*

Well, what's serious about a business lunch? The IRS assumes
you do business at one, so I will too. If women can't attend them
because restaurants are permitted to practice sex segregation, that's
a serious invasion of their rights. And believe me, in many professions the lunching, drinking, dining sessions that used to be limited
to men (the past tense of course is madly wishful) were (are) places

where candidates for promotion are put through their paces, discussed and helped on their way. Excluding women from these gatherings excludes them effectively from easy consideration for jobs, raises and steps up the ladder. In the Old Boys' Network there are few girls. No doubt you can't do away with the Old Boys' Network by legislation, but at least you can stop supporting it by legal segregation.

It isn't the beer at McSorley's that women want, any more than it's the squash courts at the Harvard Club that Radcliffe alumnae have been aiming at. It's a natural place in the natural social life of business, the professions and academia instead of the old "separate but equal" accommodations which operate against women in the same way they operate against Blacks. Picketing McSorley's may have been roundabout as well as symbolic, but it wasn't irrelevant and I even think it was kind of funny. Funnier anyway than being a female full professor who is expected to "join the ladies" when she dines at the President's house while her male colleagues settle down to a discussion of campus affairs.

You say that doesn't happen anymore? I wonder why. Could it be the effect of the Women's Movement and its humorless pursuit of women's rights?

So my first answer to the question about lack of humor in the Women's Movement is: What's so funny, anyway? Unequal wages unequal opportunities, closed doors and closed minds don't make for hilarity in the people who run into them. Instead these people tend to argue, shout and repeat themselves endlessly, which is certainly irritating and boring to the people who don't run into inequities and so, quite naturally, can't see what the fuss is all about. "Do you think there's something wrong with being a woman?" an agitated young man asked me the other day. Alas, I do, and here's a simple for-instance. In the field of teaching at elementary and secondary school level, where women are a majority and "equal wages" supposedly an enforced obligation—women working full time in 1969 averaged $7,200. Full-time male teachers pulled down $10,000. I'm willing to say with the fabled Frenchman, *"Vive la petite différence!"* But does it have to add up to $2,800, more than a third of the female wage? To me that's not so petite.

Another response, complementary to the first, is also a question: Whose sense of humor, yours or mine? Too often men's jokes about women are put-downs, often sexist and sometimes racist too. A good example is the oldie about the anthropologist who sees a Black woman pushing a baby carriage, looks inside, discovers the baby has red hair and says, "How interesting! Did the father have red hair too?"

To which the woman replies, "I don't know, Boss, he didn't take his hat off."

The funniest thing about that joke has got to be the state of mind of the man who told it to me. He clearly wasn't trying to make me laugh, but did he realize what he was doing? The urge to keep women in their place by insulting them breaks over into irrationality so fast that one can't be certain. For instance when two women from NOW went up to Yonkers to speak at the Rotary Club (by invitation), one member addressed them thus: "If my wife said anything about women's lib, I'd leave her. She's got a pocketful of credit cards. What more freedom does she need?" This genial assessment of his wife's interests and aspirations came from a retired admiral who had served as City Tax Commissioner. Isn't it odd that a man intelligent and responsible enough to hold those posts should *unhesitatingly* reveal how meanly he thinks of the woman he courted and wed? I mean, if we're going to laugh, this kind of self-exposure strikes me as funny.

Indeed there are magic moments when failure of imagination is so complete that these put-downs attain a grotesque charm. The *Sunday Times* of London has been publishing a series of them recently, under the title "Woman's Role." Here's a snatch of conversation from an audience participation program on radio:

"Good morning, Mrs. ——. It's very nice to hear from you."

"Good morning, Jimmy. Thank you."

"Tell me something about yourself. What does your husband do?"

Once alerted to this kind of unconscious male humor one finds examples everywhere. How about those two late papers on women where Freud repeatedly refers to "the fact of female castration"? What kind of a fact can that be? So far as I know, no woman in Western society has suffered even the trauma of circumcision. How about the up-to-date advice offered by Dr. Alex Comfort in *The Joy of Sex* to women about to be raped? Dr. Comfort is inclined to think that they must have done something to provoke this behavior, a well-known male view, but he suggests a way to put the rapist off if the provocateuse subsequently changes her mind: Let her have a bowel movement. Unfortunately he doesn't say how to do this.

Men, in fact, are funny people. So are women. Both often deserve to be laughed at—as people. But to laugh at people in groups is to deny them their full humanity because it denies their individual diversity. Jokes about Italians or Swedes or Chinese are intended to set these folk off in categories separate from the fun-loving human rest of us. It makes them lesser breeds without the law, whose opinions we can ignore. And so, when I pick up *A Treasury of Humorous Quotations for Speakers, Writers and Home Reference,* I am not astounded to discover that there are 105 funny things to say about women, and only 6 about men. It appears that dominant males, like Sam Goldwyn's comedies, are not to be laughed at. Which is all right with me, for I don't want to group them either. Some of them are quite nice, though even the nicest find it a bit hard to laugh at themselves.

It is this ability to laugh at oneself that is usually meant by "having a sense of humor," and I agree that it isn't a striking attribute of the Women's Movement qua Movement. One more reason, then, and that out of history. To laugh at yourself when you're top dog is appealing and humanizing. When underdogs laugh at themselves, it's different. It's a way to ease the pain of being stuck in a life situation you can't control: the sort of gallows humor which prompts Jews to tell anti-Semitic jokes. Lately a lot of underdogs have decided they don't need to be stuck. Black comics aren't telling Stepin Fetchit jokes any more, and women are laughing less at those familiar quips about women drivers, mothers-in-law and dumb blondes. Fewer and fewer are even laughing, as Dorothy Parker did, at the "normal" pain of loving a man who cheats or walks out, in the old grin-and-bear-it syndrome. The "grin" used to be part of the "bearing it"; but if you can walk out yourself, you really don't need to do either. Which doesn't necessarily mean that you'll grin less, simply that you'll enjoy it more because you'll be grinning at the oddities of the whole human condition.

Like the fascinating fact that the most popular speaker at Yale University in 1972 was a woman who was talking about chimpanzees. I'm not sure whether that's a triumph for men, women or apes (though it's certainly a tribute to an individual named Jane Goodall). Who knows? Perhaps there will come a day when the life-style of primates called women will seem as relevant to Yale men as that of chimpanzees; a day when group think and group jokes will be over, and we can sit down in all our individual differences and laugh together at the same things.

XI

Another editor's commission directed me toward a very different area of women's concern. *Ms.* asked for an article on the questions that surfaced in the minds of older women when they looked at the Liberation Movement. The whole topic of age, of the cruel fracture in the lives of both men and women when the major activities of maturity are broken off, is one we're only beginning to face honestly. The shrinkage in the time span and in the importance of woman's traditional role means that her central, normative occupation, mothering, dwindles and disappears when she is still physically and mentally at a peak of capability.

Women's liberation has a great deal to offer the middle-aged and elderly, and more of us are realizing that all the time. But the training of women who are now past their youth and the commitment many have made to traditional patterns of living and of thought make the decision to change such patterns difficult. Believing as I do that talking together and working together toward common goals is the preeminent means for building a new community among humans, I wrote this article in the hope that it would explain something about the Movement to older women, and something about older women to their daughters.

Breaking the Age Barrier

I have a problem about being nearly sixty: I keep waking up in the morning and thinking I'm thirty-one. It makes me feel like the woman in the laxative ads on TV: "You're as young as you feel!" I do not find her an acceptable role-model, but here I am, missing my real age by a generation. It's not that I want to be thirty-one, nor that I think anyone else imagines me to be thirty-one, for the first is untrue and the second is impossible. In fact, for someone who likes to think she's reality-oriented, it's a mighty silly feeling. So why do I have it?

It occurs to me that the reason may have something to do with the fact that I've worked all my life in the same field, without a series of cutoff points and new starts. Writing has given me not only a career, but a continuous identity. I wanted to be a writer in my teens, I worked at writing when I was in college and through drudge jobs that I did to make a living, I wrote when I was pregnant, I wrote when I was raising babies, I wrote while they grew up and went off to college and their own careers and marriages—in short, I wrote, I am writing and I shall (please God) bang this typewriter till the day I die. I am very lucky and I know it. My husband told me that if I wanted to write and didn't, he'd disown me, and from the minute we could afford household help, we've had it by our joint decision. Most women don't have that luck, and I know that too. I'm not sitting here saying, like a condescending idiot, "Oh, go ahead and have a career; it's easy, you can do it too." It isn't easy.

But equally, I am positive that the bonus my work has given me is not unique. Through it I gained self-confidence and a sense of self, of being a person who has some value. That is what everyone wants. It is one of the primary goals of the Women's Movement to help women acquire it. If writing gave it to me, other people have found other ways to achieve this sense of identity, of self-respect and of respect for other people that (it seems to me) goes with it. I didn't have much confidence in myself when I was young. Maybe thirty-one was the age at which I began to possess some. At any rate it's the age I was when I finished my second book and could begin to believe that writing books was really what I did, not just a lucky happenstance, one brass ring from the merry-go-round.

So if I talk from my own experience, it's because I want to work out from it to see what it can mean for other women. First, it's clear that what one does and how one feels about what one does are basic to one's self-image. The problems women have here are not, we know, just our individual problems. I want to examine some of the problems that *these* problems make, both for women —older women especially—and for the Movement itself. Difficulties can occur on both sides, unless the lived experience of older women is factored into where we are now. Betty Friedan, in *The Feminine Mystique,* made us all familiar with the depression-swamped housewives of the 1950's who simply couldn't feel that the homemaking job, being touted as so significant and essential, was either of those things. Isolated and unable to challenge the myth, each woman felt herself devalued and deviant because she couldn't find pleasure in what was supposed to be her proper work.

Indeed and indeed that's all true, but it's not the whole story. Quite a lot of women, now middle-aged, have accepted the myth that the traditional role of women is the proper one. These non-rebels accommodated to the myth and have by now a lifetime of commitment to that role. But no one can do this without tying up some of her personal image and her self-esteem in the role she has taken on. Once she's done that, it's hard for her to break away.

Roles are not simply definitions of identity. They are programs for behavior, related to activities and to social situations which involve other people. The old traditional female role directs women how to behave and how not to both in public and in private, which is very convenient. It assures us that if we follow the rules we won't be embarrassed in public, while in private we'll achieve the goal of happy-wife-and-motherdom. But it does more than that: it structures the world of women by ordering our priorities and telling us what is important—which is even more vital for us to know than what is right.

Those who accept this old role have used it to find a way to explain the world and come to an accommodation with life. It is, as women have been writing from Mary Wollstonecraft on, a crippling accommodation. But—here's my point—*it's better than none*. And if you have chosen it and committed yourself to it and tied up your self-esteem in performing your role-duties well, you are going to be very upset if someone comes along and tells you that you have made the wrong choice—because that means that you have been spending your life on nonsense.

When some older women look at the Women's Movement, this is what it seems to be saying: The goals you chose are too small. You've been satisfied with too little. You've been cheated out of your birthright and your chance at a full and meaningful life, and you let it happen. Attacks on the old role are not only frightening to women who've spent a life at it and aren't at all sure they know how to do anything else. They also appear as personal attacks on one's own judgment and self-esteem.

Self-esteem is very precious to women because it isn't easy for us to come by. The old mystique not only assures us that we are inferior beings, but that we are *properly* inferior, sentenced by God and anatomy to subordinate participation in life. A chief purpose of consciousness-raising is to restore confidence in oneself and one's capacity to judge the world and make sensible, practical decisions. It isn't until we trust ourselves that we can begin to trust each other for if I, a woman, think I'm inferior, how can I respect you, another woman? The two things go together. But the Movement, to some older women, speaks with a forked tongue, just like White Man. It's terribly easy to feel that it's saying, You made a bad mistake back there when you were young, you've put in all your waking hours on wasting time, your past doesn't mean a thing.

Now the past can't be written off that way. If your life has been made up of housewifery and rearing children, you haven't just done this, you've *reinforced* (as the psychologists say) by your day-to-day actions a belief that housewifery and child-raising are a woman's central and significant contributions to society, the crown of her life, all she need concern herself about. For if the old role tells women "You're inferior," it also offers a definition of limited but possible success. If your daughters are pretty and popular and married young, if your sons get good jobs and your husband comes home to dinner every night, you've reached your goal and you can relax. Isn't the Movement questioning this definition of success? Yes. Isn't it putting down women who have striven for such success? No. But women who are not familiar with the Movement and take their views on it from the mass media are all too likely to assume that both things are true. Even the simple statement that women want something more from life than housewifery, want a place in a wider world, can be interpreted as a criticism of women who haven't ventured outside the traditional role. A woman may know very well that she isn't getting enough out of life, and yet fear to look facts in the face, for if she does look, if she admits her unhappiness, then she is confronted with the logical next step—to change her life.

That can be terribly hard even to imagine. Daring has been trained out of many women, along with ambition and decisiveness, for it had no place in the old role. Part of the great value of the Movement is the support that women are able to offer other women through it. But on the outside looking in, that isn't apparent. Instead, subordinate, put-down women will often be afraid to change even when in fact they have little to lose. For change means learning new ways to cope with the world and, if you suspect that you are an inferior human being because you're a woman, you'll doubt your ability to do that and you'll shrink back from the demands that new approaches to the world do indeed make. How can other woman help you? They're inferior too. And men—well, they will disapprove at the least. By moving out of the old role, you'll be losing their help and inviting their mockery.

There's an extra bind on older women, too. In our society we are expected to feel inferior not only as women, but also because we are old. Where a tough old matriarch in a traditional society might feel capable of coping with the unexpected, American women have been more likely to hang back. In some cultures old women go up the pecking order to become bossy mothers-in-law and arbiters of morals and social standing. We don't, not often; not since the days of Mrs. Astor and Mrs. Potter Palmer. Older women here are apt to slide down the pecking order toward a lonely old age. And that destiny haunts women who have not had the chance to reach out and cope with life independently.

The pattern of behavior which many older women learned when young seemed to be offering just two opposing choices: you could be "womanly," that is charming, accepting, anxious to please and clever about how to do it, or you could be the opposite, which meant being tough and assertive—and disliked. It's an artificial choice, of course, a forced and unreal one. But its pressure deforms women still, by assuring us that if we turn our backs on femininity, we must expect to run into hostility from men and from other "feminine" women too. I am ashamed to confess that this makes me so mad there are times when I react to the word "femininity" the way Hermann Goering did to the word "culture"—I want to reach for a gun. Which is unfair and stupid on my part, because any woman who has bought the old role and the mystique has had to accept the humility packaged into it, and can't afford to risk the dislike of the powerful—i.e., men. I think the limits and obstacles that the old role forces on women are very often resented furiously, underneath. But resentment or not, if you feel you're inferior and weak, you can't take a chance on antagonizing the powerful. I suspect that some of the animosity expressed by some women toward the Women's Movement is a direct result of the resentment that the old roles call forth. Because this resentment can't be directed against men, out of fear of them, it's misdirected at women who seem to be defying men, breaking rules, "getting away" with something.

My experience saved me from this kind of distortion and fear because it involved me, directly and on my own, with the outer world. That's why it's worth talking about. I have had a means by which I could test, and validate, the general statements which our society makes about life. I have not had to accept world views filtered exclusively through other people's lives and judgments.

Many, many other women in middle life or aging have certainly had analogous opportunities to look at the world on their own, interact with the processes of events and arrive at their own conclusions. Over and over, in the last few years when work on my book *Man's World, Woman's Place* was raising my consciousness in a sort of self-help way, I've talked with friends looking back over their lives and finding there a strong, true pattern of reality, a continuing self, an identity stretching back over the years. As long ago as the mid-1950's, when I was writing *The Third Choice*, my tough older heroine, Diana, was doing just this, probing her past for the underlying meaning of her life. "I am the same person I was when I was eleven," she says to herself in the first scene of that book, and this sense of herself is what pulls her through a bad accident and her first realization of aging. It does not justify her actions. A good deal of the book involves her realization of where she went wrong and did wrong. But it nerves her to understand the consequences of her actions and to see herself as a fully responsible player on the stage of life.

Responsibility and dignity go together. What the Movement has to offer women (one thing, that is) which may be of particular importance to older women is the opportunity *to take themselves seriously.* If all that you are doing with your life is following the rules that your role assigns to you, you are escaping full responsibility. That reduces the importance of your actions—you're simply behaving, you're not making decisions and achieving goals. You are, in part, a programmed object. The feeling that you are leaving this behind and taking charge of your own life is one of the most thrilling experiences that any human being, male or female, can enjoy.

In response, older women who are living this experience can offer younger ones an overview of what our lives have meant to us. Self-realization is deepened by communication, and communication, of course, is a two-way street. It's still true, I'm afraid, that there are very few older women who are seen as compelling role-models for young women. We have a few heroines, but not enough yet. I was talking to two friends recently, one in her forties, one in her thirties, and we all had to say that in thinking (or dreaming, which may be more important) our futures, most of the figures we wove our ambitions around were men. True, Edna St. Vincent Millay and Elinor Wylie were writing when I was growing up, and they were career ideals for me—but life was very stingy with *behavior* models then. And this is still the case. It may take a long time for true heroines to emerge; but *in the meantime,* we older women who know we aren't heroines can offer our younger sisters, at the very least, an honest report of what we have learned and how we have grown.

I would very much hope that more and more women who have had successful careers would begin to do this. Some are; but some hold back. One gets the feeling after a while that successful women have problems with self-esteem too, just as much as do those who've stayed at home in "woman's place." I think it comes back to that choice I spoke of, in which the old role offered women only two options—to be womanly and loved, or unwomanly and disliked. Many a career woman will have opted for the latter choice but, in doing so, have bought the idea that she's losing as much as she's gaining—has to lose in order to gain.

It works this way. A woman who has made it on her own in man's world may very well derive the self-esteem she needs *from being special;* from beating "them" at their own game. If so, her specialness will last only as long as the game lasts and when it ends, so will her confidence. Now the Movement declares it wants to change the rules of the game. To such a woman, it must seem that the Movement is going to remove the whole basis of her sense of self-worth, which is tied to the status quo just as much as is that of her housewife sister. Like her sister, the female executive or top professional may also suffer from disvaluing herself as a person. Even if she has turned her back on the behavior prescribed by the old female role, she has often bought the values that go with it.

Why doesn't her own success convince her that women are not inferior beings? Is it guilt over breaking the rules? Is it self-doubt? Not surprising if it's the latter, for every woman who's fought her way up the ladder in man's world has, at one time or another, been regarded as a freak; has faced disapproval because she has not chosen to find "fulfillment" in woman's role, woman's place. She's had to find her self-confidence in career confidence. But career confidence can be shaky: what happens if you fail, if your status in man's world drops, if your rating goes down? Competitiveness gets programmed in here as a way of preserving one's own specialness, for the Bitch-Goddess Success does not patronize men only.

The suffragettes spoke of women who "hugged their chains." Success has a way of forging chains too. Power corrupts, and so does weakness, for both are isolating. A very important gift of the Movement to older women is the end of isolation, including age-grade isolation. I know some older women feel that the Movement is by and for the young, that "It will help my daughter," but "It's too late for me." I don't agree. Knowing each other and working together will help all of us. Why should we imagine that "It's too late"? Too often those words cover a reaffirmation of weakness, a choice of withdrawal into unreasonable timidity. We demean ourselves when we do that, we accept the role-judgment that women are passive and subordinate. To cite my own experience again, when I wrote *Man's World, Woman's Place* in my fifties, it was like writing a second first book. I had to read enormously, of course, but I also had to learn a quite new way of writing, with no help from the fictional skills I'd developed in the past. In a way, I think that the willingness to do something like this, to go on learning, is why I don't mock myself more for that silly wake-up delusion that I'm thirty-one. I shall certainly be proved wrong one day, but until I am, I shall think of the work I want to do, the work that lies ahead, *as if* I were thirty-one; shall be as ready to plan vast projects and tangle with new ideas.

God knows, I am not unique. Let me tell you about Vista volunteer Minerva Hathaway, aged sixty-two, of Kingsport, Tennessee. When her seven children had grown up and the last one was married, she moved to Florida to sit, as she says, "and wait to be visited." That didn't last long. She heard about Vista from a lawyer connected with the agency, decided to train for work there and went to Tennessee because she'd lived in Oak Ridge for a while when her husband was working in the A-bomb program and she had got to know and admire the independent mountain people.

Like all Vista workers, she lives among, and in the manner of, the people she is working with. She is especially committed to the very poor and the very old, the badly deprived. A minibus program she dreamed up, and got financed by the Office of Economic Opportunity, shuttled the isolated old to market and to church and other gatherings. People who don't know how to get food stamps, or even that they're eligible for them, get helped. She says she's in the protest business. It doesn't hurt that she used to be a tax consultant in Hollywood, for one bureaucracy is very like another and her earlier experience feeds in. She likes to get people together, all ages, all social strata; she likes to get them talking; she's going to work on luring more middle-aged, middle-class people into Vista; her plans for the future include desegregating senior citizens' groups and, in the meantime, getting them some chairs to sit down on while they wait in the lines that bureaucracy knows how to produce—and right on from there.

Jo-Ann Gardner was in her middle forties when she got KNOW, Inc., the feminist press, under way in Pittsburgh in 1969. Like me, she had worked most of her life, some of it drudge work: she drove a truck during the war. Like me, she has a husband who believes deeply in what she's doing. She lived in Ireland for a while in the 1950's, in deepest Woman's Role country, so she knows that scene too. She had done premed in college and when she came back here, she took a doctorate in clinical psychology—and then couldn't get a job in that malest of all psychological specialties. She switched to educational psychology, wangled herself an unpaid job, fought her way up to half-time paid work—and got fired for refusing to do something inconsistent with her professional judgment. By that time, however, KNOW was healthy, if impoverished, and there was plenty to do, for the demand for its reprints, bibliographies and publications on feminist topics was already nationwide.

Seventeen people work at KNOW now, all paid equally, but with the work divided so that those who need money most have a chance to earn most. This arrangement, like all major decisions, was made by everyone working there. Any problem that seems to be more than routine is solved by everyone meeting together, and paid for the time. If the problem is pressing, the meeting takes place at once; otherwise it comes up at a regular, scheduled session. The aim is both to spread responsibility and to practice its use, so that KNOW functions as a living organism, independent of any one person's decisiveness or drive. In the same way, everyone working there is urged to learn how to do everything needed—shipping, running the press, doing accounts and so on.

Jo-Ann sees herself as the prime mover of KNOW, but she has worked to see that it isn't "her baby." She's proud of its accomplishments, and its growth, proud that as soon as it could be done, work there became paid work, offering neither ego trips nor martyrdom. She believes that everyone there is better for being a part of it. What she gets from being active here instead of in a career is rather subtle. "I put up with put-downs at the University," she says, "including my own put-downs of me, on top of the usual situation where the men get promoted and parking slots and typists, and the women come along behind. Now I can be as active as I want and not worry about it, or feel I have to justify what I'm doing. It's different."

Maggie Kuhn, of the Gray Panthers, is another woman with a longtime career who turned it into a new channel late in life. But plenty of women who have been mostly housewives are redirecting activities and changing their scope. I know one who has made her Sunday painting into something more serious. She is selling a bit now, to galleries in New York, learning how to be "commercial" with some amusement, and feeling a new pride in her work and confidence in herself. A much older woman, not well and nearly housebound, has made herself a nerve center for the block she lives on in New York. Messages come to her, packages are delivered there, she knows where people are and she keeps an eye on street activities. Instead of being isolated and apart, the community comes in to her. She is connected and the connection sustains her identity.

While I was writing this article, I was reading Ingrid Bengis's moving book, *Combat in the Erogenous Zone*. Ms. Bengis is looking for ways to establish a trustworthy system of values in her own life. Deeper than any search for an ideology, it is a search for a way of knowing. I think, increasingly, that we validate our experience by sharing our knowledge and our emotions, opening our heads and hearts. A cliché, yes. By coincidence, a letter from Mary Douglas, the English anthropologist, that came to me this morning refers to a theory that "all great poetry consists of clichés." Perhaps what we have to do is act on those truisms, test them and extend them by our action and our probing and so turn them into the poetry of experience which enriches our lives. How much we women, old and young, have to gain by sharing!

XII

The rift in our society between art and the rest of life, art and the economic "realities," art and the material goods produced, the places we live, the ambience on which our eyes fall, day after day after day—this is not only unhealthy, but it is also a very abnormal situation. God knows in the past people lived in grinding poverty and degradation; God knows the birth of the machine and the harnessing of power through mechanical means has brought enormous good to the human race. But it has brought with it losses as well: the loss of understanding and connection with craftsmanship, loss of the everyday use of natural creativity and of the intimate, living relationship between human beings and the artful products of the human hand, expressing to the human eye and touch not only use, but the value of use, the feeling of doing and being.

There is no turning back. The movements to revive old skills and to live according to old work patterns are exercises in nostalgia. Certainly we want to preserve the human knowledge of past technologies and processes; I think they had great value, particularly the value of teaching the slow workings of process and of close relationships with other humans, with animals, with the natural world. But we can no longer *live* by them, except in privileged enclaves. The artists who today are confronting the age of mechanical man are closer to the truth than those—artists or not—who are retreating into past truths. The machine can't be dropped out, nor can we go on as we are, divided. The huge and challenging task for art today is to humanize the machine. We have to leap off the place we stand now, catch at the spiky monstrosities spawned by technology and learn how to integrate them into a human world, how to make them not only useful but truly expressive of meaning. They are not functional until they become so.

Until that time, being a practicing artist will have something isolating about it. That's a burden for artists and an impoverishment for everyone else, just as all the divisions that seem to set us apart from one another are. This address, written to be given at a conference on Women in the Arts, represents an effort to bring together what artists have to know about making images in order to ply their trade, and the present process by which women are shaping their own new image. It's directed to artists; but not exclusively. That is, it's directed also to the imaginative ingenuity and creativity that lives—at least a little—in everyone. Artists are the people who use that creativity most consciously and know most about how it works and what its processes involve; but it doesn't belong just to them. And it can be used in many ways.

Images of Woman

When I began to think about the subject of this meeting, I discovered that I was involved in a running dispute with myself even before I began to write. Before I could begin to discuss the image of woman and its relationship to art, I had to clarify a confusion in my head about another relationship. I think it is one that is germane to our topic however, and especially to any action that we may aspire to take in remaking the image of woman traditional in our society. So let me begin by stating the question that has been nagging at me: How does "image" relate to "self"? Are they the same thing? Is the image *a* way, or *the* way, in which we project the self? Or is it, perhaps, a way in which we know the self? And, if we are indeed facing the task of changing the image of woman to something more positive than it has been in the past, what will the shifting of one side of the relationship mean for the other?

Is the image the self? The idea is repugnant. Are we only what we seem to be? Surely the suggestion that we are just that is the source of a great deal of the anger and frustration that women have felt for so long and have only recently been able to bring up to consciousness and confront openly. All of us, I imagine, would deny that our true, felt, identity can be defined by an image stamped on us like a seal drawn by the outside world. We have felt for a long time that the assigned image of woman, acted out in the role-behavior expected of us, has not offered us self-fulfillment but, rather, has functioned as mask, as screen, as armor—most of all, as *barrier* between the inner self and the world. Whatever the momentary pattern of that image, every woman who has ever lived would surely cry out, "It is not I."

But in a curious way this alienation between the self and the image, necessary though it may be for the very survival of the self, has contributed to the continuing life of the image. We are, as Simone de Beauvoir saw and said so well, not only the second sex, but the *other* sex. Our alienation has sustained this otherness. Perceptive men have spoken for centuries of the mysterious woman, the female enigma, hiding her inner qualities from the world. Upon this blank space, this turned-away face of the self, they have projected their desires and fancies, time out of mind. Fertility fetish from the caves of the Stone Age, virgin goddess, all-giving mother, demoniac maenad, sibylline prophetess, malign witch, angel in the house, golden-hearted whore—we have been all these things and more. When Virginia Woolf's father was courting her mother he wrote her, "You must let me tell you that I do and always shall feel for you something which I can only call reverence as well as love. You see, I have not got any saints and you must not be angry if I put you in the place where my saints ought to be." Perhaps Julia Duckworth, whose warm, loving portrait her daughter drew in *To the Lighthouse* as Mrs. Ramsay, knitting away on a sock for one of the children, might have preferred to be a plain human being, but Leslie Stephen decreed otherwise. Sainthood was thrust upon her, and we can only admire her ability to carry off the role.

And indeed many women have carried off unexpected and probably less welcome roles while they hid their own inner qualities from the world. Often, I think, they must have hugged to themselves, as their greatest treasure, the unknown self within the image, the sensitive, feeling mind. On occasion that mind has surely seen the world more clearly and realistically than a man can do, for often *his* mind is entangled with the sentiment and principle that appears to be needed by those charged with sustaining and justifying the structure of an imperfect world; the sentiments and principles and prejudices embodied in the mythology of any society. Imprisoned in her image, the feminine mind has sometimes questioned that mythology, turning on it a gaze so bleak, so cynical, if you will, that men who have felt its penetration have drawn back in terror. For this is a view removed from the possibility of action, and therefore from the need to justify that action by setting up pious reasons for its validity. It is the view of she who is not doer, but done-to; and done-to, acted-upon, manipulated by the rationale of others, what revenge can the passive observer hope for except to see clearly, with mordant, unwavering gaze, the way it is, the course that action takes? If we can do nothing but *see,* then our unused energies will force us to see to the bottom, to the last grain of vanity and self-deceit and vain aspiration in those who act. We will follow sardonically the course of action, unmoved ourselves by failure or success since we have had no hand in achieving either one and know only that all action ends at last in the grave. Women have been blamed for that view often enough, told they are disloyal and, of course, "deadlier than the male." So we can be satisfied that it is part of our image too.

I believe it is a very important part of the image because it is an expression of the irreducible self, and I believe further that our first task in remaking or re-creating the image of woman is to call on the energy and the reality of the self within the image. So I ask you, for a moment, to consider with me that silent observer within her interior tower. Even to other women she is hesitant to make herself known save by an occasional complicitous glance, but she is there within us, casting her cold eye at the horsemen of the passing scene, whether we admit her presence or not. She is what bears and endures and survives, knowing and accepting with mocking amusement her distance and difference from the exterior image, whatever it may be: dutiful daughter, loving wife, nurturing mother. She is the thing that the image has bound but not murdered. I wish I knew what to call her. Yeats called her "Crazy Jane," and perhaps that will do for now since his poems incorporate both the loneliness of her existence and the sense that it is the world which is insane, not Jane herself. But in the end, it is women who will have to name her, if we want to acknowledge her right not only to judge the world, but also to act upon it.

For this Jane of ours cannot stand apart in total isolation from her image, self-enclosed and self-sufficient. She cannot retreat into craziness and still be human. Repugnant as it may be to see ourselves in the image assigned to us by others, we cannot deny that vision entirely. No one can live alone. We human beings are social creatures in a very special sense, not simply because we depend on others for protection, like herd animals, but because we need other eyes and other minds to know our world, and ourselves. How can we understand the world at all and learn its working connections and processes, how can we ascribe significance to events, except through the teaching of those who were here when we were born? For we are born not just into a natural world as the animals are, but into the whole enormous expanse of a cultural heritage, a heritage that has to be learned, by every child, from the preexistent system of imagery that our ancestors began to make when the first hand shaped the first tool.

It is the transmission of this heritage, of all the artifacts of the mind, of mythologies and conceptual structures, of science and technology, of ways of seeing and knowing from Kant to Castaneda, which makes us human and distinguishes man from beast. Indeed without our culture we are not even animals but mere naked abortions, for we have lost the inborn instincts which are given to animals for their journey through life. We have replaced these preprogrammed instructions in the genes with something

quite else and quite different—with an ability to learn and also
to *teach*, which means the ability to change both our world and
ourselves. This capacity to learn, and then to pass on what we
have learned by means of language, is uniquely human. It is the
reason why we are not imperial animals or naked apes, bound to
the slow and random mutations which produce the means of physical evolution. Darwinian we may be in our bodies, like the rest
of the animal kingdom, but we are Lamarckian in our minds,
for we are capable of rearing children who can profit by our lived
experience, by mutations recorded not in the genetic code, but
in our continuing and collective memories. We have escaped from
the prison of instincts that binds our animal cousins, first by our
ability to structure and restructure the world around us through
the instruments of our thoughts and, second, by our capacity to
speak to others and thus to break down the isolation of the individual mind within its brain cage. In the human, social world,
we cannot be only selves, for that world is held together by the
fact that we know and communicate with each other, and this we
do through our representations, our images, the aspects of the
self that are seen and recognized by the other inhabitants of our
world.

Let us think of images, then, not just as expressive of the self,
but as communications, as messages to other selves. The image
which is not the self, but which passes for it in public, fixes the
self in social reality because it can be recognized. What I am saying is that the confusion with which I began my thinking on this
question is in fact part of the question. For we cannot cut ourselves off from the images others bestow on us even when they
seem false to us. Unless those others who share the world with
us can point to an image which represents the selves we are, they
cannot see us at all. And without this label of image, the self becomes a jibbering ghost, immured in its watchtower, unable to
reach the world. Self and image are not the same, but they cannot
live apart from each other. Each acts continually on the other in a
constant tension, for while the private self is the only source of
authentic experience, this experience can only be stated and understood through the public image; and we are, in a way, depen-

dent on being understood if we are to be able to value for ourselves the experience we have known.

To women the valuation of others has come to seem false in terms of our experience, but we cannot simply turn away from the false image without paying a price, the price of alienation. By withdrawing behind the image and nursing the secret self, women have left the false images in command and control. Now, such a withdrawal is natural enough in creatures who have been taught that passivity is proper to them while the attempt to exercise power is not. Perhaps I should pause to remark that I mean it is natural as a learned response of the weak to the powerful whatever sex the weak may have been born with, and not as an innate, genetic mark of femininity. Men who have been born into a status of dependence have found themselves fighting as hard as women to overcome the learned response of passivity and servility. The Black men demanding Black Power today remember the Uncle Toms of the past all too well, remember the entertainers and jokesters and flatterers who survived by amusing, pleasing and toadying to the powerful. They are striving now to wipe that shadow of the phantom slave out of the backgrounds of their minds. Like them, we have learned passivity and the behavior proper to weakness and have learned, with these attitudes, to disvalue ourselves. Perhaps we hug these selves to us as treasures because they are the only things we can call our own. At the same time, we ask ourselves, Who are we to judge comparative values? If these are our treasures, if we take ourselves so seriously when so obviously the world does not—isn't that just another sign of our foolishness? And consequently isn't it another reason for sitting still in our woman's place and minding our manners, holding our peace, making do with what we know but never say?

That may have been so once but it is so no longer. Like the men who shout that "Black is beautiful," it is time for us to change our images by speaking out. We have withdrawn too long into a private world and by so doing have refused to vivify the image of woman with the authentic pulse and breath of women's lives. The result is a disastrous spate of false images, of cheats which are cheats for men too, which fail even in the social world, so that public reality itself is coming unstuck. The traditional images had some dignity at least, some "redeeming social value," to quote the old Supreme Court on permissible pornography—but these have degenerated into bloodless mechanical puppets. They represent not loving women, but Bunnies for Playboys; not laughing, energetic mothers capable of teaching daughters and sons the ways of the world, but frightened, clutching Moms; not venturesome young explorers, but resentful daughters finding no values in a plastic world to replace the plastic values they have rejected. Because women have let the false images stand as our representatives, we have failed ourselves, diminished ourselves, chosen to divide ourselves and exist in a hopeless, endless stasis, unable either to act truly or to be ourselves in freedom and enjoyment.

What can we do? We must change our image instead of merely withdrawing inside it and denying that it represents the self. Now I think this can be done, but in our new task of image-making, we will have to take account of both the difficulties inherent in such a change and the opportunities which have newly arisen to make the change possible. These opportunities stem from a process of change that has long been under way and that has already produced notable shifts in our world. They are familiar enough, taken one by one. It is only when we put them together that we realize what an extraordinary effect they have had overall. Let's list a few. Item: we can choose when and whether to have children. Because we can, most of us will outlive the period in which we are involved in active child-rearing by something like half our lives. Item: more and more of us not only know we can earn a living, but we are doing so, and planning to do so. Only twenty-five years ago the dean of American sociology was writing that the choice of a husband was far and away the most important decision that a woman ever made. It's still important, but it's not the only vital decision for women today. Vital too is the choice of vocation; and the certainty that without a husband we can still look after ourselves also influences the husband-choice. We no longer need to grab the first man who proposes or face a life as an old-maid aunt.

At the same time that social change has given us these freedoms, it has taken some away. Item: women who work, whether out of choice or out of need, face a bind that was rarer for their mothers and grandmothers. The extended family, the close neighborhood, the supportive community, the possibility of good and loving domestic help in raising children—all are gone. The motherhood years may be shorter than they used to be, but they are often busier and more hectic and wearing. Item: social mobility picks up families and puts them down a thousand miles from home and roots. At the very time they need more community support, they are getting less.

Then there are changes which don't simply alter our traditional roles, but make them specifically more like those of men. Item: the educations we can get and the work we can do after we get them are more and more similar to men's. Which means that our our experience of life is growing closer to that of men, so that the identities we learn from our everyday living may be more like those of our brothers and husbands than they have been in the past. Again, these similarities can be bad as well as good. The work identities we achieve can be broken off and fragmented by technological obsolescence as much as men's can.

Overall, however, there is a powerful positive value in these shifts. They can be extremely upsetting *but* the future shock we are living with is a force that tells us we must change the old roles and the old image. History may be dragging us by the scruff of the neck into the future—but it is on our side once we realize the need for change. Even inflation is on the side of change. The two-income family is becoming a necessity at many levels of society. Social historians are well aware, even the MCPs among them, that women have worked throughout the centuries at many a difficult and laborious task, but in the past they have been able to do this work largely within the bosom of the family, on the subsistence farm or in the family workshop. Today we live in a cash economy, and women who work get paid. Now, there are certainly higher and more spiritual values in life than a paycheck, but it's remarkable how much easier it is to think of them once one has got a paycheck in the pocket, and the spiritual value of freedom becomes conceivable.

There is one more point to be made in the historical context.

Social change is shaking up not only the lives of women, but the structure of the world around us. For us, change is needed. It may also be easier than ever before because old shibboleths have lost their validity and old processes of life have been drained away. That is often a loss and an impoverishment, but it loosens bonds that have been restrictive too. Consequently, when we think of changing roles and images today, we are much less wishful than we were even fifty years ago. I want to dwell on this point for a moment, because nobody is going to work hard to change anything unless there exists some feeble chance of success. The first feminist wave, which achieved the vote for women, was probably the first generation that could have done it. Technology was giving some women the leisure to fight for more than a living, higher education was giving some women a chance to seize opportunities and others to imagine that their ambitions could be fulfilled and—on the negative side—the factory system was pooling women together and subjecting them to the same pressures in the same place at the same time. The pressures and the opportunities together, plus, remember always, the loosening of social context created by World War I and the draft of men to fight, bonded women together enough to win our first big victory.

Then, like God on the seventh day, we all sat down and rested for a while. That lull between the first and the second waves of feminism will be a fascinating period to explore someday. Here, let me just say that I believe we were waiting until women's lived experience again changed enough to force another effort on us, while at the same time, the historical context produced the opportunities for change to come. That has happened now, and that is where we are today. So I shall say farewell for the moment to history and return to the topic of our conference.

But I hope you will understand why I have made this digression when I say that I believe the only way we can create a new and valid image of women is out of our lived experience, our confrontation with history. That experience has always modified the stereotypes of sex and class. In the past, however, personal life and public life ran closer together. Big families and small communities where men and women lived close to their roots guaranteed that people knew each other well over long stretches of their lives. Stereotypes of behavior certainly existed, but they were continually being adjusted to match the personalities of people whom one knew in an intimate, long-term way. Think of Chaucer's women, think of Shakespeare's. Over and over vivid, speaking reality bursts through the image to illuminate it with immediate reactions to everyday life. Which means that if today we once again call on the resources of the self and its felt experience to help us create a new image, we are following a known path.

Today, however, we must do it more consciously and on a grander scale. And here we come right to the heart of the matter of our meeting, to the connection between women and the arts. For I believe that the way we use personal experience to create a new image of woman is closely allied to the work of the artist. Within art we can find the finished creations of the insightful mind which will act as guides to the future, and that is a great deal. But even more vital, we can find in art the very process of creativity itself which we shall be using to reshape our image. For art is the way in which internal experience is formed into the image which is comprehensible to others. It is a basic process of communication, which establishes for one human being the interior reality, the lived experience of another; and this is what is demanded of us today.

Let me say that in formulating this definition of art and creativity I am indebted to a very great philosopher who happens to be a woman, Susanne Langer. She is also the only philosopher of art of whom I know who is read with passion and delight by practicing artists: writers, musicians and painters have all told me so. In her book *Feeling and Form* Langer offers a simple definition of art. It is, she says, "the creation of forms symbolic of human feeling." Again, in a later work, *Mind: An Essay on Human Feeling,* she writes: "Artistic conception . . . is not a transitional phase of mental evolution, but a final symbolic form making revelation of truths about actual life." And these truths are communicable. I quote again: "[The artist] creates an image of that phase of events which only the organism wherein they occur ever knows. This image, however, serves two purposes in human culture, one individual, and one social: it articulates our own life of feeling so that we become conscious of its elements and its intricate and subtle fabric, and it reveals the fact that the basic forms of feeling are common to most people at least within a culture, and often far beyond it. . . . Art is the surest affidavit that feeling, despite its absolute privacy, repeats itself in each individual life." It is, moreover, the only form of communication which can convey the truths of internal feelings. "The facts which it makes conceivable are precisely those which literal statement distorts."

In creating a new image, then, we shall have to proceed as if we were artists. For us, art is both guide and paradigm. I hope that isn't a frightening idea. It shouldn't be. Creativity is not really a rare gift, it is just one that we have rather systematically pushed out of our lives for a while. But it is present not just in the high arts of music and drama and dance and literature and painting and sculpture; it is present in folk art too. The quilts our great-grandmothers made, the knitting patterns they adapted, the embroidery with which they enlivened simple traditional styles of clothing, were all products of creativity. So were folks songs and work songs and country dances, weaving and pottery-making and all the crafts that were in earlier days a necessary part of life. We haven't lost the ability to create just because we've let it slide: creativity is one thing human beings are born with. And since we also possess the capacity to learn, we can relearn and reuse old skills, the skills which show us how to transmute the feeling of life into the expressive image which will represent us truly in the social, human world.

How do we begin? First, before everything, by listening to ourselves, listening to our experience as an artist listens to a work that is trying to be born; by listening deeply and listening humbly, but with a sense of trust and confidence that we can understand what our experience shows we require, for that is what the new image must incorporate. Let me emphasize that element of confidence, for the old image of woman is going to rise at once to dispute it; and the old image of woman, of the good woman, is still far from dead. She is still very influential, still felt by many of us to be an important and proper model when she tells us that our central characteristic is devotion to others and that our very capacity for feeling—which we are trying to use for our own ends in remaking our image—is misused unless we forget *our* feelings and put others first.

But this is what we cannot do as creators. The image of the good woman is thoroughly ambivalent, which is to say that there are indeed still valuable elements within it; that we do certainly want to be open to others and receptive and giving in personal relationships. But we must be more. The old model of the good woman has become insufficient for life today, and it is especially inappropriate in the struggle for the expression of experience that we face in creating the new image which will enlarge the old. The old image has grown so small and so narrow that it has cut out a whole range of feeling and, by so doing, it makes our responses smaller and less valuable than they should be. Let us put the old image gently aside and see ourselves not as good *women,* but as good *artists,* for the job we are tackling is simply a larger, social form of the artist's work. And every artist knows that an intuitive sense of the reality and the worth of others must be matched with a kind of sublime faith in one's own ability to conceive a new truth and embody it in the right, revealing symbols, a faith which at times approaches arrogance. If a writer, painter, composer, doesn't know what is true and necessary in his vision and isn't prepared to hold on to that knowledge in the teeth of everyone else's opinion, he had better go into some other business. Equally, if women are not prepared to believe that they understand their own lives better than do men, they will not have the courage and stamina to change them. And change them we must.

So, we listen. And one of the people we listen to is certainly Crazy Jane. She is a good antidote to the old model of the good woman and her obligatory dedication to others. Jane will tell us to beware of old ideas, most notably the idea that women are possessed of finer, nobler, less aggressive and more nurturant qualities than men. Not only can no one prove that, but the mere existence of the belief is hampering to women. It invites a sort of emotional snobbery, akin to the intellectual snobbery which blinds those who suffer from it to new ideas because they are so sure they know best that they don't have to listen. But we have to listen and we have to look, with Jane's cold eye, at all the experience we have turned our backs on in the past because it wasn't proper

for good women. We have a great deal to learn about coping
with man's world. For instance I am sure we need to know more
about the positive value of aggression, and stubbornness, and decisiveness and daring, when these qualities are called for. They
happen to be called for now, because they are the qualities that
allow the artist to control the stuff he is working with.

We must not be put off by the idea that these qualities are
selfish. So they are, in a special, a primary, way: it is ourselves
which we must be willing to explore in our search for the true
experience we must use in our creative task. But this selfishness is
quite different from the selfishness that is a product of vicarious
living. That sort is exclusive, possessive, mean-minded. It says, if
I can't have the world, if I can't reach for what I need, then I'll
snatch at what's left, I'll take this and hold it so tightly that no
one can share.

Primary selfishness, on the other hand, is for sharing because
it is based on enjoyment, on one's own enjoyment, and is not simply a reaction to the enjoyment of others. It is a form of self-en-
richment, which is again sharable, generous. Women very much
need to know what pleases them immediately, because our enjoyment has been filtered through others for so long. We are pleased
at being thought well of: at wolf whistles on the street, or five
invitations for Saturday night, or the symbols of celebrity—our
name on an office door. These things are not what I mean when
I say we will find out who we are, and therefore how our image
should be shaped, by discovering enjoyment. I mean a sense of
connection with the world, and pleasure flowing from the world,
and discrimination about that pleasure even as you feel it; so that
you hear music that turns the world to gold, remember it and
know whose it is; know whose poetry explodes in your head,
whose books ride with you through life as guides and comforters.
I mean what paintings and sculptures you call on when you come
back to Paris or Athens or Basel or Washington or Boston; what
makes you laugh and, equally, what doesn't. I mean what sports
you love, for they partake of the aesthetic qualities we assign too
narrowly to high art. I mean the pleasures of good food and fine
weather and the rise and fall of certain landscapes and animals
moving and children on a beach, and half a hundred things more

at least, things that color the world and teach us to discriminate.

To discriminate, again, on our own, so that it is our own personal experience that tells us what is pleasant and what is painful, for it is only by learning this *on our own* that we can trust ourselves to discriminate further, so that we go on, with equal confidence, to say this is good and that is bad, this is just and that is oppression, this is true and that is false. We need to know these things for ourselves and not through mediators, because we must trust ourselves and our knowledge. That trust, that confidence, is the instrument of the creator, and no one can work without it.

But this immediate, discriminating knowledge of the validity of experience is also the ground beneath the social structure. Our image is not for ourselves alone, it is a message, a communication of truth. Our society is in bad trouble today because too many messages have been falsified, too few of us rely on our experience to validate our lives. Let me remind you of a recent example of what I'm talking about from a field quite apart from art, or from women either. Do you remember when Sam Ervin was asked, during the Watergate hearings, by someone, Ehrlichman's lawyer, I think, how he—Ervin, that is—knew what Section so-and-so of Title this-or-that of the Criminal Code meant, and Ervin answered in utter astonishment, "How do I know? Because I understand the English language. It's my mother tongue."

Now, Senator Ervin did not mean that he was born knowing English. Like all of us, he learned his mother tongue. So let us note, at once, that this intuitive, subliminal knowledge *can be learned.* Once learned, this immediacy, developed through a lifetime of connection and response, is the way that the self knows valid experience. *Experience* is our mother tongue; but if we are to trust it, we must be open to it ourselves, take it in by ourselves, and not through mediators.

And if we are going to change the false image which represents women to the world, this sort of trust in what we know and feel, this responsiveness which doesn't quibble about how we know at the moment of knowledge, which uses the self by forgetting the self, is the fundamental means through which we can do our work. It is just here that we shall find the touchstone of authenticity which will help us in this formidable task. We cannot undertake to change our image in any halfhearted way, distracted by caveats from the past, from the old assigned image. We shall have to engage the individual personalities of hundreds, thousands, millions of women, each of whom will know the necessity of the task within herself. What we have on our side is already the statement by history that it is necessary, that social change demands it. But if we are to create not just a different, but a true, image we need more than the knowledge of necessity. We need the motivation of joy in creation, of delight and connection with life. We need more than a push from history, we need a pull from the possible future.

The creative process, implicit in art, can help us imagine that future, can help us test it against our own actual experience and then, by showing us the reality of other human feelings as embodied in art, it can extend our experience, so that we know we do not speak for the odd, individual self alone. In art, the self speaks through the image *and is recognized*. Crazy Jane, so long alone, will finally find her name; and in so doing she will become more than the cold, passive observer. Because she is recognizable, because singular experience has been transformed into an image which can be shared and understood, the image affects the interior lives of its audience until they become—Jane and all of us, or the Jane in all of us—not just audience, but participants. This is the task we are undertaking today, the creation of a true symbol of ourselves out of our special, lived experience, which will explain our identities, both to others and to ourselves. We shall find ourselves here, just as the artist finds, as he finishes his work, what the work means and says. Let me say again, art is a guide for us not just to the image, but to the *making* of the image; and the making will shape the image, for we shall learn, as we work, who we are. The process will tell us what the symbol must be, for the very work itself will enlarge and enrich the image we are making. We must live not just as women, but as artists, open and daring but always alive to our own experience, listening and assertive both, trying out our newfound voices but knowing, as we do, that the music we are making will not be just ours, but that of a great chorus.

One last word. Last year I found myself asked why a group of women, of whom I was one, had discussed the place of women in the world and the significance of women's experience and, as we did so, had referred to women not as "we" but as "they." I think there were many reasons for this. One of them was certainly that we all happened to be writers, and writers tend to keep a distance between themselves and their work (*their* work, you see, not *our* work; I don't fall into this distancing only in speaking of women), because this distance imposes impersonality and keeps individual crankiness from getting in the way of abstraction. But another reason, I felt, was that for me, at any rate, there is a larger "we" than women. That "we" is humankind.

I bring this up because I think it is important for us to realize how vital a new image of women is for humanity as a whole. We live in a divided society. In our society art and feeling have both been assigned to women for a long time. Dealing with practical events has been reserved for men, and has thus been separated from the expression of feeling. And now we are discovering the price exacted for that division—I mean "we" there, I mean humankind. The Western world is sick with a great malaise that stems from this division. You can find it in the disturbing statistics on job alienation, with their evidence of working men and women who go to their jobs in a spirit of disgust and boredom and hate. You can see it reflected in the determined refusal of young people to project lives conforming to the orthodoxies of Western society, of respect for work, the system, the country where one was born. All the old patterns of life that should be familiar and sustaining have come to seem a cheap, mocking show. You can hear it in the defiled language of the Watergate witnesses whose words and grammar and syntax all seem intended not to express the truth of authentic experience, but to disguise it, so that they mouth one thing and mean another. And it has happened because the world of events, man's world, has been drained of feeling and has lost, therefore, a sense of human dimensions of life, both great and small, and of real human requirements.

It is very necessary that this division be healed, so that feeling and action can once more flow together. A new image of woman as active participant in society does not mean that women will desert the emotional validity of personal relations as we move into the world of action. We will bring it along with us, to a place where it is badly needed.

XIII

The women's movement toward equality in the world of action necessarily involves them in the use of power. Women are very conscious of this. Many women's organizations are experimenting with different ways of structuring themselves: different, more consensual, processes for arriving at decisions, less hierarchy and a great deal less respect for it. In every period of social change, philosophic arguments for anarchy are heard. Millenarian sects, dating back to the early Christians, have given voice to them over and over. They are worth listening to because they always point to unused, overlooked human qualities, because they insist on the equal worth and equal reality of every individual.

A sense of the equal worth of others has to be part of the exercise of power, if power is not to be corrupted; but of course power has to be exercised, and exercised through an instrument which must in the end be a human agency. Decisions have to be taken and acted on; and part of every decision is some degree of tension between what we want and what we can have, between what is and what ought to be. Increasing this internal tension is the expected public response to action. The agent will be held responsible for what follows from the deed he has committed or sanctioned.

It is worth talking about these axioms of behavior because they not only affect women's attitudes toward the use of power (and these attitudes reflect the long exile of women to a relatively powerless state), but they also affect the way men think about women as power-users, decision-makers. One such male attitude can be summed up as "You'll be sorry." After a shorter version of the article which follows was published in *The Atlantic*, an eleven-page letter from a disturbed male warned me (among other things) to look out or I might become part of a future Establishment, defending its values from other, later, rebels and questioners. As I told him, I wouldn't mind that at all. If women want power, they must accept the responsibility for the actions they will have to undertake and be willing to explain why they did so. Whether I or any other individual woman would be a *good* executive or not—and writers tend not to be because we get distracted by the continuing pressures of events and ideas—has nothing to do with the principle. Responsibility follows action. It follows inaction too, of course, in cases where action is called for.

What my correspondent had in mind, however, is clearly that responsibility is undesirable; and that attitude is very informative indeed about our present situation. Many people feel that. I believe they do so because it is so difficult to know what repercussions may follow from an action in a society as complex as ours and, more discouraging, difficult to know whether any effect will be felt at all. Why act if nothing happens? Why lay yourself open to censure if your action gets nowhere? Better to do nothing at all; which is a doctrine very useful to the power structure, for it discourages any challenges. But even more interesting is the fact that the power structure itself talks this way. Its members are aping the perquisites of the weak, to be guiltless because they cannot exercise power. It seems as if the powerful want the weak to sympathize with them in their plight—as if they are assuring us that they can do nothing with the world.

Which means it's out of control. No one can do anything. So no one can be blamed.

When the power structure says that, perhaps it's time for them to move over. Naturally one must reckon with the chance that its members are abdicating only in name and will hand the dirty chores to the eager minority aspirants crowding the outskirts of the Establishment citadel while they themselves hold on to the central keep. I guess we have to take that chance. No one says that our chores have to be confined to dirty work; and maybe the central keep isn't all that important. One remembers the powerless Merovingian kings of realms run by the Mayor of the Palace, the powerless Japanese emperors whose state was administered by the Shogun. Politics is the art of the possible, the old saw goes. More things are possible today than are thought of in many a philosophy.

The Weak Are the Second Sex

The title of my last book, *Man's World, Woman's Place,* was taken from two old sayings, "It's a man's world" and "Woman's place is in the home." As I hoped to make clear by my subtitle, *A Study in Social Mythology,* I didn't and don't believe that either statement is true, but I began with a study of woman's role because it is more limited, and therefore better defined and easier to study. And the fallacy of the old statement was clear. As a matter of factual description, the number of women who never, at any time, work outside their homes is approaching the vanishing point. At some period in their lives more than 90 percent of American women are "in the labor force"; that is, in the official job market, outside the house. Since 1940, more and more of them have stayed there longer. Today there is not just one peak of female employment among girls and young married women, followed by a steady drop. If women quit to have children, they now tend to start looking for jobs as soon as, sometimes even before, the children are of school age. Since fewer children are born to younger mothers—the average age of a mother at the time of her last child's birth is now twenty-seven—the number of working wives has been rising steadily to a second, later peak as high as the first. The amount of income they bring in has become a greater and greater factor in our economy and, of course, in the ability of a family to stay ahead of inflationary pressures. We are two-income families now and the second income is almost always the wife's, not that of an older child still living at home.

But my effort to examine the fallacy inherent in the contention that "Woman's place is in the home" was based on the conviction that such an investigation would, in addition, help me understand the overall effect of social myth on our capacity for dealing with change. Consequently I did not want to neglect, but only curtail, my consideration of the other old saw about its being "man's world." I wish now to turn more specifically to this bit of mythic wisdom, and particularly to what it tells us about the structure of our contemporary Establishment.

We can't, of course, separate the two statements entirely, for they support each other. To declare that women belong at home not only leaves the rest of the world in men's possession, but it justifies that possession. Pragmatically it means that women who chose to leave the cloister of their "inner space," and wander out into the world of events have no one to blame but themselves if they get into trouble. Now, this is a useful conclusion for the powers-that-be, because it absolves them of responsibility for women in men's world. But another conclusion is at least as valuable. Divide the world into two by sex, grouping all men together. Demonstrate what is inarguable, that power resides within this group since women are declared a limited (and therefore inferior) caste. Will you not, then, persuade the members of your male moiety that they all have some share in the ownership of the world, in the power which is held by their group?

It is power I want to talk about, and some other assets that we currently associate with it, like dominance and celebrity—or, if you can tolerate the word, charisma. We don't talk about power much in our society and, as Sherlock Holmes said about the dog that didn't bark in the night, this silence is extremely significant. Americans are nervous about power—it's a dirty word. Just consider, for example, the dedication of Lyndon Baines Johnson, a connoisseur of power, to the public slogan of consensus. Few men can have taken more real, almost physical, pleasure in wielding power than LBJ did, but he didn't like to be seen brandishing it in his own mailed fist. He greatly preferred to present the appearance of operating as the devoted tribune of the people, expressing a near-unanimous common desire. We will come to the reasons for this kind of camouflage later, but let us for the moment note the simple fact: it is common form to waffle about wanting and exercising power, even among those who are totally aware that it exists under their noses and that, as long as it does, it will be wielded by somebody.

Looked at in this way, we see how misleading is the statement about its being man's world. As always, *the world belongs to the powerful* and though, almost universally, the powerful are male, we can't reverse that statement. Males are not almost universally powerful. The lives of most men—well, we know what Thoreau said. In any case, they are almost as limited as women's, though the limits fall in rather different places and though the daydreams which so often pass for goals are different too. These differences are the result of social training and we need do no more than glance at the daily paper to see how effective and continuous that training is. Men are interested in sports, women in recipes and fashion, and the sports pages and fashion news are as firmly sex-directed as the anterior parental urges to give a little boy a ball to play with, give a little girl a doll to dress.

But underneath the difference is a common ground uniting these sex-specific areas. *Neither of them has anything to do with the exercise of power.* Like bread and circuses, they serve to direct the attention of men and women alike away from the interests of the powerful which, naturally, center on the holding and use of power. Obviously, then, sex difference is not the only way to divide the world in two. Another division sets off the weak from the powerful, and it may well be the older, it may be the more profound.

Now the idea that society is made up of two parts, haves and have-nots, is a commonplace of political theory. Perhaps Lenin stated it most clearly when he said that the question of power comes down to *"kto kovo?"* That is, who has the ability to use another and who gives in? Just as familiar is the observation that women belong to the have-nots, and the radical feminists base their belief on the necessity for revolution just here: there will never be equality for women until the politics of their abasement is done away with. True enough. But the question then arises of the relationship between women and the men who fall outside the company of the elite, which of course means most men. I do not believe we can begin to understand the effect on men of the demands for equality made by the Women's Movement unless we consider *together* the two human divisions, male and female, weak and powerful and, more, the way in which these two splits can foster hostility just because they threaten to run into each other. More important, I believe that a study of these conjoint and disruptive splits will illuminate the use of power in the abstract.

What happens if we join the two divisions into one? If we do, we come up with a statement that may or may not be factual in any particular society but that expresses a mythic and terrifying possibility: *the weak are the second sex.* It is this equation of weakness and femininity in its sexual aspect that underlies a great deal of masculine reaction to a redefinition of woman's role, and it does so because such a redefinition necessarily involves a shift not just in sex relations, but in power relations too. If the weak are the second sex, the subordination of women is not simply the result of sexual difference, but is typical of the realities of dominance, of elementary power as exerted by one person over another. Unlimited dominance allows—indeed, may entrain—sexual exploitation of the weak by the strong, whether the weak be physiologically male or female. If the powerful are powerful enough and the weak are weak enough, nondominant men and women will tend to be treated alike, as a caste of "the weak," and their submission is potentially total—that is, spiritual and physical too: ordinary, everyday, normal, expected.

If this is a valuable hypothesis, it will illuminate some problems that have not been easy to solve without it, and it will also be testable in the real world. I believe it does both. In fact, I think we know already, below the tops of our minds, that the weak are the second sex, and considerable experience exists to validate it. It's just that in our society the physical exploitation of the weak is thought of as aberrant. But the buggered prisoners in their jail cells know that buggery is normal in an aberrant situation, as Kate Millett perceived when she claimed Gênet as a speaker for the underdog of sexual politics. If our culture, even to its revolutionary dogma, has hesitated to include sexual use and abuse as part of the doing between *"kto"* and *"kovo,"* this is in large part an accident of history.

Certainly the sexual component comes to the surface in societies living closer to the disaster line than ours, where weakness can mean degradation and death and survival depends on pleasing the powerful. There, physiological differences are subordinate to those of dominance. The indiscriminate use of boys or women to satisfy the desires of grandees recurs throughout history. Indeed, clever and ambitious men have become female impersonators of such éclat that they outdo the sex they imitate. Flaubert, in his travel notes from Egypt, records one such, the dancer Hasan, with whom the most accomplished women performers had a hard time competing. "It's too beautiful to be exciting," Flaubert wrote a friend after seeing Hasan dance, but added with characteristic honesty, "I had a headache for the rest of the day."

By contrast, the economics of affluence, the politics of democracy and the religion of the Protestant ethic (put them in whatever order you wish) have, among us, combined to defuse—and to diffuse—the concentration of power by decreasing the physical abasement of the weak. In addition, our middle-class norms of behavior (and they have always been the directive ones in America), were for a long time puritanical enough to suppress overt manifestations of any sort of sexuality. At the most, sexual exploitation has seemed no more than a metaphor for the powerful/weak relationship, as in the common-speech use of "fuck," which connotes a power relationship at least as often as it does a sexual one and thus mingles the former with the latter. Nonetheless, it has remained a haunting analogy. When James Dickey called up the reality in his novel, *Deliverance,* it gave the book an inner core of force, and a justification of violence which certainly resonated in the minds of its readers. It was argued there that the ultimate physical attack (in Dickey's terms), male rape of a male, can and must be answered by murder.

Dickey successfully tapped a still potent myth, but in fact compared to the rest of the world and to much of the history of our own culture, not very many men in America today feel dominance as in any way personal. Our bureaucratic society is so intricate that its very complications turn power into an abstraction. The boss, the baron and the bullying priest have given way to an impersonal machine and what the weak chiefly feel is just this impersonality: limits and barriers ordained by—no one we know. By "Them," but they are faceless. We are governed, we say with some pride, by laws, not by men. Well, that is no doubt an advance over individual caprice, but we might note that it has its own advantages for the powerful, for it functions as a deterrent to the desire for power among the weak. By donning anonymity and institutionalizing themselves, the dominant conceal the pleasures of privilege and so avoid the arousal of envy. The machine distances us from the figures at the top and grays the emotions we feel for them. Political hatred and devotion are still commonplace in areas of personal rule, in Uganda for example, and Northern Ireland, but they have not been widely and passionately felt in America for many a long year.

For within the second sex of the weak, that part of it which is male is not much interested in power in America today. We are a violent but not a rebellious society, and what we chiefly want is not power over others but a different sort of life for ourselves. We are still rich enough to be more interested in pleasure than in power, and our felt want is for lives which will seem more real, significant, authentic; offering more meaningful experiences, more rewarding pleasures. Expressed in clichés though they be, these are aesthetic qualities of profound importance. Without them, the flame of identity within each of us dwindles. But human needs of any real importance cannot be totally divorced from politics because they demand social change to satisfy them. I note however that the idea that such changes can only be achieved for the many by reworking the power structure, a matter requiring much thought and effort, is singularly little discussed. It sometimes seems as if even our revolutionaries expect "Them," the anonymous powerful, to make the revolution against themselves, while the rest of us follow it on television. Of course, effective politics has always known how to use show business, but seldom have the two things been so confused as they are today. The impersonality of governance conceals the human processes involved in effective action, and by concealing them it confuses our understanding of causality, tends to equate gesture or rhetoric with action and leaves us imagining that when we express emotion—when we "demonstrate" —we have actually done something. But a "happening" is not an event.

One aspect of this muddle is that it is not the powerful who are envied today by the weak, but the celebrated. It's star quality we admire, charisma, not authority. One reason is certainly the impersonality and anonymity of much of contemporary life. To be celebrated is to be *known*. One's identity is validated by public recognition. In the past, title and rank identified the powerful, vocation or craft the middling, and the lower sort at least possessed an attachment to a special region, spoke the language thereof and knew whom they could call *landsman* or *paysan*. Reisman calls our ancestors "tradition-directed," and so they were. But it was the familiar group, transmitting the traditions, which provided human warmth and a group identity and thus "placed" our fathers in their own experience. Narrow as these lives were, what happened within them remained relevant to present and future, and therefore preserved a unified identity.

Now such supports have been largely swept away. Life has become a lottery in which we are unmarked counters. Struggle as we may to establish the value we should bear, fate can overrule us and change our status in a minute. In such a situation, it's easy to see how power and celebrity get mixed up with each other. In a lottery, causality and process are meaningless. Celebrity is the stamp of fate, touching this one or that, chancy and unpredictable. Working for it is useless; it's just as sensible and a lot easier simply to wish. The prize will come or it won't and, this being so, action won't help while gesture may—putting oneself forward, waving at the camera. Celebrity is a kind of magical "mana." Some of the desperate horde imagine that it may rub off on them if they can just get close enough, touch it, rip its shirt, go to bed with it, shoot it. Our assassinations, these last ten years at least, and some of our earlier ones too, have not been political. They have been magical, reminiscent of the belief that the king's touch could heal, that contact with the great of any sort can transmit greatness.

The dangers of celebrity, however, are few compared to the

burdens of power, for if one is powerful, one is responsible. One must act and, having acted, accept the consequences—which may be unpleasant. This difficulty surely had something to do with Lyndon Johnson's devotion to the idea of consensus, for consensus gets the wielder of power off the hook. He's not just doing what he wants or thinks wise, he's operating as an agent for The People, and responsibility can thus be extended to them. Celebrities, however, are in even better shape, for they need accept no share at all in responsibility; they simply bow to the cheering crowd and introduce the speaker. If the powerful are cheered, and on occasion they are for they do have some celebrity value, they are also booed. Does anyone like to be booed? Very few; but I suspect that in the past, the great and secure minded it less than they do today. They were more certain in their identities. "The public be damned," said Commodore Vanderbilt, hardly a laudable statement, but one that was authentically his own, not dictated by a public relations counselor who had been reading polls.

But the public shame of booing is not the only disadvantage that shadows power in our eyes. More off-putting still is the prospect of private guilt. Lord Acton has something to answer for, I think. Power tends to corrupt, said he, and so it does. But when the good are so fearful of corruption that they refuse to take part in the use of power, they are resigning power to the evil. One might as well say that because fire burns we will have nothing to do with it. The conscious refusal of power can be just as corrupting as its use, just as grave a moral decision, or why do we remember Pontius Pilate?

The impersonality of life comes in here once again, acting to decrease the apparent advantages of holding power. Not only are guilt and shame feared, but there appears to be little or no offsetting factor of reward to be gained by seizing power. If the individual were persuaded that he could actually change anything by grasping the nettle, he would be more willing to take on the dangerous task. But to the extent that men feel themselves featureless and interchangeable cogs in a machine; to the extent that they look for satisfactions in leisure and private life and expect less and less from their work; to the extent, also, that their ignorance of the operation of the power structure persuades them that "You can't fight City Hall," the urge to reach for power is weakened. The weaker the urge becomes the less "normal" it seems and the greater the implausibility of trying to act out a Horatio Alger story. Result: nondominant males may be discontented, but they are not discontented enough to be willing to do much about it.

If you choose to do nothing about an unpleasant situation, however, you certainly don't want to *hear* about it. It's damned hard to feel both impotent and guilty, and human nature will attempt to avoid such a bind whenever it can. We might name this reaction the Watergate Syndrome; but it is equally apparent in the general reaction of nondominant males to the Women's Movement. Demands for equal rights for women have produced, first, a flurry of joking and, next, some irritation and anger, but mainly and fundamentally a determination to pay no attention: a simple, almost animal, retreat into not listening. Not argument, hardly even refusal to argue, but something even closer to an instinctive reflex—a refusal to *hear*.

"Playing possum" is a defensive mechanism which has often proved a useful tool for surviving. Women have been doing it for millennia as a defense against wanting to act when they are sure they can't, in a situation where raised consciousnesses are liabilities. Ignorance is bliss in a case like that. But it becomes less delightful if the difficulties increase and the situation becomes more abrasive. Most men still don't want to hear about the Women's Movement—but the buzzing goes on. A little is getting through, willy-nilly.

I think it is only natural that what is heard is largely misunderstood and what is passed on (by the men in whose hands lies the distribution of news) is mostly misrepresented because it is misunderstood. And a good deal of the time, too, the Women's Movement is still talking to itself. No doubt that's a necessary step in the formation of any movement: intercommunication helps to bond the group together and give it a cohesive identity, and since women are a group who have not, in recent history, had much to hold them together as a group (except outside pressure) they stand in need of a chance to learn sisterhood. Besides, talking to men who have made up their minds not to listen is a great waste of

energy; and I speak as one who has addressed both listening male
audiences and retreating male backs. I don't think this situation
is incurable but there will have to be motion on both sides before
women talk in terms men find it easy to understand, and men
listen hard enough to follow women's arguments without closing
their minds after the first three sentences.

But right now as the result of these understandable psychological processes, we are in the middle of a mire of contradictions
and rationalizations. If we look at men's reactions to the Women's
Movement we find it described on the one hand as absurd, and
on the other as threatening. It will undermine and destroy normal
relationships of all kinds, and it will also disappear tomorrow
morning by ten o'clock. Its adherents are sex-mad orgiasts who
(contrariwise) want to castrate men. It's a hilarious joke with no
sense of humor. Women are plotting to turn the tables on men
and subject them to hideous indignities; but the whole fuss is
really over who washes the dishes. Anyhow, most women don't
believe in the "Movement" at all, it's the plaything of a handful
of highly publicized exhibitionists. Black women and working-
class women aren't interested, all feminists are rich, white and
bored, and my secretary likes to make me coffee just as my wife
wants to stay home. And if she didn't, I'd (a) fire her and (b)
divorce her.

Allowing for exaggeration by journalists who like a good story,
a lot of men say they believe a lot of these non sequiturs. Emotionally this operates as a comforting statement, since it points to
the conclusion that the Women's Movement is lunatic and up-
holds the decision not to listen to it. But pragmatically it does
nothing at all to deal with the situation. For these contradictory
descripions don't attempt serious opposition to the feminist positions. They are, rather, justifications for ignoring the whole thing.
I don't set them down to argue with them, for one can't, any
more than one can argue with upholders of the Flat Earth theory,
if they still exist. The real meat for examination lies in their
provenance. If women are going to respond intelligently, they
will need to understand the psychic sources of these disorderly
reactions. Where do they come from? Why are they verbalized in
these forms? What do they tell us about the distress and uneasi-

ness which women's apparently rather understandable desire for equality raises in the male breast?

I believe they tell us a great deal and, I repeat, not simply about male/female relationships and mutual images, but about power relationships too; and thus about the fundamental sociopolitical structure of our society and the dynamics of change and potential change within it. I do not believe that one can (leave "should" aside) make a Case for Women and *only* for women, and I believe that until women see this they will waste time and energy fighting all men as if every issue that arises between them were political. Politicizing personal problems may make them easier to understand, but it usually makes them harder to deal with because it imports principles into a private situation and turns teapots into tempests. Vice versa, it can trivialize politics, to a point where all issues are seen as personal. In my view, the case for women is a paradigm, a brief in a class action for subordinated groups as a whole against a clumsy, inefficient and stupidly solipsistic power center. But I would say too that making a case for women provides a particularly useful field for study because it is novel. And thus it brings to the surface hitherto undisturbed layers of mythic mental entanglements and self-serving slogans, like the old one I began with, "It's a man's world."

If we start with the most conscious and rational opposition to women's desire to leave their place and move into man's world, we find that this world is being defined in a distinctly pejorative way: it's a rat race. This is the premise to quite a good argument, a kind of Catch-23, which goes like this: If women are daft enough to want to get out of the house and into the rat race, that in itself is a very good reason for refusing them a shot at decision-making. If they can't tell when they're well off—at home, protected, guaranteed a status, a role and an identity (while men struggle for all three in the chaos of the world of activity)—then obviously their tiny minds can't be trusted to handle the work of the world. Leave us men alone in our rat race where we are sacrificing ourselves to keep you women happy.

Quite a few men find this a satisfying formula and, at first blush, it does have a sort of specious plausibility. But it won't quite

stand up. *Is* the world really a rat race, for the great as well as
the weak? If it is, men must be credited with superhuman magnanimity. If man's world offers nothing but strain and unpleasure,
it seems remarkable that more men wouldn't welcome help in
coping with it. In fact, when women do get out of their place,
they are almost universally assigned to the rattiest part of the race,
the drudge work at the bottom. Male magnanimity seems to end
at home, and the argument for keeping women there somehow
slides over to their limitations per se, instead of basing itself on
the unpleasant features of the male world they seek to enter.

At once we are back in a contradictory muddle, for the limitations of woman's nature as usually presented oppose each other.
The female sex is defined on the one hand as too gentle and fine
to do man's work, and on the other as too indecisive, slow and
self-centered. If the two objections are lumped together to say
simply that women aren't fitted for man's world, we are still faced
with a contradiction from another familiar argument, that their
competition will be tough enough to take jobs away from deserving men. A tangle of contradictions like this suggests that
rationalization has usurped the place of reason. I think we must
conclude that causality has got itself twisted around and that these
arguments follow on a purpose; an already agreed-on answer. Men
want to see women as bundles of contradictions ("What do they
want?") because this image of woman as an unresolvable enigma
serves to exclude her from man's world. When men say, "You
don't belong here," they mean "We don't want you here." I am
not surprised that women get angry at that (though it is the first
time in history that they have got angry at it, which is one reason
men are surprised and discountenanced), and their anger will
help to reinforce their desire for change. But no one can work
effectively for change simply by looking at her own side of the
question. If the opposition to equality for women is contradictory,
that means its roots run deep and straightforward argument won't
change anything, by itself. If men would be better off listening
to women, women would be better off seeing their cause in its
full emotional context.

Of course the concept of woman as mystery, woman as "other,"
is not the only justification in men's minds for their opposition

to equality between the sexes. Certainly it's a primary obstacle, as Simone de Beauvoir saw and said long ago. But there's another catch which is less familiar and perhaps less obvious because it is contained within the very term "equality." What does reaching equality mean? For women, it is a *step up,* to a level where, like men, one will be in better control of one's life and find one's ambitions limited by fewer a priori barriers.

Unfortunately, and women don't often see this, a step up for them will be seen by many men in reverse, as a step *down* to an inferior level, woman's level. To these men, and they are a vast majority, equality doesn't mean "A woman is as good as I am," it means "I'm no better than she is." Equality *for* women brings more competition, but for those who think of themselves as fair competitors, that isn't shattering. Equality *with* women, however, is something else. If you have been brought up to know, with every nerve in your body, that women are inferior—deservedly inferior—how can you accept that? It's shocking, it's insulting, it's UNFAIR.

Worse still—and here we come back to the hidden terror haunting men—doesn't an acceptance of this inferior-equality cut men off (most men, nondominant men) from their alliance with the powerful which that handy old slogan "It's a man's world" seems to validate? To divide the world by sex allies both weak and powerful males together by means of the destiny of anatomy. Take that alliance away and equate the men who stand outside the elite with women, and you are telling them that they can expect to be treated *like* women, to become objects and "others," not doers but done-to; and done-to, yes, right down to sexual doing. The effect of closing the male/female split is to turn the one that separates the weak from the powerful into an abyss.

Alliance with women removes from men the protection of maleness against rape by the powerful. Note the premise underlying this fear: if power has no bounds, it will extend to physical misuse. The paradigmatic act of the powerful, performed upon the weak, is rape.

Now, rape need not always be performed by force. In fact, one of the charms of pornography is that it records session after session of guiltless rape in which the powerful are licensed to have their will of the weak because the weak "really like it that way." *Last Tango in Paris* offers a contemporary example which makes brilliant use of currently resonant themes. It is a story of an encounter between strangers, which is a fundamental and haunting situation for us today. It is also a situation that invites mythic interpretation because the individual personalities of the man and woman involved are erased, leaving only the central nub of their sexual presence. Only symbolic rape is present here, because the woman accepts subordination and asks for abuse; but we can regard it as psychologically equivalent to physical rape because the relationship involves dominance of female by male to the point which our society usually considers degrading. This is not a matter of moral judgment, but of aesthetics. There is no doubt that the audience is intended to be shocked, and is shocked, by the man's demands and the woman's acquiescence. The heroine, and she is not presented as an individual but rather as a mythic projection of "what they really like," is depicted as wanting degradation and returning willingly to the male in order to receive it.

The element of myth is further underlined by the fact that the man has nothing to sustain his superiority except his maleness, which is depicted as his ability to dominate-to-degradation the girl he meets by chance, and the depersonalized universality of the situation is increased by his insistence on anonymity between them. We are down on bedrock, says this demanding and brilliant film, on physical confrontation outside social structures, a confrontation that can stand for any encounter between man and woman. The lesson of the film is that male superiority is based on dominance over the female, an idyll acted out in a vacuum in obedience to transcendent and magical law. Social status doesn't count. She is young, beautiful, better-class—indeed, privileged— and none of that matters. In the idyll, in the myth, her pleasure is his power, and his power is shown by her degradation: she wants it that way. Note, also, how her everyday relationship with her fiancé reinforces this statement by the way *it* states a commentary. In the documentary film he is making of her, she is being asked to assume an identity, to be an individual instead of the mythic partner of the dominant male—and she doesn't like it, doesn't want it. It's amusing, I think, that this "identity" is presented not as anything of the girl's, but as an image projected by another man. She is really nothing, no one. Her choice is which image she accepts.

In the end, actuality begins to break in, with the threat of the end of anonymity in the mythic idyll: "he" will tell his name, he will follow her home, he will identify her. Life-as-it-is (or, rather, life-as-it-is according to the film) rises up against life-as-it-ought-to-be. In life-as-it-is, the woman must release herself from the submission she really desires. But she is not strong enough to do so by merely sending her lover away. He is dominant. He won't go. She can free herself only by violence. Even her privileged and protected position cannot make her his equal, and she can win back her autonomy and find her own identity only by breaking the law which is not strong enough to protect her; by killing him. Which leaves us with the moral that it is a law of nature that men are dominant over women and the only means by which woman can, even temporarily, reverse this edict is by murder. Or, to say it the other way around, equality is nonsense, and women who ask for it are liars who will end by slaughtering men. In any case, there can be no equilibrium of shared power, only a hierarchy of dominance.

If we try to sort out this visceral response to the Women's Movement I think we can discern three stages of opposition. The first results from the fact that the Movement raises the question of power. It is not simply, or even fundamentally, the demand that women be given a share in power that upsets men, it is the review this demand forces upon men of their own position. If women are announcing themselves ready to storm the bastions of the Establishment, where does that leave the men who have failed to do so? Who have settled down to live out their lives in submission and resignation? Suddenly past the doors of their cells, bursting out of the slave quarters, come women-the-inferiors, invading the corridors of power as if, by merely being human, they had a right to be there. But most men have given up that right in return for a quiet life and some sense of security, for government by law as an acceptable bargain between the weak and the powerful. The idea that women are now refusing to accept this bargain acts as a terrifying, a paralyzing, challenge to men. Either they too must revolt or they must acknowledge themselves lacking in the courage and ambition being shown by their traditionally inferior sisters.

Role-changing, I wrote in *Man's World, Woman's Place,* is hard on everyone but hardest on those members of a relationship who have not themselves initiated the changes in the role-relations which they share. It's true that role-changers have troubles. To-day women who are attempting new roles still find it a daunting challenge to value themselves and their experience and ambitions as seriously as they do those of men. Doubting themselves, they can make unnerving mistakes, fall into negation and the mere reversal of old attitudes instead of working out creative new approaches to the demands of changed reality, and sometimes they despair. But men are worse handicapped by the fact that, in to-day's shifts in sex-roles, they are not the initiators. Women are motivated and often very strongly so. To the extent that they can contain and control the drive and anger they feel, it helps them. Men, however, would rather have had things left as they were; which means that in the present situation they are actually experiencing the unpleasant sensation of being done-to instead of doing, and the anger they perceive among women is frightening. They don't understand that it comes out of past frustration and assume, naturally enough, that it is an augury of future dominance. More-over, there is this further point: the changes women demand are compelling men to rethink their relationship not just to women, but to the whole power structure of our society. It is a hard and unwelcome task.

There is also the very real problem that women's demands mean different things to men from what they mean to women. We have seen how that works with the apparently fair demand for equality. The same difficulty dogs another seemingly uncomplicated statement made by women, of their similarity as human beings. We are not "others," say women, we are human beings like you in whom there exists merely a happenstantial sex difference. We acknowledge that difference, but why should it apply to more than sex? Why should it signify across-the-board differences of nature and capability? Anatomy is not destiny, it is simply anatomy. Let us be whole human beings together, accepting differences between us as individual excellences or defects, not determinants of character. Even if they are anatomical, why should they be much more important than, say, the fact that Corelli and Siepi have a lower vocal range than that of Sutherland and Sills? What is important is that all of these four people sing superbly, and this likeness is the significant fact, while the sex difference between them does no more than determine the repertory each commands.

But the ability of women to see themselves as human beings first and females only second is the product of a change in women's life experience which has not yet, at any rate, been matched by a corresponding change in men's lives. The acceptance by women of a self-image which is totally different from the male is diminishing as their life-styles become more like those of men. Psychological shifts of this kind are hard to trace, particularly because they are masked by words which remain the same on the surface while their content changes. To be "feminine" for example is still very important to most women. But what exactly do we mean by feminine? We don't mean what our grandparents and great-grandparents meant, and the simplest research makes that clear. In the last few months I have gone over a mass of newspaper clippings culled from *The New York Times* in the years from the 1860's to the present, relating to women and their activities. Of course that isn't the whole story, but it does offer a representative image of women which would be recognizable and acceptable to the ordinary reader. The long-term trend reveals a marked shift in this image: women are more and more seen as approaching the capable, active, involved human norm and leaving "otherness" behind. Their interests grow wider. They are assumed to arrive at their own decisions more frequently. They stop being adjuncts of parents or husbands. The jobs open to them shift from the most menial (salesgirls, domestics working for pittances, seamstresses, factory operatives, addressers of envelopes) toward the white-collar area, and then beyond it. Eighty years ago, marriage was not just the goal presented as proper to every young girl, marriage without parental consent might well involve elopement: which means that a marriageable girl was still something of an object of barter between father and husband. Fifty years ago, a daring middle-class girl could become a secretary without being immediately declassed. The advantage she gained, however, was not independence, but rather freedom from the absolute necessity of accepting the first man who asked her hand in marriage. Her job was not thought of as a career, but as a chance to build up a dowry for herself and gain her a better choice of marriage partner. Career women were things apart, and not expected to marry at all. These are certainly middle-class stereotypes but, let me repeat, America has been shaped by middle-class ideals and aims.

Today, as a current attack on the Women's Movement for being middle class makes clear, middle-class women are very much somewhere else. I have talked to enough of them in the last few years, in cities and small towns across the country, to bear witness to the transformation. If middle-class ideals are still influential, we must factor into American attitudes the idea that growing up and getting married to Mr. Right is now a very old-fashioned dream. It's a nice idea, but it isn't enough. The normal expectation now includes some kind of career-vocation-job which will continue to occupy and interest one throughout life. Which is simply to say that women now see their lives as being much more like the lives of men than they ever have before.

This shift of image is not a matter of wishful thinking. It is given force by the actual change in women's lived experience, a change that began years ago. Again, this is important for men to understand in their assessment of the Women's Movement. One of the statements in that tangle of contradictions I cited is that women's lib is a fad which was played up for a couple of years and is now on the way out. Thus, student revolutionaries were "hot" in 1968, feminist rhetoric was "hot" in 1970 and 1971, and both are over the hill today. But this generalized parallel overlooks the very different context of these movements. Student protests grew out of the war and the draft, and that threat has indeed passed. But the Women's Movement is a response to fundamental social and economic changes, long-term, continuing and affecting women's lives both inside and outside the home. The number and the proportion of women in the labor force grows every year. It now stands at 40 percent and gives the push to climb the ladder toward upper-level jobs a nonbiodegradable base that didn't exist at the time of the first feminist wave. Young women are moving into the professions at a faster and faster clip. The step-up in women law students that began in 1970 is hitting the job market now and will become more obvious every year. Applications to medical school have begun the same kind of rise. Young women in industry are less and less willing to be shunted off into lower-management jobs, with top-level promotion going to a token few. In politics, women are increasingly active at neighborhood level, county level and municipal level, where they are able to command a power base that is not dependent on tactical appointment by male bosses. In time, they will move up.

This is the experience behind the questioning of happy-wife-and-motherdom as a total goal. Underlining the experience is the reason for it. Most of these women workers are not out in man's world primarily to find self-fulfillment. They are working because their families need the money. Very few men really grasp the fact that few working women have an option to work or not. Too many discussions of women at work assume they could all stay home if they wanted to. But six million women are heads of households, and at least sixteen million more bring in the wages that keep their families above the poverty line. With prices of food and fuel and housing and transport and education climbing steadily, more and more families are coming to depend on a second paycheck. Publicly rather than privately, the income of working wives has been a very important source of economic growth in America since the war, perhaps the most important. If a growth economy makes jobs, which is a fundamental tenet of our American creed, these working women are making jobs for men and other women, not cutting men out of the labor force.

It's true that most women at work are working in women's jobs, which are definable as routine, dead-end and low-paid. But they are jobs in man's world, and that means that women's lives are coming more and more to approximate men's lives. Especially, of course, the lives of nondominant men who are also likely to hold the more routine and lower-paid jobs. The effect on women is to reduce their sense of themselves as deserving that label of "other." In the workaday world, they are not "other" in terms of

sex difference, but rather in terms of power difference. Which, to
them, would appear to bring them closer to the men who fall on
the same side of the powerful-weak division.

It doesn't—in men's minds. Some of the toughest opposition to
the Equal Rights Amendment has been mounted by unions, and
it wasn't till 1973 that the AFL-CIO convention voted support
and changed its own constitution to conform. Which supplies an
interesting yardstick to the depth of the repugnance within nondominant men toward equality with women. Union leaders who
prefer a divided labor movement to giving women equality (and
a shot at overtime pay) are clearly motivated by forces beyond the
reach of logic.

The third aspect of the opposition by nondominant men to
women's demands is grounded in men's need to retain the image
of woman as "other." That's connected of course with the idea of
woman as inferior, most obviously (as de Beauvoir pointed out)
because if you are the *first* sex, you will be the setter of norms, not
the deviates who must be defined in "other" terms. But being
"other" signifies a great many things besides being inferior, and
these aspects of "otherness" quite often seem to men to have positive values. Women who want to be regarded as human beings
first and female only incidentally—they are upsetting the old, long-
standing value system in what seems to men an ungracious and
ungrateful way. This lapse is what provokes all those jokes about
opening doors and pulling out chairs and rising when a woman
enters the room, for these gestures have been the honorifics, so
to speak, of the traditional male/female relationship, pointing up
the sex difference. All this to-do about minor manners seems non-
sensical to rational women, but when we maintain that, we are
being simpleminded, not rational. This kind of to-do is a clue to
the meaning of myth. Minor manners could give rise to such a fuss
only by symbolizing something else, something important. Indeed,
Professor Laurel Richardson Walum of Ohio State enlivened the
proceedings of last fall's meeting of the American Sociological
Association by delivering a paper on "The Changing Door Ceremony." Professor Walum's students were enlisted to invade public places and deliberately violate the regular ritual of door open-

ing, in which the female modestly steps aside, "demonstrating frailty, ineptitude and a need for protection," and waits till the male opens the door, thus displaying "the male virtues of physical strength, mechanical ability, worldliness, self-confidence and efficiency." Who would have thought so much could be read from door ritual? But its violation produced confusion and embarrassment, and allowed Professor Walum to conclude that "the hand that holds the door-knob rules the world." And sociological jokiness aside, we can't deal with the distress occasioned by variations in such day-to-day actions unless we see that they are symbols of proper attitudes and behavior.

But why do men need to have women accept the role of "other"? What positive value can there be to such a position? I believe that the value lies not just in pushing women out of competition in man's world, but in the fact that this apartness serves to keep alive a different system of values, another set of norms and goods. "Others" (women) serve as repositories for ideals and life-styles which men feel they cannot themselves take on but which, they suspect, may have some potential usefulness. These values have been significant in the past and sometimes are still given lip service as virtues. Such ideals don't answer in the contemporary arena of day-to-day activity, but one doesn't quite like to kill them off.

Let us glance at one. In an earlier age when most normal human beings (i.e., men) were unable to disguise from themselves the fact of their inequality with the power elite, when such inequality was an everywhere evident aspect of daily life, Christian humility was a socially useful ideal, often preached and sometimes practiced. For the oppressed, it justified their oppression and thus allowed those who might otherwise have floundered in shame to support lives they could not change.

If it is argued that they could have changed their lives by successful determined revolt, and that Christian humility functioned to keep them from revolting, I can counter only by saying that, in fact, it didn't. Other, millennial Christian ideals nurtured a long series of peasant rebellions, all of which were ultimately unsuccessful. As long as rebellions were doomed to failure, the ideal of humility had the positive value of shielding those who had failed from seeing themselves as nothing but failures. At the point when modern times and modern technology made it possible for rebellions to succeed—sometime in the eighteenth century—humility became a virtue not so much of the weak per se as of women. And since it may become useful once again, at some future date, it remains a part of the female hoard of virtues, stored for safekeeping till needed. Indeed, since women today have not yet rebelled successfully, it continues to support the identity of those who would otherwise have to name themselves failures. Whether we consider that a good thing or a bad thing will depend on how sanguine we are about women's chances of successful revolt.

One function of "otherness," then, is social, to keep archaic attitudes and once-useful character traits in being against a day when they may once more meet a need. Concomitantly the personal use to men of woman-as-other (and honor again to de Beauvoir for her exposition of the point) is as locus for projection by the First Sex of its desires, needs and fears, so that emotions which can't be allowed full play in "real life" can be somehow absorbed or transformed. All wives and most secretaries expect to be dumped on now and then, not just as confidantes to whom frustrations can be reported but as surrogates on whom they can be vented. Not, of course, that all the emotions projected onto women by men are angry, any more than they are all lustful urges toward sex objects. Woman-as-other provides a focus for many needs and yearnings: for tenderness, given and asked for; for maternal protection; for divine assurance; for support against forces of depersonalization; for evidence of the existence of self-sacrifice and loving-kindness. Women are thought of by men (and thus they are instructed to be) upholders and transmitters of high virtues and values. They are validators of emotions and interpreters of experience. To men, this seems a role of great dignity and nobility, an elevation. Why do women refuse the pedestal?

How very hard it is for women to make clear that to the extent that one's life is spent as only a terribly necessary aspect of someone else's life, one ceases to be a person in oneself. To accept that one is "other" rather than human is to deny one's identity *as a* human and feel one's own personality as obtrusive, clouding the mirror one is supposed to be.

And how very hard it is for men to accept women's need to take on the unworthy (it seems to them) everydayness of mere human personality! For if women are simply people, no better and no worse than men, where are men's dreams to roost? Who will forgive them for their trespasses? Who will accept the sins they cannot accept themselves, minister to the needs that shame them, reflect their view of the world back to them unchanged and so make it real, echo their curses and confirm their creeds? Isn't that power? men ask. What more do they want?

And here we see, I think, a convergence not just of sex and power, but of our current need, in this post-Christian world, for affirmation of meaning and significance in life which is disturbingly absent. The Sacred has deserted us. We have no central Church to explain the world inarguably, only religious splinters. Though they may support and illuminate those who believe and practice their rites, they lack the authority of earlier times. They are defiant or defensive rather than confident. Outside the churches other seekers rummage through debris from the occult, hoping for clues to a mystic order which will illuminate the ordinary jangle of events. Common as this is, its importance is still very marginal, and marginal too is the drug road to transcendence. Our approved drug, alcohol, is not in fact used for transcendent experience at all, but simply for private easement. Other cultures have used drugs in religious rites, but it's a very alien practice for us and remains either an incidental counterculture affair, or the product of a totally different culture, like the Navajo peyote ceremonies. Even our current interest in reaching "a drugless high" appears to envisage these experiences as private, mystic connections, not public ceremonies. They are apparently thought of as substitutes for drug use, not communal celebrations.

Given the decline in religion as a common road to transcendence and the tie of drugs to aberration, the importance of sex as a way out of the drabness of everyday living, as a blameless joyful extension of experience, becomes very great. Obviously,

it is as great for women as for men, but I am not at the moment
arguing their case. I am instead attempting to understand and
explore the dismay of men who find themselves confronted by
an unexpected shift in the way their partners in this enriching
experience behave and ask to be regarded. When women demand
equal status with men and insist that they are simply human
beings, they are (in men's eyes) not refusing a subordinate role
at all, they are refusing the awesome status of priestess, mediator
between the human and the sacred sphere.

Woman-as-other, they repeat, is woman-on-a-pedestal. If she is
limited by her position, her limitations echo those of the priest-
kings of the past who could not be allowed common humanity
because they embodied the whole tribe's connection to another
sacred and significant world which irradiated the ordinary. Evidence of human failing could not be tolerated in such figures, and
with the high honor given them went the duty to accept death
before age could disfigure or weaken them. The doom of a region
ruled by an ailing Fisher King still makes us shiver when Eliot
invokes it in *The Wasteland.* And just so, an eerie uneasiness in
the depths of the mind is roused by women when they insist on
abdicating their role as mediating "other." If they do that and
"become men"—that is, merely human—they leave men alone in
the face of a threatening universe.

To come back for a moment to *Last Tango in Paris,* we should
regard it not just as a counterassertion against women's demands,
but as an expression of need. It declares that the acquiescence of
women in men's sexual acts—that is, in their desperate reach for
transcendence and a connection to the sacred—is the way men
validate their sense of themselves, of their very right to exist and
enforce demands and be assuaged of pain and anger and frustration, and that this right is paramount, essential to life. The existence of power depends on the right to dominate. Take it away,
and men will cease to be men. Which means that by "becoming
men" women are threatening men with "becoming women"—that
is, with having to acknowledge no identity except that shared one
of weakness.

For the powerful male, of course, is granted easy dominance and
shielded from constant frustration. It is the weak who suffer daily

hurt, who do indeed know what is it to be inferior. For them, women have become the only territory on which their daring and drive can prove itself. And so, for them, women must be "other," a nameless and faceless creature with the right to say Yes, but not No. We see these fantasies spelled out in *Playboy* and *Penthouse* and the other magazines of this nature. They normalize the premises of pornography and assure their readers that dominance is right, by surrounding these battered egos with a world full of female puppets who can be clothed in dreams and desires without intruding unwelcome personalities. The Women's Movement can see all that, but have we paid enough attention in our strategies, I wonder, to the need behind it, the terrible need to dominate *something?* If your sense of inferiority persuades you that you can't successfully dominate another human being, you are going to try to find a puppet.

Thus, when women say, "We do not want to be puppets anymore," and they have been saying that since Nora slammed the door, the obvious fairness of this cry mustn't be taken as obvious to men. To many men, these women seem to be saying, "We refuse any longer to receive and act out your hopes and dreams." The dreams are what men see, and women's refusal to respond to them appears a brusque and undeserved rejection of a very precious gift, the gift of oneself, of trust, made by asking for something one needs so badly. The idea that they are reducing women to puppets and denying them individual identities by forcing *their,* male, dreams on women is equally overlooked by men. And the greater the need for acceptance and reflection of these desires, the harder it is for the men who harbor them to understand why they should be rejected.

In Baton Rouge, Louisiana, where I visited this past flood season, the Equal Rights Amendment was coming up for discussion in the legislature. Its support is largely respectable and middle class—rational, I guess you'd say. Its opposition runs a gamut, but it certainly reaches beyond the rational. The night before I arrived in town, a furious female opponent had taken to the airwaves and castigated the local chapter of the National Organization for Women (which in Baton Rouge is about as radical as the League of Women Voters) for upholding homosexuality and aiming to castrate normal males. The members of NOW whom I met were almost more astounded by the attack than they were angry, and one saw—as with Nixon's henchmen when Watergate brought them to the surface—how useful the numbing shock effect of calculated effrontery can be. But Mme. X was not simply outrageous, she was aiming her outrages well; for she invoked the deep fear that equality for women means that men will be treated *like* women, will be faced with the alternatives of choosing to act the woman's sexual role (homosexuality) or being turned into eunuchs by castration. To admit one's equality with women means taking on membership in the second sex among creatures who are not quite human, who are not protected by bonds of fellow feeling, whose alliance with the powerful has been lost and, with it, their protection against use and misuse and abuse of all sorts. It means sporting a badge as engulfing of hope and possibilities as the yellow star Jews wore in Hitler's Germany.

Put at its simplest, men whose experience has taught them that equality between weak and powerful doesn't exist find it intensely difficult to imagine that admitting women to equality (and what that means is unclear to them at best) will not somehow jeopardize their own insecure position. The idea that joining with women to oppose the power structure might be profitable is regarded as ludicrous: how could you profit by taking on an ally weaker than yourself? Your losses, on the contrary, are clear: the only sure security you have is that guaranteed by women's inferior place. Dissolving the sex difference will accentuate the power difference. It will drop you into the limbo where exploitation doesn't just happen, but is sanctioned.

To say these are nightmare fears doesn't make them easier to deal with. Can they be dealt with at all? Or is the nascent Women's Movement going to spawn a bitter and disruptive backlash that will stop it in its tracks? There is, of course, no easy answer. We are certainly going to get some backlash, though more important than verbal attack by mythic pronouncements will be the continuance of inaction which the attacks serve to justify. The idea that women are going to climb easily into positions of power because fairness demands that they be represented according to their numbers is naive; and, in fact, few women take seriously Government rulings on equal employment as effective in themselves. They will have to be invoked and enforced by repeated court action. But despair over the prospect is at least as naive, because so much has already happened. The economic and technological base for a world polarized by sex into dual systems of occupation and behavior began to vanish years ago. The strength of the Women's Movement doesn't lie in its rhetoric, but in the fact that it is a response (diverse and unorganized still, and the better for it) to changed realities.

One such reality is a very different kind of family structure from that we still frame as ideal, much reduced in sheer numbers, reduced in necessary or useful activities, in specialness—the tide of television gives children a common, nonfamily-related world of experience as soon as they can talk—and greatly reduced in active relations to a wider community. Such relations are now individual, not made as a family group.

Economic needs now pull families apart instead of supporting their existence as working groups. Working mothers and wives aren't new, but today they must leave the home to earn, and though that too began years ago, only in the last generation has support to working mothers from relatives, neighbors and hired help dwindled to practically zero. The demand for child-care centers (for example) is forced on women by the present situation. For most working mothers the alternative is untrained baby-sitters, custodial day-care with other untrained women in their homes— or the street and an empty (except for TV) apartment.

Equally, the isolation of the family has reinforced the effort to bring fathers closer into child care and housework. It's a response (good in itself but inadequate) to the lack of community support for the family and to our American social mobility that separates young couples from their families. Communes and cluster-living may help in time, but they are not only still disapproved socially, they also seem to many to involve too great a loss of privacy. To be brief, a great many of our widespread contemporary problems have surfaced first, or in slightly different but acute form, in women's lives because they affect the family drastically. All too often they have been seen exclusively as family problems, personal dilemmas. The isolation of women from one another, each tucked away in her nuclear family, leaves a woman to grope with difficulties that may well have been thrust on her by society in the belief that she can solve them individually. One real reward that the Women's Movement has brought us all is the increasing realization that a lot of family upsets are not unique, but are instead the result of social dislocations. Understanding their nature makes them easier to cope with because it not only brings in the social context, but also gets rid of personal guilt.

Women can't solve these problems by themselves, or by male/female argument. They are bound up with the accepted social system as sustained by the power structure. But women at least are aware of them. I believe that intelligent men will start listening harder to what women are telling them about the realities they find themselves facing once they understand that these are offshoots of larger difficulties that show themselves in other areas. Polarization in society, alienation at work, isolation of families, the irrelevance of much current education, the fragmentation of life between work and leisure, the questioning of old values, including the astonishingly swift change in sex mores and practices —men as well as women are aware of these problems. None of them is unconnected with the social processes that are producing changes in women's role, for all of them (at the simplest level) affect the structure of the family and the norms by which children are raised.

For what it's worth, my own feeling about the future of the sexes is hopeful. Partly my optimism is based on as objective and historical-minded a judgment as I can come to. The fact that men's and women's lives are becoming more alike seems to me to open doors to understanding and affectionate friendship between them. In addition the increased ability of women to look after themselves as independent beings suggests that when they give love, it will be real love, not a hypocritical sham exacted by their dependence and often hiding secret resentment. I don't at all believe, as Erich Fromm does, that polarization of the sexes is necessary for a sound relationship between them. At any rate, it doesn't guarantee it, or how explain the large amount of homosexuality present in two such polarized societies as Periclean Greece and Victorian England? No, it seems to me that getting rid of sexual stereotypes can only enlarge the variety of *"petites différences"* which add a spice to affection.

Beyond objectivity, I find myself unable to ignore my old novelist's sense of mood. I have met an awful lot of liberated women in the last three years, and the constant impression they make is sheer enjoyment of life and good-feeling with each other. That is indeed a personal reaction, but it may be worth recording as an offset to the constant recurrence of sad tales about unhappy and lonesome women who have chosen feminism and therefore (!) left their mates, to their everlasting regret. God knows there's trouble enough in women's lives. I don't want to belittle the difficulties that social change and the need to deal with it have bestowed on women. But even Pandora's box included more than trouble: it offered hope too. In women's lives today there is more than trouble; there is courage and confidence in one's ability to deal with the world, there is reliance on trustworthy friendship and a sense of alliance with others in a common task. Women used to be very lonely. They are less so now, and I don't mean just in the cities of the "advanced" East, but in Arkansas, Wisconsin, Louisiana, and Iowa; in Oregon, Missouri, Virginia, Tennessee, Delaware, Michigan, Massachusetts, western Pennsylvania, upstate New York and places in between. Most of the women I have run into and talked with are married, or see no reason why they may not be. Lots of them have children; they are coping with jobs or with studies too; and they have been overwhelmingly energetic, cheerful, funny and good-natured. They were also, those I met, of all ages, many backgrounds and several colors. Discount my impression by all means, by whatever amount you desire, but it was everywhere the same, and everywhere positive.

Out of this experience and cogitation let me make two recommendations for future discourse between the sexes. I think women would do well to widen the context in which they see their needs and present their demands. A change in sex roles is a challenge to personal dominance and to political power both; to men as individuals and to a male caste which has a stake in separating itself from women, or at least thinks it has. I believe also that women would profit by a study of power and its workings. They might even produce some effective new techniques just because they come fresh to macropolitics, but they also need to see how such political action differs from private tussles over domination in the personal sphere.

As for men, I suggest that more of them listen more to women, and listen with the possibility in mind that some of what women say may not only be serious but even sensible. For the first time in history, perhaps, it is women's experience which is changing faster and more radically than that of men. In itself that bears witness to the profundity of the changes and it might alert men to the value of taking a look at them. Certainly it will not be easy to overcome men's fears of the effects of change in woman's role and image, but these fears are grounded in a mythology that is less and less in tune with social actuality. Mythologies do change as their support falls away, and perhaps we might find some cheer in the fact that men who habitually work with women, as equals in man's world, seem to be less disturbed by the ideas of equality for women than men who don't. In part, men's fear of equality is based on ignorance of how such a situation would work in practice. Our best evidence that the situation can work comes from the experience of those who have been living with it, and that seems to me realistically heartening.

XIV

Reviewing books is good exercise for a writer of books if only because it involves an exercise in role-reversal. A writer-reviewer turns into a reader for a while and must think analytically about processes which are largely unconscious when one is writing: how to communicate experience as fully as possible, how to produce an intended emotion, how to use the instruments of language and literary device to create a simulacrum of reality which will seem plausible and moving to the reader. Beyond this, reviewers know that many nascent ideas, not yet solid enough for full, coherent expression in an independent form, will first come to light by attaching themselves to the words and ideas of others. A bell rings there, an echo resonates in one's own mind. Out of the hundreds of reviews I seem to have written over the last quarter-century, I've culled here a handful in which my own thinking about women surfaced clearly.

I add them to the very contemporary material which makes up the rest of this book for two reasons. First, they offer a view of one woman awakening; for though women's potentialities and capabilities had always been part of my awareness, it still took time and change to make clear the *importance* for society of seeing women's equality with men accepted and established. Second, it may hearten readers to find that women were thinking, twenty years ago, in terms that are not too different from those in use today; to find, that is, an historical base of counteropinion present even in the palmy days of the feminine mystique. If the century's early surge of feminist action and writing was reduced to a trickle, still the trickle never entirely dried up. The fact that it managed to survive stubbornly, and to reach an audience in a variety of publications, is evidence of its strength and vitality. It makes me happy to think that I was, in small part, a channel for its expression. Even my own 1969 reaction to the reviving Women's Movement, as being frivolous and gestural, may serve as a useful reminder that minds can change and clarify with time and experience, and is left as written for this purpose.

The reviews that follow run in date from 1953 to 1974 and appeared in *The New Leader, The New York Times, The Saturday Review, Harper's, The Atlantic* and *The Civil Liberties Review.*

Reviews: Books on Women, on Images

1. A Woman Examines Dr. Kinsey

Sexual Behavior in the Human Female. By Alfred C. Kinsey et al. Philadelphia, Saunders. 842 pp., $8.00.

The big news about the second Kinsey Report is that it doesn't seem to be news. As a human female, I find this, on the whole, more amusing than upsetting. It is really only what one might have expected: out comes the book on men, and the country goes wild, leaps up and down, debates and discusses and points with indignation. Fine! Dr. Kinsey, stunned but happy, goes back to his coded questionnaires and his discreet interviews, years pass, thousands of females answer hundreds of questions, the press pants at the heels of innocent members of the University of Indiana faculty, the book is unveiled in advance in a more than Pentecostal atmosphere, finally—shrouded in the obscurity of a bright yellow wrapper—it is put on sale. And what happens?

Nothing. Nothing at all. Nobody really gives a damn. About men, yes. Men care very deeply whether or not they enjoy themselves; and women care, too, because if men are not enjoying themselves, they will go and look for other women to enjoy themselves with.

But women enjoying themselves? Why, even the women don't care very much. At least, they care about other things first.

This is an irritating statement, I know, and I apologize to women for making it. It is not intended to express an eternal truth about women as against men, but only a fundamental truth about women in American society today. In many ways, it is a tribute to women's adaptability and grasp on reality. We still live in a male-first culture, if not in a patriarchal one, and in a Darwinian sense women are quite right to put survival and reproduction ahead of personal emotion—or, in Freudian terminology, to live by the reality principle rather than the pleasure principle. The surprising thing is that so many do it so successfully.

As for Dr. Kinsey's book, it is enormous, dull and—I would say —entirely true. The two major facts which emerge from it are valid and obvious. (Not that I wish to belittle Dr. Kinsey's work: Quantitative data are necessary to evaluate qualitative change.) The first, historical, fact is that the generations of women born after 1900 are able to respond better and to enjoy sexual experience more than the previous generations. Women who are not cramped by so many external restrictions—that is, who can earn their own livings, hold stimulating jobs and vote—are much less apt to be short-circuited sexually by inner restrictions. Liberty and the pursuit of happiness are closely tied together.

Dr. Kinsey's second great fact is that men and women are still by no means perfectly adjusted sexually. Of this conclusion, too, it is possible to say: *Si monumentum requiris, circumspice.* There are other ways in which they are not perfectly adjusted, nor do we dwell in a world in which perfect adjustment to life is either possible or particularly desirable. Still, the less energy that a human being, male or female, has to spend on adjustment—on repression, sublimation, the holding in check of neurotic anxieties and impulses—the more energy exists to feed sensible and generous action in the external world. Dr. Kinsey's differing curves of sexual activity among men and women—peaking for men in the 'teens, rising more slowly for women to a long plateau—are his most interesting contribution.

So far, the most general response to these unhappy curves has been anguished head-clasping—a regular egghead reaction, if I may say so, of despairing resignation, and not at all the stuff to feed the troops. Dr. Kinsey maintains that there is a millennia-old basis for human sexuality which can be traced in other mammalian species. Here I would argue: Man is, to such a much greater degree than any other, a social animal, and Dr. Kinsey has indicated so clearly a change in sexual kinetics based on social change that any mammalian fundamentals would seem not—or at least not yet—thoroughly established as unchangeable limits. The double standard—still operative—may appeal to biological fact as its authority, but it is nonetheless essentially a social, not a physiological, force. Our society accentuates any physiological differences that may exist between male and female responsiveness. I see no reason to assume that another type of culture might not all but damp out these differences.

For girls are still brought up to be—or rather to seem—chaste, and the human psyche is plastic enough for there to be considerable cooperation. The difficulty—as not only Dr. Kinsey has pointed out—is that marriage is supposed to convert a girl who says No into a woman whose response to her husband is immediate and appreciative. This is asking a good deal of the human psyche, particularly since the marriage ceremony has ceased to be a magical and mystical ritual: its catalytic power is not what it was. Naturally girls have been going around left end and saying Yes instead of No. Dr. Kinsey's confirmation of this well-known truth is again of interest quantitatively rather than qualitatively.

But the chief value of Dr. Kinsey's stupendous, repetitious and humorless effort is that it takes seriously the idea that women have a right to enjoy sexual experience—not just a right to the experience, but a right to the enjoyment. Embedded in our cultural consciousness is the sad and crippling idea that women use sex as a weapon. Too many of them do. The dreary adolescent dilemma, "How can I be popular if I don't pet, but won't I make myself cheap if I do?" is founded on just this premise—that sex is a tool to be used for domination, or security or some kind of egotistic end.

This assumption, of course, takes its toll in frigidity and misunderstanding and anxiety. Sex is not a tool. Equally, it is not merely an end in itself. Its value is both its own pleasure and release, and that, in addition, it can—enjoyed freely—blossom into affection and generosity and abiding joy. Dr. Kinsey has been accused of ignoring these values. Of course they are not what he is writing about, and indeed are not susceptible of statistical study. But Dr. Kinsey is against *Angst* and the *Angst*-makers, and however we may joke about the ponderous mountain of his research, it is not a mouse that he has brought forth.

The New Leader
November 16, 1953

2. A Woman's Role

The Better Half: The Emancipation of the American Woman.
By Andrew Sinclair. Illustrated. New York, Harper & Row. 401 pp., $6.95.
The Flight From Woman. By Karl Stern. New York, Farrar, Straus & Giroux. 310 pp., $4.95.

Books on Woman are getting to be nearly as large a sector of the publishing business as books on cooking. Andrew Sinclair, a thirty-year-old Englishman who is bucking for the degree of American Specialist and the mantle of D. W. Brogan, has written quite a sensible one. It is a historical study of the feminist movement in America which can stand beside his earlier volume of social history, *Prohibition: The Era of Excess*. It is well documented, if not really scholarly. Mr. Sinclair has obviously spent time in good libraries (he lists seven in the introduction to his notes) and has read not only the relevant books, back to John Knox at least, but also many of the unpublished journals and letters in the Library of Congress and the Woman's Archive at Radcliffe College.

Overall, he deserves a B+ for his work, which pulls much material together and should become a useful source for anyone wanting to trace the shifts of power and priorities within the Women's Movement from the days of Lucretia Mott to those of Carrie Chapman Catt. (Mr. Sinclair persists in denying Mrs. Catt her middle name, though, which is a bit like referring to the politics of David George, or the writings of Robert Warren and Katherine Porter. All in all, I suspect that this rare slip is due to his age rather than to his country of origin.)

If Mr. Sinclair doesn't earn an A with this book, it is largely because his research has been cobbled together in a number of places, and the stitches show. He has got hold of a wealth of material, but it is not sufficiently organized into one whole. There are areas of puzzlement and apparent contradiction where his conclusions do not quite gibe with each other. No doubt it is often a matter of emphasis, with one argument taking priority here and another there. But the effect is to make the book anecdotal and journalistic. Still, much of Mr. Sinclair's material is revealing in itself, and quite a bit has been pulled together skillfully enough to illuminate other aspects of history.

From the beginning, the Women's Movement had to choose whether to make alliances with other reformers, or to go it alone. Before the Civil War the Woman's Righters and the Abolitionists felt a natural sympathy, but neither could agree to a full working partnership. "We have good cause to be grateful to the slave," wrote the feminist and abolitionist Abby Kelley, "for the benefit we have received to *ourselves* in working for *him*. In striving to strike his irons off, we found most surely that *we* were manacled *ourselves*." (Miss Kelley's italics.) Nevertheless, each group included those who felt that to work against both evils was to tie them inextricably together and invite prejudice to reject both. There were conservative ladies (not all Southern) who were readier to pray for the slave than to admit his equality. Equally, the women remembered the Negro delegate to an antislavery convention in England who spoke against seating American women delegates. The majority agreed with him and exiled the women to the gallery.

Later, the suffrage movement had to choose whether to join the early trade unionists and the temperance workers. It was plagued by regional divisions, with the conservative eastern wing, under Lucy Stone, fighting, and then splitting from, the more radical Midwesterners led by Elizabeth Cady Stanton and Susan B. Anthony. Both groups were attacked as advocating free love and both did, in fact, get themselves involved in contemporary scandals. The Conservatives elected Henry Ward Beecher as first president of the American Suffrage Association just in time to sit out his trial for "misconduct"—i.e., the seduction of Mrs. Theodore Tilton, one of his parishioners. At the same time, the National Woman Suffrage Association, led by Mrs. Stanton and Miss Anthony, had taken Victoria Woodhull to its heart when, as Mr. Sinclair puts it "this charismatic clairvoyant, stockbroker and courtesan . . . appeared on the scene of woman's rights." Mrs. Woodhull and her sister, Tennessee Claflin, were happy to add suffrage to the list of causes, which already included spiritualism and free love, defended by their not too savory *Woman's Journal*. It was estimated that these unfortunate events and relationships set the Women's Movement back twenty years by costing it the support of the respectable.

About this Mr. Sinclair is somewhat skeptical. Indeed he declares (and here he is unambiguous) that it wasn't until "working women became organized in trade unions and threw their support behind the suffragettes [that] all American adult women received the vote." This came with the passage of the Nineteenth Amendment in 1920, the year that saw Warren G. Harding elected President and ushered in the decade of Flaming Youth. The moral, perhaps, is that you can't win anything important if you're worried about respectability.

There is a great deal more lively reporting and anecdote in Mr. Sinclair's book, and there are the beginnings of some interesting theses on the origins of American reform movements, on the celebrated influence of the frontier and on the changing relationships between American cities and small towns. I am sorry that they are not worked out more clearly and thoroughly, for Mr.

Sinclair has an inquiring mind and his book is free of most of the dubious cant which so often infects authors who have decided to answer the Woman Question. My husband once phrased this question as "Does the author of that book believe women are men or cows?" In his last chapter, Mr. Sinclair comes down on the side of woman as man: which is certainly better than a vote for woman as cow.

Dr. Karl Stern, on the other hand, in *Flight From Woman,* believes that the polarity of the sexes is more important than the equivalence between men and women as human beings. He believes that woman is tied "deeply to the life of nature, to the pulse beat of the Cosmos." He believes that it is significant that "the words for *mother* and *matter,* for *mater* and *materia,* are etymologically related." As he puts it: "If there had been female Bachs or Newtons, no power on earth could have kept them from producing. Having been barred from the basic training is no argument." He quotes approvingly from Ortega y Gasset:

> The more of a man one is, the more he is filled to the brim with rationality. Everything he does and achieves, he does and achieves for a reason, especially for a practical reason. A woman's love, that divine surrender of her ultra-inner being which the impassioned woman makes, is perhaps the only thing which is not achieved by reasoning. The core of the feminine mind, no matter how intelligent the woman may be, is occupied by an irrational power. If the male is the rational being, the female is the irrational being.

Now, I am not trying to prove here that the rational male mind of Dr. Stern can, like the White Queen, believe six impossible things before breakfast. I am trying to offer a sample of his method, because his method embodies his thesis. Actually, what he wants to talk about is not so much the difference between men and women, but a subject that he associates with this difference: the current overvaluation of analytical thinking (scientific, male) and the corresponding undervaluation of intuitive perception (poetic, female).

Dr. Stern is certainly right in thinking that the scientific method is being applied in areas where it does not clarify but obfuscates. In addition, he sees it as having invaded the world of personal relationships to produce, on the one hand, frantic activism with no real end in view, and on the other, that well-known phenomenon, the alienated soul. Here I think he has confused the scientific method with its present results, and is moreover judging these results only on their defects. It is surely within the bounds of possibility that science can build a less divisive, more coherent world than the one we inhabit at the moment.

Again, there is indeed a difference between analytical thinking and intuitive perception, and each is useful according to what one's aim is. But Dr. Stern seems to have gone as far in the other direction as the misusers of analytical thinking have. He is using intuitive perception to try to make an argument, and it is just as unsuited for this purpose as analysis is for making poetry. Again and again he falls into nominalism; it is surely not significant *as a fact* that the words for mother and matter are related; it is significant as an indication of how the human mind works.

Again and again, too, he takes metaphor literally and makes superstition of it: "To the ancients . . . the relationship between things human and things beyond the human was part of an intrinsic order of the world. . . . The Elizabethans had a keen sense of this: a famous statement of it is Ulysses's speech on 'degree' in 'Troilus and Cressida.' Hamlet's first reflection, on hearing of his family's tragedy, is: 'The time is out of joint.' . . . All it means is that between the spiritual order and order in the human family, between things ontological and the microcosm of everyday life, there exists a correspondence." This last sentence is not to be attributed to Hamlet or, to the ancients. It is Dr. Stern speaking.

Dr. Stern is a psychiatrist, presently practicing in Montreal. The substance of his book is a series of psychoaesthetic critiques of some writers and some characters. His chapters are headed: Descartes, Schopenhauer, Sartre, Hedda Gabler and Her Companions, Tolstoy, Kierkegaard, Goethe. Now, criticism is a perfectly valid field for intuitive perception—as a beginning. But even here it is not enough. How can one persuade the good doctor that, simply because one perceives something intuitively, it is not necessarily so? That it should be laid out on the counter of the mind and compared, by reason, to other perceptions? And that even the most deeply felt perception may not have much meaning for anyone else? "Schopenhauer opened up that vast unredeemed world of the irrational which gave birth to Wagner and Nietzsche." "Something had gone wrong with Love itself in the world into which [Kierkegaard] was born." What can we make of such sentences? Dr. Stern may have made a discovery, but he does not manage to pass much of it on.

I don't believe that it is impossible to write a good book about the situation of women in the present world; though I believe that anyone starting with this subject will find himself moving away both from the present and from women into a discussion of the future of humanity, as he follows the trail of his questions and his discoveries toward some tentative hypotheses. But I do believe that to write such a book would be difficult in any case, and is quite impossible for anyone approaching his subject with a ready-made thesis. Naturally, the people who want to undertake such a vast project are likely to be those who are fired and fueled by a thesis. Women are thus, men on the contrary are so, the only way to fulfillment is via the the nursery. And yet, how flexible, how malleable, humanity is! How capable still of evolution! To lock even one sex to a pattern of behavior is wasteful and burdensome. Besides—it won't stay there.

The New York Times
August 1, 1965

3. The Lives of Four Women

Titania. By Permenia Migel. New York, Random House, $8.95.
The Last Years of a Rebel, A Memoir of Edith Sitwell. By Elizabeth Salter. Boston, Houghton Mifflin, $5.00.

Too Strong For Fantasy. By Marcia Davenport. New York, Charles Scribner's Sons, $8.95.

Twenty Letters to a Friend. By Svetlana Allilueva. New York, Harper & Row, English, $5.95. Russian, 7.95 (and worth the difference).

Here are the lives of four women. Two tell their own stories, two are the subject of biographies by friends close to them in their later years. Svetlana Allilueva is forty-one, Marcia Davenport sixty-four. Edith Sitwell died in December 1964 at seventy-seven, Isak Dinesen in 1962 at the same age. How much of the world in our century they have seen between them! Is it a world that differs in any way from that seen by men?

I think so, although it is not the private household world one thinks of as being "feminine." These women have lived and worked in the great world as much as any man has. They are all able, all capable of decision and action. They have fought to be responsible for themselves; and yet not one of them has controlled her own life in the way that men of equal talent expect to do. When they acted, it was out of necessity. The decisions they made resolved dilemmas instead of being arrived at by free choice. Not one of them made a "successful" marriage, though each loved one man deeply and passionately. All of them outlived their lovers, too, two of whom died violently. There is very little humor and much tragedy in these books, and above all a sense of struggle.

By contrast, two recent autobiographies of distinguished men, Bertrand Russell and Harold Nicholson, breathe a very different atmosphere. Wit, humor, easy control of life and freely taken decisions mark them. Russell and Nicholson were certainly as serious in their attitude toward their work, but it was by comparison a straightforward approach, simple and untormented. Russell writes of the exhausting years during which he strove to complete the *Principia Mathematica,* but nothing stood between him and the struggle. He had no need to justify it to himself or anyone else. None of these women was able to approach a career with such simplicity.

This lack of control over and space in life is not necessarily "a bad thing," for one may very well see more, do more and become more out of compulsion than by one's own intentions.

But it accounts for the lack of humor and play in these stories. There was little room for it, and little psychic energy left for such indulgence. Edith Sitwell's wit was famous, of course, but there was nothing playful about it. It was a weapon, used on the theory that the best defense is the offense. No doubt successful men are as busy, and sometimes feel as driven, as women with careers, but somehow they ride life more easily and with less effort. I suspect this is due to nurture, not nature, habit, not instinct—but that's another subject. At any rate, the twentieth century as witnessed by these four women is a tormenting, tragic and overwhelming epoch.

Isak Dinesen, the oldest and probably the most widely read, is represented by the least good book. I have never, myself, found her work particularly sympathetic, but I don't think this influences my opinion that Permenia Migel's lengthy biography is wooden and pedestrian. *That* Isak Dinesen's own books are not. (I find them baroquely, sentimentally banal.) Her life is recounted here in relentless, imperceptive detail, and she comes to life as a person only rarely. Then it is usually when she is being unpleasant. On a trip to New York, for instance, she told friends that she particularly wanted to meet Pearl Buck, and a luncheon was arranged. Miss Dinesen came late and talked steadily. Her desired guest was quite left out. "Was that really Pearl Buck?" she asked later. "She certainly didn't say much!" Of course Miss Buck had received the Nobel Prize, and Miss Dinesen had not. Her vanity, her need for adoration from young men, the unending demands she made on those around her, these details live; whereas her undoubted courage, the insight and verve which won her such a range of friends in Europe, Africa and America, her untiring interest in life and the welcome she extended to the young must be surmised.

Karen Blixen was born into an old, well-to-do but not aristocratic Danish family. Her heritage, however, was not the settled upper-middle-class *Gemütlichkeit* this might imply. Her father, an idealistic liberal, was a wanderer—he came to America and lived among the Indians for two years in the 1870's—and something of a soldier of fortune. His daughter adored him—and he shot himself when she was ten years old.

It was the first note of tragedy, but not the last. Brought up in a household which demanded intellectual daring and conventional behavior, Karen (or Tania, as she was called) married in order to gain independence. The marriage took her to East Africa, which she came to love deeply, but in every other way it was disastrous. Except that to survive at all, she had to make herself a life. She did. Her best book, *Out of Africa*, tells much of that story. She spent seventeen years there of glory, misery, danger, drudgery, disillusion and fulfillment, divorced her husband, fought to make her coffee plantation a going concern, formed deeply affectionate relationships with many Africans and met her great love. This was Denys Finch-Hatton, an Elizabethan Englishman born out of his time. In the end, circumstances defeated her. The plantation could not be kept up and, numb with misery, she sold it and prepared to leave Africa. Just before she sailed, Finch-Hatton was killed when his plane crashed on take-off.

She had married to get away from boredom and the restrictions of her home life. Back in Denmark, she began to write her way out of despair. Her first book, *Seven Gothic Tales*, cast back to the world of her ancestors. Perhaps its artifices stem from her need to hold reality at bay. Its publication in America brought her instant fame, and her career began. But the events of her personal life were over—except for the crippling encroachment of the ugly disease which was the only lasting gift her husband had made her. Unfortunately, the book Mrs. Migel has written is largely devoted to these later years of work and fame and minor friendships and minor feuding. It makes dull reading.

One might expect the same thing to be true of the short memoir of Dame Edith Sitwell (she was very insistent on the use of her title) by her secretary, Elizabeth Salter, but it is not so. Of course this is not in the same class with Dame Edith's own book on her life, *Taken Care Of,* or her brother's magnificent quartet of volumes on their wildly erratic parents, but then—who writes like a Sitwell? Only another Sitwell. Mrs. Salter has produced a warm, acute and affectionate portrait of a remarkable woman. The chronicling is kept to a minimum, and if a television interview is reported in detail, it is because the details tell us a great deal about Dame Edith.

Mrs. Salter was devoted to her, but not blindly. She came as a stranger, but their relationship grew steadily in intimacy and trust. Her help in the production of Dame Edith's own volume of memoirs is acknowledged there, and beyond that, she was a pillar of good sense and responsibility in the personal life of her employer, who became her friend. She tried to make sense of Dame Edith's finances (which were complicated on one side by debts to the Inland Revenue, and on the other by the lady's feudal generosity), she found apartments and nurses, she took her around the world, she knew which furious letters to send, which to amend and which to suppress, and with it all she maintained her own dignity and kept her own work going—she is a detective novelist of skill. She records her memories with grace and precision, to make of Dame Edith a living presence, sharp-tongued, haughty, witty and warm, indomitable, stubborn, generous, vain, creative and appealing.

She was six feet tall and astonishing-looking, with a great beak of a nose, broad forehead and receding chin. She maintained that she looked like Queen Elizabeth, having inherited the same Plantagenet blood through her mother's family, and indeed the monument to Elizabeth in Westminster Abbey (reproduced here) supports that claim. Alice Toklas described her as the height of a grenadier, and once some Parisian children pursued her, crying, "Soldat anglais!" "Edith turned on them with great dignity," writes Mrs. Salter, "and answered, 'Sans les soldats anglais, vous n'auriez pas gagné la guerre.'" It is typical that she should speak to historical fact and ignore personal implications. Pavel Tchelitchew, whom she loved deeply, painted her six times, and wonderfully; but so powerful was her personality and so unique her appearance that even news photographs could not blur or obscure her.

Her own autobiography tells the story of her childhood with parents whose behavior to each other and to their children makes the word "eccentric" grow pale and stammer. Her father, "indescribably mean . . . resembled a portrait of one of the Borgias. . . . Apart from the fact that he had married my mother, [his] principal worry was that the world did not understand that it had been created in order to prove his theories." As for her mother, she was wont to remark "with a faraway, idealistic look in her eyes . . . 'Of course, what I would *really* like would be to get your father put in a lunatic asylum.' " Edith was the oldest child by some years, and growing up in the power of this pair must have sent weaker characters into lifelong madness. She was saved, one supposes, by the inner resource of her talent and by the alliance of admiring affection which existed between herself and her brothers. Finally, at the start of World War I, a particularly sordid domestic contretemps gave her the opportunity to move out of her parents' home. Her independent life began, never easy, sometimes catastrophic, but in its own way, triumphant. Read Mrs. Salter's book for a vivid summing up of Edith Sitwell's achievement, and for a speaking likeness of this fascinating creature.

The two women who tell their own stories both begin by declaring that they were writing less about themselves than about the people who shaped their lives. Marcia Davenport is the daughter of Alma Gluck by her first marriage. Mrs. Davenport barely remembers her father, and doesn't mention his name. Her mother married very young. She loved to sing, but had no idea that she possessed the kind of voice that is remembered fifty years later by those who heard her concerts. A friend, coming for dinner, overheard Mme. Gluck singing. An opera lover, he steered her to a good teacher, and she moved into her career with the natural ease of a swan breasting water. The man she had married faded from the picture, and Marcia Davenport's early world was completely centered on the mother she adored.

Alma Gluck was also a mother from whom one had to recover, though not in the same way as was Lady Sitwell. Loving her mother and longing for freedom, Gluck's daughter was pulled two ways. The contest went on all through her childhood, past her own hasty first marriage (to a man whose name she doesn't mention), and into the years when she was making a good income at *The New Yorker* and living with Russell Davenport. (She married him later.) Her mother (long since the heroine of a happy second marriage to Efrem Zimbalist) disapproved of her daughter's unconventional life, and one day she said so, ending with the words, "I won't have it!" "You won't?" replied her daughter. "Just what can you do about it?" After a moment Mme. Gluck burst into laughter, and Marcia felt herself finally independent.

This is a long book, full of gossip about personalities. Mme. Gluck, Toscanini and Max Perkins play the leading roles, but there are many supporting parts. For a good deal of the time, this book too suffers from the need to chronicle. Mrs. Davenport's novels are the old-fashioned kind, and her style is to have no style but to get everything in. Her autobiography is written in the same way and few readers can care about all the things Mrs. Davenport cares about quite as much as she does. One slogs along, bowing to Harry Luce and Wendell Willkie as they appear, with other land-marks of the time, and reflecting that Mrs. Davenport did indeed go many places and meet many people.

Then she met Jan Masaryk. The whole story changes tone and deepens. He was the love of her life, and as everyone remembers (or should) he met a tragic and horrible end when the Commu-nists took power in Czechoslovakia in 1948. He was Foreign Min-ister in the coalition government under Benes when he and Mrs. Davenport met, and the struggle to keep the Communists from gaining complete control of the country was already bitter. She brought him warmth and comfort in his personal life at a time when his public situation was desperately difficult. They planned to marry, but never quite got to it. She bought an apartment in Prague, which she had known and loved before the war, and was there often. Indeed, it was easier to face the future there than to be in New York where their friends would urge Masaryk, when he came to the UN, to leave the government. Loyalty to the memory of his father, who had founded the Czech state, kept him in office, and the feeling that his presence was the only thing that stiffened Benes's will to resist. Then Benes had a stroke, and the Communist faction moved in for the kill. Mrs. Davenport left for London. Three days later Masaryk was found dead in the court-yard under the windows of his official residence. It was given out as suicide, but many doubted it then, and Mrs. Davenport is cer-tain it was assassination.

In the summer of 1947 Masaryk went to Moscow with a Czech delegation to see Stalin. He came back stunned, looking ill. Mrs. Davenport made it a rule not to question him on politics, unless he spoke first, but one evening she did ask, "How does Stalin treat you?"

"Oh, he's very gracious," Masaryk answered. "Of course he'd kill me if he could. But very gracious."

About a month after that visit, Stalin's daughter, Svetlana Allilueva, spent three weeks with her father at the Black Sea resort of Sochi. It was the first time that they had been together for years, for he had bitterly disapproved of her first marriage to Grigory Morozov. This had ended, however, and Stalin's attitude had somewhat softened though, his daughter records, she was still a source of irritation to him. Here is her account of him at that time.

> He was difficult to talk to. Strange as it may seem, we had nothing to say to each other. When we were alone, I'd rack my brain trying to think of something to talk about. I always felt as though I were standing at the foot of a high mountain. He was up above and I was shouting at him, but an isolated word here or there was all that was getting through. Only scattered words of his got through to me, too, and you can't have much of a conversation that way. . . . He had aged. He wanted peace and quiet. Rather, he didn't know himself just what it was he wanted. . . . The whole crowd would come for dinner, Beria, Malenkov, Zhdanov, Bulganin and the rest. I found it dull and exhausting to sit three or four hours at the table listening to the same old stories as if there were no news and nothing whatever going on in the world.

Perhaps the most fascinating revelation (if it can be called that) of this fascinating book is how true are all the legends of power, all the morality plays, all the myths. Stalin's situation at the end was one of total isolation. He might have been Tolkien's Lord of the Rings, alone on his dark tower, under the never-shifting shadow of his own taboo. In the last months of his life, *he had no doctor.* The only one he had trusted, Vinogradov, had been arrested, and he would let no other near him. He dosed himself. His secretary had been arrested too, and so had the old petty demon, Vlasik, who had commanded the domestic staff since the days of the GPU. Personal ties had been broken long ago. "It was as though my father was at the center of a black circle," writes

Mme. Allilueva, "and anyone who ventured inside vanished or perished or was destroyed in one way or another."

This book will be read for many reasons, but whatever brings readers to it, they will profit; most of all, perhaps, by discovering that the ogre had a human child for a daughter, whose nature obeyed the simplest human laws. Anyone who has been touched by affection for Russian culture has felt that there is a kind of noble simplicity and grandeur of feeling possible, indeed characteristic, in that country (along with a great many less attractive qualities, of course). This simplicity and sincerity shines everywhere in Mme. Allilueva's book. It is written with candor and breadth of spirit, and an utter lack of artifice.

Indeed she humanizes even her ogre-father, though not because she offers an apologia for him. What she does is make clear the nature of the terrible flaw which corrupted him and, like the sickness of the Fisher King, brought plague and paralysis to his country. Stalin was a very intelligent man, very perceptive, of course strong-willed, hard and courageous, completely puritanical about material things, who lacked that first virtue which underlies all fruitful growth—the ability to trust others. He expected to be betrayed.

Shakespeare made a tragedy out of the flaw. Stalin was shrewder and more cunning than Othello, but he found his Iago in Beria. That one became, Mme. Allilueva believes, Stalin's evil genius because he knew how to represent disagreement as betrayal. Once that word had been spoken, Stalin's heart chilled, and he turned away implacably from those who had been closest to him. It was Beria, she believes, who arranged the murder of Kirov, and so set in motion the New Inquisition and the purges. But even before the advent of Beria, when Svetlana's mother killed herself in 1934, Stalin rejected the thought that his wife's suicide was a reproach to him. He came to see that too as a betrayal.

How the child Svetlana survived her mother's death—she did not know it was suicide till ten years later when she was sixteen—and became the honest and magnanimous human being one meets in these pages is also a story out of legend or fairy tale. Quite simply, she was saved by her nurse; not from physical danger, but from the moral disaster which overtook her brother Vasily and sent him to an unmourned drunkard's grave. Alexandra Bychkov nursed Svetlana from the time she was born, and after her mother's death, she "was the only stable, unchanging thing left . . . the bulwark of home and family, of what, if it hadn't been for her, would have gone out of my life forever. . . . It was to her kisses and her words that I fell asleep at night [and] I started off each day in her cheery capable hands." The translation tends to level down and make ordinary the terse and vivid simplicity of the original, but in the Russian, Mme. Allilueva speaks of her nurse as being like "a huge good stove"; and again, describes her as "a bountiful, healthy, rustling-leaved tree of life, with boughs full of birds, washed by the rains and glinting in the sun." When she died, the child she had raised mourned her as the very nearest kin she had.

"We are all responsible for everything that happened," Svetlana Allilueva writes at the end of her book (though interestingly enough the sentence does not appear in the Russian text). It is of course what Father Zossima preached and what Alyosha Karamazov held to, in the face of his brother's tale of the Grand Inquisitor: that we are each responsible to all for all, and if men knew it, the world would become paradise. Neither Dostoevski nor Mme. Allilueva, I am sure, meant to limit that "we" to the Russian people. The lives of all of us are intertwined, and the similarities which echo in these books are correspondences, not coincidences.

Harper's
November 1967

4. Meg, Jo, Beth, Amy and Louisa

Meg, Jo, Beth and Amy are 100 years old on October 3, and except for Natasha Rostova, who is almost exactly their contemporary (*War and Peace* appeared over the years 1865 to 1869), the Marches must be the most read about and cried over young women of their years. In my time we read *Little Women* of course, but we liked to think it was because our sentimental mothers had loved the book so and urged it on us. For all I know, this is still the cover story today, but just the same, the answer to "Have you read *Little Women*?" is still "Of course." In the last week I've heard it from three Americans, an Italian and an English girl, all in their twenties—the English girl quoted the whole opening: "Christmas won't be Christmas without any presents," it begins, in case you've forgotten—and a mother of teen-agers assured me that her daughters were even now devouring the works of Miss Alcott. Read *Little Women*? Of course.

Why? It is dated and sentimental and full of preaching and moralizing, and some snobbery about the lower classes that is positively breathtaking in its horror: that moment, for instance, when old Mr. Laurence is improbably discovered in a fishmarket, and bestows his charity on a starving Irish woman by hooking a large fish on the end of his cane, and depositing it, to her gasping gratitude, in her arms. It is as often smug as it is snug, and its high-mindedness tends to be that peculiar sort that pays. Brigid Brophy, writing in *The New York Times Book Review* a few years ago, called it a dreadful masterpiece, and the judgment stands (though not, I think, quite on Miss Brophy's grounds). And yet, here it is in a new and handsome centennial edition, as compulsively readable as it was a century ago when publisher Thomas Niles's nieces overrode their uncle's doubts and urged him to bring it out.

Its faults we can see in a moment. They cry to heaven, and when

Miss Brophy dwelt at length on the literary sin of sentimentality which falsifies emotion and manipulates the process of life, she hardly had to cite evidence. *Little Women* does harp on our nerves, does play on our feelings, does stack the cards to bring about undeserved happy outcomes here and undeserved come-uppance there. But that is not the whole story, and couldn't be, or there wouldn't be all those girls with their noses in the book right now, and all those women who remember the supreme shock of the moment when Jo sold her hair; when Beth was discovered on the medicine chest in the closet with scarlet fever coming on; when Meg let the Moffats dress her up; when Amy was packed off, pro-testing and bargaining, to Aunt March's stiff house.

No, *Little Women* does manipulate life, but it is also *about* life, and life that is recognizable in human terms today. Miss Alcott preached, and the conclusions she came to are frequently too good to be true; but the facts of emotion that she started with were real. She might end by softening the ways to deal with them, but she began by looking them in the eye. Her girls were jealous, mean, silly and lazy; and for 100 years jealous, mean, silly and lazy girls have been ardently grateful for the chance to read about them-selves. If Miss Alcott's prescriptions for curing their sins are too simple, it doesn't alter the fact that her diagnoses are clear, un-equivocal and humanly right. When her girls are good, they are apt to be painful; but when they are bad, they are bad just the way we all are, and over the same things. It must have been a heavenly relief 100 years ago to learn that one's faults were not unique. Today I suspect that it is a relief to be told to take them seriously and struggle with them; that it is important to be good.

This general background of human interest makes *Little Women* still plausible, but it is hardly enough to keep it a peren-nial classic. The real attraction is not the book as a whole, but its heroine, Jo, and Jo is a unique creation: the one young woman in nineteenth-century fiction who maintains her individual inde-pendence, who gives up no part of her autonomy as payment for being born a woman—and who gets away with it. Jo is the tomboy dream come true, the dream of growing up into full humanity with all its potentialities instead of into limited femininity: of looking after oneself and paying one's way and doing effective work in the real world instead of learning how to please a man who will look after you, as Meg and Amy both do with pious pleasure. (So, by the way, does Natasha.) It's no secret that Jo's story is the heart of *Little Women*, but just what that story represents has not, to my knowledge, been explored, and I think it is worth looking at.

We shall have to work back and forth from Louisa May Alcott's life to her book, but no one has ever denied that Jo is Louisa and that a great deal of her story is autobiographical. The very fact that *Little Women* was written so quickly makes that conclusion inescapable: two and a half months for the first part and two months for the second. More clearly in life, but clearly enough in her book, Louisa-Jo wanted to become the head of the family. In part, this was necessity. Bronson Alcott suffered from a kind of obsessional generosity that appears at times to have verged on *folie de grandeur;* and his wife and daughters learned early to shift for themselves, for Papa's plans not only went astray, they were apt to ignore the existence of his family completely.

Then there came a time—Louisa was eleven—when Bronson Alcott all but deserted his wife and daughters and went off to join a Shaker colony with his English friend, Charles Lane, who (as his wife put it) had almost hypnotic power over him. In the end he did not go, but suffered so powerfully from the crisis that he did in fact abdicate the father's role in the family. In that frequent nineteenth-century gesture of despair, he took to his bed and turned his face to the wall. None of this was hidden from Louisa. She and her older sister Anna made part of the family council which discussed Mr. Alcott's decision to go off with his friend to the celibate Shakers or to stay.

This clumsy agony is glossed over in *Little Women,* where absent Mr. March is away as a chaplain during the Civil War. But the pressure on Jo to hold her family together by working and earning is all there, and so is the emotion of the one who aspires to play the role of responsibility when it has become vacant. When Meg is falling in love, Jo blurts out in fury, "I just wish I could marry Meg myself, and keep her safe in the family." This is, of course, treated as a joke, though anthropologist students of the incest taboo in the nuclear family would find it of interest. It is, at any rate, indicative of Jo's desire to become the responsible head of the household, and the last half of the book is devoted to her effort to achieve this end, which, in her life, she did achieve.

This aim explains her refusal to marry handsome Laurie, the next-door hero. Their relationship has always been that of two equals, which in nineteenth-century America (and in some places today) implies two equals of the same sex. Twice at least Laurie suggests that they run off together, not for lovemaking, but for adventure; very much in the manner and mood in which Tom Sawyer and Huck Finn plan to run away from comfort and civilization. Again when Jo speaks to her mother about the possibility of marriage to Laurie, Mrs. March is against it "because you two are too much alike." So they are, and so—with no explanations ever given—Jo refuses Laurie, and the reader knows she is right, for Jo and Laurie are dear friends, competitors and not in the least a couple. It is worth noting that the two other adored nineteenth-century heroines who say No to the hero's proposal give way in the end, when circumstances and the hero have changed: Elizabeth Bennet and Jane Eyre. But Jo says No and does not shift.

The subtlety of Miss Alcott's character drawing (or self-knowledge, if you will) comes through here, for Jo is a tomboy, but never a masculinized or lesbian figure. She is, somehow, an idealized "New Woman," capable of male virtues but not, as the Victorians would have said, "unsexed." Or perhaps she is really archaic woman, recreated out of some New-World-frontier necessity when patriarchy breaks down. For Jo marries (as we all know! Who can forget that last great self-indulgent burst of tears when Professor Bhaer stops, under the umbrella, and asks "Heart's dearest, why do you cry?") Yes, Jo marries and becomes, please note, not a sweet little wife but a matriarch: mistress of the professor's school, mother of healthy sons (while Amy and Laurie have only one sickly daughter), and cheerful, active manager of events and people. For this Victorian moral tract, sentimental and preachy, was written by a secret rebel against the order of the world and woman's place in it, and all the girls who ever read it know it.

The New York Times Book Review
September 29, 1968

5. The Subordinate Sex

An essay review of *Everyone Was Brave: The Rise and Fall of Feminism in America*. By William L. O'Neill. New York, Quadrangle, 369 pp., $7.95.

Half the human race is female. It is sometimes difficult to remember this, even for a female; and never more difficult than when reading history. Until late yesterday afternoon (speaking in terms of historical time) women intruded so rarely on the course of events that their total omission would hardly be noticeable. When they did appear, it was almost always in passive roles: a princess whose dowry set off a war, a wife whose sterility brought her husband into conflict with the church, a mistress whose influence can be traced now and then in a general appointed or an artist favored.

Naturally, these scanty appearances at the summit have no connection with the work women did where it was taken for granted and forgotten, as the work of the great mass of humanity has always been taken for granted and forgotten. But the absence of women from history has a special effect. True, the rest of the eternal, ubiquitous crowd of dependents, serfs, slaves and servants are seldom identified, though we know the names of a few of the rebels among them who challenged the way things were "supposed to be." But enough social history has been written for us to remember that they were there and had to be reckoned with, whether as starving peasants, victims of the plague, millenarian heretics or political revolutionaries.

This is not true of women. For most of history and for most historians, they are not only anonymous as individuals, but they don't even exist as a group. Ants in the ant heap, their separate identity is not only unimagined but largely unimaginable. Anthropologists and archeologists, approaching societies other than their own, are well aware of the importance of understanding the position ascribed to women—their duties, products, place in the kinship structure and in religious ceremony—for an overall comprehension of these unfamiliar social systems. Yet in the annals of their own people, women have—or have had—no history. Lacking it, they have been wreathed in myth, the myth of their special place in man's world, their special attributes and failings, their special abilities and the special dangers they pose.

The trouble with myth is not that it is false, but that it is partly true; true, that is, to what we want to believe. If it didn't embody desires and satisfy needs, we could get rid of it much more easily. But when rational argument manages to clear away untenable foundations, there is no sure guarantee that the myth they supported will die. Sexual discrimination and racial discrimination have both been sustained, over the last century, first on the basis of biblical revelation (God's curse on Eve, God's curse on Ham), then on the evidence of "psychological" tenets and tests whose assumptions came straight out of the realm of unprovable fixed ideas, and now on the "researches" of neo-Lamarckian ethologists. Give us the facts, they cry (baboons hunt in groups, men join political clubs), and never mind the logic that gets us from the one to the other.

Whatever the authority for discrimination, the effect is the same: some people are different not just because of social pressures or training or clever individual adaptation to patterns of life, but irredeemably, by the will of God or of Science. When these fountainheads of wisdom say "humanity" they are, however, referring less to fact than to some general concept of the norm. Oddly enough, the norm consistently turns out to be exemplified by white heterosexual males, with the corollary that anyone else is abnormal and had better go away quietly and cease to make trouble by disrupting hypotheses. Thus, the myth (which always speaks in the imperative mood).

One can sympathize with its believers without wanting to condone the belief. It is very difficult to change one's mind and the

larger, more amorphous and diffuse the belief, the harder it is to
dig it all out. Books like William O'Neill's, therefore, are valuable
not only in themselves, but because they bring women into history
and out of the region of myth. Arguing with mythic statements, as
John Donne remarked apropos of another matter, is like going to
sea for no reason but to get sick. The best history doesn't argue;
it takes its stand on another ground. Thus, Mr. O'Neill is not trying to prove that the position of women ought to be this, or that,
or anything else. He is writing about what happened. But his study
of the Women's Movement in America from the mid-nineteenth
century on, of the problems it ran into, of how the Movement
achieved its successes and stumbled into its failures, has an interesting by-product. By recording what happened his factual chronicle
reduces the plausibility of the women-myths since what happened
doesn't fit the myths.

The myths begin with the assumption that women's behavior is
innately, unchangeably, and by predestination different from
men's because their anatomy is. "Why can't a woman," cried Professor Henry Higgins, "be more like a man?" Whatever the answer
he expected, it was surely not the one that Professor O'Neill provides. Nevertheless, the message of this book is unmistakable:
"Dear Henry," it runs, "she *is* like a man, right down to her capacity to make the same mistakes when she meets the same problems."
Put her in a political situation and she will learn politics. Offer
her a choice between reform and revolution, and she will debate
the possibilities with her sisters on just the same grounds as have
males. Confront her with the question of ends versus means, of
seeking allies or going it alone, of attacking the Washington establishment or appeasing it in order to lobby legislation through
Congress, and her maneuvers will be indistinguishable from those
of men with a cause. The really remarkable thing about the Wom-
en's Movement of the nineteenth and twentieth centuries is how
typical feminism was of other reform movements, and of its historical period.

Its first considerable gathering and first real achievement, in
fact, occurred typically in that *annus mirabilis* of reform and
revolution, 1848. In that year the original Woman's Rights Convention was held at Seneca Falls, New York, and the cause it cham-

pioned won a limited but prophetic victory when the New York State Legislature passed the Married Women's Property Act, which secured their possessions to all women, not simply to those whose canny fathers had drawn up marriage settlements that kept their dowries out of their husbands' hands. From that time forward the movement for women's rights pretty well rose and fell with the social climate. When reform was in the air, this reform movement thrived. When reaction or indifference held sway, the mood inhibited women's efforts too.

But as Professor O'Neill is well aware, the existence of good weather for reform does not mean that all reforms will prosper equally, or that it is necessarily wise for reformers to join hands and go forward together. Central to his discussion is a question that continually plagued the councils of the feminists: should they concentrate on getting the vote, or should their aims be broader? If so, how broad? Were Victoria Woodhull and Charlotte Perkins Gilman right in attacking (in very different ways) the whole institution of marriage? Was Vida Scudder correct in declaring that only socialism could bring sex equality along with class equality? Was Carrie Chapman Catt more sensible than Jane Addams because she concentrated her energies on fighting for suffrage instead of diffusing them in work for the poor and for pacifism? Or did the ultrapragmatics narrow their attack until they became nothing but an interest group, all too willing to compromise on any issue? Here, in the pages of *Everyone Was Brave* and widening it far beyond a purely feminine audience, is an extraordinarily perceptive analysis of how social aims can achieve political success; and how the desire for political success affects social aims.

The crusade for women's rights surfaced in the second quarter of the nineteenth century. Mr. O'Neill touches very briefly on its causes, which is wise; an exhaustive study would have involved him in writing another book. I don't myself agree with his emphasis and think he has rather misinterpreted the very interesting and suggestive findings of Philippe Ariès, but that is really neither here nor there, for the antecedents of the organized Women's Movement lie outside his field. In some fashion, at any rate, the social and economic changes let loose by the technological revolution, by the Enlightenment and the Evangelical reaction against

it, and by the political ideology of egalitarianism combined to produce a ferment of questioning whose currents undermined the
foundations of orthodoxy. For centuries, probably for millennia,
perhaps forever, mankind (or most of it) had believed that whatever was, was right—or at least unavoidable. Now Renaissance,
Reformation and revolution began to assert that whatever was
might not only be wrong but, even more important, might be
subject to change. People's lives were changing fast enough for
them to be aware of it. Why not work for the changes one wanted,
then, instead of simply submitting to those that came? So with the
consciousness of process was born the idea of progress.

In America feminism and abolitionism arose together. The
Grimké sisters, daughters of a slave-holding South Carolina plan-
tation-owner, were eloquent in both causes. Reforming women
were quick to see the analogy between racial and sexual discrimination, and many of them seized on slavery as a metaphor for
their own condition. Women's bondage, wrote Elizabeth Cady
Stanton to Lucy Stone in 1856, "though it differs from that of the
Negro slave, frets and chafes her just the same. She too sighs and
groans in her chains." Men like William Lloyd Garrison and
Theodore Tilton were willing to work for both causes. And yet,
the alliance was uneasy from the beginning. For, as in all political
alliances, each member had to decide for himself which aim to put
first. In 1840, women delegates to an antislavery convention in
London were denied seats on the floor and relegated to the bal-
cony as mere spectators. Horace Greeley battled suffragists who
hoped the New York State Constitution would give them the vote
by striking out the qualifying word "male" when it struck out the
word "white." Negro men, Mrs. Stanton found, did not all see the
connection between slavery and the limitations placed on women
as clearly as she did: some of them believed that men should dominate women, and that white women were their worst enemies.
So she reported in 1869, and such sentiments are not unheard a
century later.

The Civil War inaugurated (more in letter than in spirit) the
incorporation of minority groups into the American mainstream.
Both for women and Negroes there were forward steps and later
retreats. Women nursed and did other war work. Some of the

universities opened their doors to girls because male students were lacking. These were not great advances, but, they were not lost when, in the 1870's, reaction set in, as the first Negro advances vanished with the end of Reconstruction. The stultifying atmosphere of the Gilded Age slowed down the Women's Movement; Victorian prudery gave it a massive and debilitating dose of purity; but, no doubt because feminism was less threatening than the drive for Negro rights, the former was not brought completely to a halt.

It did, however, suffer a confusion of aims. The apparent success of Abolitionism removed the original allies of the feminist movement, and the times confronted women with the dilemma of settling what they were working toward. Was it the vote, the vote first, the vote alone, with all other desirable reforms to flow from a cohesive and centralized Female Power group? Or were crying social abuses to be attacked along the way? What about education for women? What about working hours? What about child labor? What about sweatshops? What about pacifism? Americanization of immigrant familes? Settlement houses? Temperance? The double standard? Free love? There simply was no answer to any of these questions that was not, in some way, divisive. Victoria Woodhull, champion of free love, candidate for the Presidency of the United States in 1872, protégée of Elizabeth Cady Stanton *and* Commodore Vanderbilt (whom she advised on financial matters with the aid of clairvoyance), instigator of Theodore Tilton's famous suit for adultery against Henry Ward Beecher, can't be said to be typical of anything. But the fact that she found a home in the suffrage movement after the Civil War does indicate the problems from which it suffered. Without clear-cut goals and continuous evaluation of the methods required to reach them, the drive for women's rights came down with a bad case of the Sillies.

Let us not assume that this is a disease that attacks only female organizations. The American backcountry had seen the growth of any number of weird sects, both religious and political and often both. The Abolitionists had had their extremists, and the nascent labor movement grappled with theirs. Its leaders, like the suffragists after the Woodhull debacle, swung to the right, fearing that the anarchists and the IWW would raise the country against them.

Indeed, they went even further, for the AFL found most women reformers too radical for their taste, and women workers (as the Lawrence, Massachusetts, textile strike made all too clear) hardly worth organizing on the remarkable grounds that they did not earn enough to pay full union dues. The dilemma of choosing what aims and which means is one that every reform movement has faced, and the feminists were no exception.

It is Mr. O'Neill's contention that, in the end, they came down too hard on the side of pragmatism and reform and lost their relevance and usefulness by abjuring more revolutionary methods and more idealistic goals. It is a well-reasoned argument. "Woman's suffrage," O'Neill writes, "was not just another political movement; it was above all a great moral enterprise. . . . The first duty of a reformer is to secure the substance, not just the appearance, of change." By deciding to concentrate on getting the vote, the suffragists had to defer work for other causes. How could this be justified? Only by claiming too much for the vote. Let women reach the polls, ran the claim, and their votes would bring the millennium; would end corruption, purify morals, put a stop to oppression, and prevent war. Weren't they against all these evils? Weren't they—and here we find the mythic tide rising within their own camp—weren't they better, purer, finer and more moral than men? So the myth of women's fundamental difference from men contributed to their acting in just the same way as men. For the vote made no difference. They won it in the social upheaval of World War I, as the Negroes won it, in theory, through the upheaval and change of the Civil War. And then nothing happened.

Or, rather, disillusion set in. The Women's Movement, after it achieved the vote, became something of a joke. It is still. The freedoms people wanted in the 1920's and the freedoms they want now are pretty much human freedoms. The Women's Liberation Movement, burning bras and girdles on the Atlantic City boardwalk to protest the Miss America contest, is not much less foolish than the Miss America contest itself. But that isn't really the point. If the Women's Movement has caught a case of the Sillies again, it is not because it is a Women's Movement, but because it is not working, at the moment, in the mainstream, nor attracting the energy and intelligence that it profited from in the early years of the century. This can happen to any cause. The years of advance won success, but they shaped the feminist drive to the success which they won.

All groups that suffer from social disadvantages have got to find out how to overcome them politically. The feminists did, and it was a big step. Their victories and their defeats are highly instructive. What is particularly valuable in O'Neill's explication of events is that he faces the influence of political action on moral problems, and of moral imperatives, as they were felt at the time, on political judgments. Let us remember, however, that the two things are juxtaposed in a serious way *only* when social dislocations get big enough and upsetting enough to call for political action. Small social problems attract cranks, or are swept into corners by moral imperatives. The decline of feminism is partly due to its hubris in accepting the myth that women are different from men, and exploiting the myth for its own ends. But political success can halt a process too. Witness the way in which the drive to end the war in Vietnam has been slowed to a crawl by its political success in getting Lyndon Johnson out of the White House.

Let me conclude by recommending Mr. O'Neill's book heartily, not only as a valuable volume of history, but also as a sound and perceptive analysis of political verities. These, he tells us, are the choices that the context of events offered the suffragists within their times. The alliances they made, the methods they used, the chances of history—all affected the way the feminists went after what they wanted. These were the women who wrought the changes, he reports, giving us vivid thumbnail sketches of some of the leaders. These were the organizations that were drawn into the campaign, and again we have a useful description of the suffrage associations—the Women's Trade Union League, the Consumers League, the settlement groups and many others. But best of all, we have a truly intelligent discussion of what the issues were, and how the decision to work in this area and not in that affected the outcome of the whole Movement. From it, we can draw our own conclusions about political processes and how they are likely to use, or be used by, those who are now seeking reforms or facing the choice of more revolutionary methods. Mr. O'Neill has not tried to write a parable for our times, but he has given us much food for thought in the historical example of the Women's Movement.

The Saturday Review
October 11, 1969

6. Provide, Provide!

The Coming of Age. By Simone de Beauvoir. New York. Putnam's, $10.00

Simone de Beauvoir's study of old age was published in France as *La Vieillesse,* and in England under an exact translation: *Old Age.* How amused Mlle. de Beauvoir must be to find her suspicions of America's hypocritical readers confirmed by the name bestowed on her book here: *The Coming of Age!* As far as the title goes, her 572 pages (plus index) might be addressed to those members of the younger generation who face, or have recently passed, their eighteenth birthday. The change neatly underlines her point: no one, not even the aged themselves, *really* wants to hear or think about the grim last days of life, narrowing down to the grave; when, as Robert Frost reminded us in the poem whose title I have borrowed, the "beauty Abishag, the picture pride of Hollywood," has become the withered hag who comes with rag and pail to wash the steps.

It is one of Mlle. de Beauvoir's strengths that she does not wince away from the unpleasant. Nor—another strength—does she wallow in it. She is, above all else, a just judge of the great issues of life, at once compassionate and objective. Her sympathies are engaged by the old, but so is her mind, and it is a powerful mind;

best, I have always thought, when grappling with issues of a profound moral nature. Here she is discussing the treatment and the image, including the self-image, of the old imposed by society; but the purpose of her book is to examine society as it is revealed by treatment and image, not simply to describe and deplore the valuation set on the aged.

So this is (as was *The Second Sex*) a book about power; for any examination of how society works must come down to Lenin's question, Who does what to whom? (How one regrets the succinct Russian, "*Kto kovo?*" which fits so well into Mlle. de Beauvoir's opposing categories of "subject" and "object.") What society does to the old is to label them "objects." They lose their freedom of action and with it, their dignity. In her introduction, Mlle. de Beauvoir quotes Grimm's chilling tale about the peasant who makes his old father eat out of a small wooden trough, apart from the rest of the family. One day he finds his son fitting little boards together. "It's for you when you're old," says the child.

The tension between generations has always existed. The young challenge the old, the old fear the young's attack. But when we say this, we are blurring an important distinction. To the young, the older generations blend together: "Don't trust anyone over thirty." But the grandfathers differ from the fathers, the really aged from the mature who hold the power of action and control. When we talk of old age we are almost always talking of those who have passed beyond the wielding of power. But, as Mlle. de Beauvoir makes clear, citing examples from anthropology and from history, the attitudes of younger adults toward the aged have always been founded earlier. The memory of past power provokes a present urge of revenge or mockery. The adult generation remembers the power of its fathers and so, as that power wanes, the adults react. Treatment of the aged by adults reflects the treatment of yesterday's children by yesterday's parents.

Such treatment is deeply affected by economic possibilities and by social norms. "I have come across only one [ethnological example]," writes Mlle. de Beauvoir, "in which happy children turn into adults who are cruel to their fathers and mothers—the Ojibway. Whereas the Yakut and the Ainu, who are badly treated as children, neglect the old most brutally, the Yaghan and Aleut, who live in almost the same conditions but among whom the child is king, honor their old people. Yet the aged," she pauses to remind us, "are often the victims of a vicious circle: extreme poverty obliges the adults to feed their children badly and to neglect them." How much freedom and respect the powerful can allow the weak, then, is dependent on what is available for all. We need not be surprised to discover that the most hard-pressed communities practice both infanticide and the abandonment of the old. One provides for the future or remembers the past only after one has eaten today.

Against such threats, of course, the old have their weapons. The first is memory. In a stable society, experience increases useful knowledge. The old know the patterns of the weather, the movements of animals and the skills of husbandry. Besides, stable societies tend to respect traditions and these the old know too and can expound. Another weapon is magic. Tradition often blends into "knowledge" of how to control the supernatural. But, more than that, the old can be seen as prenatal ghosts. If death is no more than a rite of passage and the reborn old man returns to haunt his former home, it will be *his* turn to take revenge on those who mistreated him. Certainly rites for the dead around the world emphasize the need to propitiate the ghost, to feed him well and speed him on his way, lest he linger close at hand, for if he lingers, it will only be with malicious intent. Who listens for a loving ghost?

When literacy appears, memory loses much of its value. Fear of the supernatural comes and goes. But the third weapon of the old has never lost its weight: property. Die early and avoid the fate of the ruined beauty, Abishag. Frost advises his readers,

> Or if predestined to die late,
> Make up your mind to die in state.
> Make the whole stock exchange your own!
> If need be occupy a throne. . . .

In short, since this is a question of power, hold on to what you have of it. "Boughten friendship" will not save you from mockery and hate, but it will protect you from their effects, at least from their immediate effects.

The powerful, stubborn, hardfisted old, the frustrated, ambitious, resentful young—this confrontation has passed into the deepest reaches of our social awareness. These figures are part of the furniture of our minds: Fedor Karamazov, Lyndon Johnson, Chaucer's old January with his bought bride, May, Pétain challenged by De Gaulle, who later suffered a similar challenge, the old generals of World War I and the young poets in the trenches, the marching students of Paris in May, 1968, the impudent lovers of Congreve and Molière who conspire against their miserly parents, we know them all. They speak to us with a double authority, that of fact and that of myth. Hostility between generations confirms the prophecy each angry child makes to himself of the revenge he will take when his time comes, And then—

And then, even for the powerful, power passes again. What does it feel like inside, to be old when one was young, weak when one was strong? The second part of Mlle. de Beauvoir's book explores the interior world whose existence the first part has documented. Like the very rich, in Fitzgerald's well-known aperçu, the old are different from you and, maybe, me. How? And how do they perceive this difference?

In the external world, old people become objects instead of agents. Heretofore I have spoken of the wielders of power, but really this is a very small percentage of adult human beings. The poor and subordinate have always been objects, moved about by economic forces and social demands. But because they have participated in the work of the world, most of them have had the illusion that they have some control over their actions. They imagine a future; though, as psychologists have shown, the ability to plan for a future is closely tied to economic and sexual status. Women, subordinates and the poor tend to live in the present. The coming of old age closes off the future to all. For the powerful, this is a stunning and disheartening shock. For the powerless, says Mlle. de Beauvoir, it is an equally stunning revelation of betrayal. Is this all? they are left to ask of their past lives, their *whole* lives. In today's industrial society, their hard-won skills are useless, their memories are irrelevant, ties with home and kin have withered or broken, customs have changed or vanished, ahead lie isolation, disregard and a death among strangers. Was it for this they lived out the busy years? The devalued present calls the past into question, and the answer is mocking.

In the interior world inside each graying head there is an equally unsettling confrontation. One's old identity is somehow no longer acceptable on public exchange. One may feel nineteen or thirty-one or no age at all, but those out there get up and offer a seat on the bus, listen for a moment, laugh and go on talking, or don't listen at all. One is faced with the task—if one wants to keep in touch with reality—of remaking one's sense of oneself; and remaking it downwards, to incorporate that unflattering figure seen in the eyes of those others, the young and the powerful. One lives between lies—the inner feeling of youth, the outer judgment of age, which is true? To accept the outer judgment, one must be false to oneself; falseness, then, can spread to all one feels or knows. "Old age," writes Mlle. de Beauvoir, "is life's parody." Again, her documentation of this bitter conclusion has compelling weight.

I must speak of one omission which is understandable, though, I think, mistaken. But first I want to praise the insight, the candor, the subtle vision, and the unflinching objectivity of this whole enterprise. Reading this book took on the aspect of conducting an interior orchestra. I found myself leaping up again and again to leaf through Yeats, or Susanne Langer's analysis of the comic and tragic modes of drama in *Feeling and Form,* to re-read Erik Erikson's vision of the last crisis of life as one moves from maturity to age, or Victor Turner's brilliant analysis of rites of passage in *The Ritual Process,* to recall a dozen more examples of my own touchstones of validity in human experience. Far from being depressing, *The Coming of Age* is a life-giving book. Published passages devoted to the sexual activities of the old are almost vulgarly misleading: in the book they illuminate the connection between vitality, creativity and libido with considerable force, and indicate the effect on personal life of societal status, roles, and role-reversals. One can't abstract from a book like this without diminishing what is selected, for, by so doing, one cuts conections. Any whole is greater than the sum of its parts, and this is a noble whole. The life of the poor, the life of the mind, the triumphs and the failures of statesmen, the trials of artists, writers and composers, myth, legend and drama, absurdity, despair, dedication and joy are woven together so that the many vivid examples and quotations that Mlle. de Beauvoir uses light up the conclusions she draws and keep them from seeming doctrinaire or insistent. Pedantic? Well, yes. She's a little pedantic. In her, it becomes a virtue. She supplies a baker's dozen of facts, she provides exhaustive analyses. Astonishingly, they are always interesting.

Then, what is missing? Something I would not have looked for myself until, toward the end of the book, I began to be aware, from a sentence or two of Mlle. de Beauvoir's, that she had excluded it from consideration: religion. Perhaps she is right, for considering religion without debating it as sacred truth may be more disruptive of reasoned argument than not considering it at all. But I would like to suggest that what religion *does* (leaving aside what it *is*—that is, true or not true) is posit an alternative reality to that figured forth in our daily lives. She speaks of the deadening effect on the old of having the *idea* of a future removed, of there being no more room in which to project plans or imagine action. Again, she remarks on the way in which the reality of old age shows up the assumed reality of earlier life and reveals it as a cheat. "The promises have been kept," she quotes herself from an earlier book, *La force des choses,* and ends, "I have been swindled."

Now, what religion tells us is that everyday reality is indeed untrue and invalid—a swindle—unless it is invaded and transfigured by the sacred. Can we believe this ambivalent statement? Such a question can only be argued, never decided. It will and has been *used,* taken as a directive to put up with everyday life and its horrors because they are false and will be wiped away in a better world. Alas, that does not dispose of the proposition that there may be a better world. And if one is caught in falsity, as the old are caught between "self" and "image," faith in another reality offers an alternative framework of value to which the self may be attached. But how can one ask questions like these without their seeming to be pious banalities inviting a like response?

Can one ask them at all unless one asks sincerely (that is, without
judging), and does this not imply one's own belief? The anthropologist can question believers in other faiths on the psychological aspects of their systems, for he is a stranger. Can a fellow
member of Western society approach believers in the same way?
Will his presence not, in itself, disturb the experimental equilibrium? At any rate, understandably, they are not asked.

But the problem is heightened by the fact that those old who
seem to manage best (as cited here) often appear to make a connection with a reality outside that of ordinary life. Religion is
not always a comfort. Victor Hugo kept his faith to the end, along
with an abiding interest in young girls. To a friend he said, "I
am old; I am going to die. I shall see God . . . Talk to him!
What a tremendous event! What shall I say to him?" He never
wondered, Mlle. de Beauvoir notes acerbly, what God might say
to *him*. Michelangelo, retaining his faith and losing his skill with
advanced age, felt that God was reproving him for wasting his
time on art instead of worship. Other artists have been sustained
by joy in their continuing power to create: their connection, that
is, with the "other reality" of art, Yeats's "artifice of eternity."
Mlle. de Beauvoir's own advice is "to go on pursuing ends that
give our existence a meaning," which she then sums up rather an-
ticlimactically as "devotion to individuals, to groups or to causes,
social, political, intellectual or creative work."

In the end, I suppose, one can only accept that other being,
the aged image in another's eyes, as oneself if there is somehow
room in one's self to take the creature in. Of all the teeming
examples in this bountiful book of such a confrontation, the most
useful for our shaken and frightened age seems to me an anecdote
about the aged Goya, who had lived through terror, revolution,
invasion and counterterror, had painted the protagonists of all
these systems and then retired from life. Or so it seemed. But
when he was eighty, he drew a self-portrait, "an ancient man
propped on two sticks, with a great mass of white hair and beard
all over his face, and the inscription 'I am still learning.' Goya,"
writes Mlle. de Beauvoir, "was making fun of himself and his
eagerness for everything new." No doubt. But what an unexpected, toe-of-the-Christmas-stocking gift to find as one's best pro-

vision for survival—the eagerness to know: "I am still learning."
There's a thing to say to God!

The Atlantic
June 1972

7. About Women

A Different Woman. By Jane Howard. New York, E. P. Dutton, 1973,
413 pp., $7.95.

Changing Women in a Changing Society. Edited by Joan Huber.
Chicago, The University of Chicago Press, 1973, 295 pp., $7.95.

Radical Feminism. Edited by Anne Koedt, Ellen Levine and Anita
Rapone. New York, Quadrangle Books, 1973, 424 pp., $10.00.

Woman's Fate. By Claudia Dreyfus. New York, Bantam Books, 1973,
277 pp., $1.25.

Unlearning the Lie: Sexism in School. By Barbara Grizzuti Harrison.
New York, Liveright, 1973, 176 pp., $6.95.

Women in Prison. By Kathryn Watterson Burkhart. Garden City, New
York, Doubleday, 1973, 465 pp., $10.00.

Sex Roles in Law and Society. By Leo Kanowitz. Albuquerque, University of New Mexico Press, 1973, 706 pp., $20.00.

The Subordinate Sex. By Vern L. Bullough, with the assistance of
Bonnie Bullough. Urbana, Chicago, London, University of Illinois
Press, 1973, 375 pp., $10.95.

Not in God's Image. Edited by Julia O'Faolain and Lauro Martines.
New York, Harper & Row, 1973, 362 pp., $15.00.

By a Woman Writt. Edited by Joan Goulianos. Indianapolis, Bobbs-
Merrill, 1972, 379 pp., $14.95.

Discrimination Against Women. Edited by Dr. Catharine R. Stimpson.
New York, R. R. Bowker Company, 1973, 558 pp., $12.50.

The Inferior Sex. By Wallace Reyburn. Englewood Cliffs, New Jersey,
Prentice-Hall, 1973, 235 pp., $5.95.

The Inevitability of Patriarchy. By Steven Goldberg. New York, William Morrow, 1973, 256 pp., $6.95.

Sexual Suicide. By George Gilder. New York, Quadrangle Books, 1973, 308 pp., $7.95.

Toward a Recognition of Androgyny. By Carolyn Heilbrun. New York, Alfred A. Knopf, 1973, 189 pp., $6.95.

"The Woman Question," as Tolstoy called it a century ago, is perhaps most easily seen in an objective light if it is considered as a paradigm of social change, and of human reaction thereto. All social change confronts its subjects with two queries. The more disruptive is felt first: "What am I losing?" Since any change involves loss, it is easy to see all change as overthrow and revolution, break rather than continuity—"Things will never be the same!" Thus the first emotional reaction will often be one of horror and despair.

But the second question can apply its own tough therapy: "What do I stand to lose by *not* changing or accepting change?" It is when the price of succumbing to future shock is assessed as being too high that our brains will, at last and no doubt reluctantly, begin to control our emotions, so that we can forge the links that will provide continuity between past and future by means of action in the present. We are, I believe, finally at work weaving this web of connection across the break in our perceptions of woman's image.

The old image and ideal of "the good woman" was the symbol of an ascribed social role, not one which was chosen by those who exemplified it though it may have been acquiesced in often enough. The very attributes of the role make this clear. Woman as wife and mother, as helpmeet and nurturing provider, is obviously being defined in relationship to someone else, someone who is allowed to be active and primary in a sense that she is not. To be "the second sex" signifies that someone else comes first and sets the norms and goals of humanity. Secondness implies otherness, what men are not but feel themselves in need of. Responsiveness to the standards and desires of others, then, complementarity and subordination, these have defined the outer limits and the inner purposes of the lives of good women since time immemorial. Until today.

Perhaps the clearest connection between the new aims of women and the principle of civil liberty lies just here. Women today, really for the first time in history, are seeking to define themselves rather than merely accepting the definition of their place, role and identity offered by others. What right can be more fundamental than the freedom to name one's own goals, find and use one's own capabilities, fail or succeed on one's own, to take one's rank and status by dint of one's own actions? It has been just this freedom which the old, ascribed role denied, the liberty to be fully oneself as an individual—indeed, the liberty simply to try out individuality.

Such liberation, it should be stated at once, can no more free women from social bonds or the obligations of family relationships than does the long-accepted freedom for men to enjoy life and liberty and to pursue happiness as they conceive it. What it does is open the door to mature, motivated responsibility; to partnership in life instead of protected inferiority. If this step brings with it the right to make one's own mistakes—as it does—and the obligation to pay for them, it offers society in return the use of hitherto untapped talent and resources and of a wider life experience than it has had access to. In addition, breaking the stereotype of woman's role, now both binding and outdated, may well bring a further bonus. The old masculine stereotype is just as outdated and limiting, as compulsive and irrelevant in its own way. Enlarging it can also refresh society by enlisting disregarded male energies.

To this extent, the Women's Movement can (it seems to me) be seen as a civil-libertarian demiurge at work in an area where public duties and private wants overlap. The Movement is both young and diverse, diverse at times to the point of apparent contradiction. It is anything but regimented and restrictive. Above all, it is not contained or containable in ideologies. Its essence is the testing of new potentialities in the actual world as individual humans confront the demands made on them by social change.

Not so long ago the idea that the position of women was a proper subject for study by the social sciences was regarded as ludicrous and untenable. "Can you really teach a whole semester on the history of women?" a friend of mine was asked when an early course was being projected. Now of course books on the woman question are coming in spate.

Out of this year's flood I have chosen some representative productions to report on here, with an eye directed toward their usefulness for the process of evolutionary adaptation to change which we are now undergoing. They are diverse both in content and in the audiences they address. Some are literate, well-researched, even scholarly. Some provide excellent reportage. Some light up dark patches of life, hitherto ignored. Some present male reactions of varying degrees of sense and seriousness. Some purvey the standard sludge which the publishing industry can be trusted to present in the third year of any trendy topic. A few are aglint with real imagination and insight. And none of them would have seen the light of day (or, probably, have surfaced as possibilities in the authors' minds) a decade ago, in the year when Betty Friedan published *The Feminine Mystique*.

Shall we begin with where we are now? Then for the general reader, dimly and rather uneasily aware that something called "women's lib" has not only surfaced but appears to be resisting arrest, I recommend Jane Howard's amusing and very readable transcontinental reporting, *A Different Woman*. Ms. Howard, whose articles used to enliven *LIFE*, and whose book on encounter groups, *Please Touch*, was widely praised and read, spent two years traversing America and talking with women of all ages and many conditions of life. She has produced an up-to-date, full-length version of *How America Lives*, and middle-class America should find it as diverting and informative as the *Ladies' Home Journal* articles of the same name were a generation ago. Especially valuable is the feeling it gives of the diversity of women's lives and goals. Thus we meet a California fisherman (as she calls herself), Doris, who works level with men, and "Darn right I get paid the same. . . . I unload the pots and do rebaiting." She's fished the Pacific "from the Bering Sea down to Chile," when shark liver brought ninety cents a pound. Married to a fisherman, mother of four—"I've got two in college now and three next year, and you know what they cost"—Doris works nights in a cafe as well. "I've just always worked," she says, but did put in two years at college in Skagit, Washington, when her father was fishing there. "I studied sociology of all things. Ain't that something? No, I didn't want to stay longer. I wanted just what I got: to get married and raise my family." Jane Howard matches Doris with a woman engineer fighting a class-action suit to be allowed to work on site in a tunnel from which male superstition bars her; with West Coast lawyers and mountain wives deep in Appalachia; with cat breeders, professors and students of all ages; with dwellers in communes and dwellers in nuclear families and with her own ongoing experience. Her reflections on her own life are not profound enough to give her book any philosophic depth, but it's splendid, vivid reporting, full of glimpses of real life and scraps of lively conversation.

Changing Women in a Changing Society, edited by Joan Huber, provides another sort of look at where we are now. This collection of articles appeared first as a special issue of the *American Journal of Sociology* and includes reminiscences of her career by pioneering Jessie Bernard, an excellent brief history of the Women's Movement by Jo Freeman and a wealth of valuable work by leading women sociologists (and several men). Hannah Papanek's discussion of "two-person careers" investigates a familiar phenomenon with great insight. Mirra Komarovsky reports on current student attitudes, with emphasis on the male view (still damn stodgy as of 1971, when the research was done). Cynthia Epstein takes a look at the women who've climbed two barriers, the Black professionals. I've found myself quoting from these and other excellent contributions here over and over again. The book is a never-failing resource.

Another collection, *Radical Feminism,* is a good deal more uneven. Its editors, Anne Koedt, Ellen Levine and Anita Rapone, are probably aware of this. They are addressing themselves to women already in touch with the Movement and are, in this sense, talking as insiders with insiders. Their intent is to include classic articles which have played a part in raising individual consciousness and in general discussion of political ends. This is a book about what it feels like inside—inside "femininity," inside a mind that is realizing the limits that have been set up against its aspirations, inside angry spirits undertaking rebellion and seeking help and validation of their own experience, inside a defiant forward edge which is both aware of its defiance, and reacting with strong emotion to it. To some extent, the book already dates. Many issues raised here have been followed up more extensively elsewhere. But it has value as a record of women coming to know themselves and to evaluate their situation.

Another book addressed to women is *Woman's Fate* by Claudia Dreyfus, a collection of conversations among members of a consciousness-raising group. As such, it's a test case. It will either send you screaming up the wall, or tell you a lot about the sheer daily experience of being a woman, uncertain not just of what she can properly ask of life, but even of what it is that is happening to her. It's material for a soap opera—until you realize that the people trapped in that afternoon serial are real, just as human and sensitive as lucky educated you and I who can turn with certainty to accepted standards of judgment. I can imagine it meaning a lot to many young women groping toward some sense of their place and value in the world. Speaking voices help, perhaps most of all when they talk of common emotions leaping up in the mush and chaos of everydayness, illuminating one's loneliness with a shared light.

And now three excellent books on special aspects of where we are now for the serious readers. *Unlearning the Lie: Sexism in School,* by Barbara Grizzuti Harrison, also is about everydayness, but the author continually relates the particulars of her subject to the major issues of growing up in America, of valuing oneself truly, of trusting and working with others, of problematic priorities in very human situations. She has turned a private experience into an enlightening case history by pointing out its public implications. Ms. Harrison is the mother of a boy and a girl who attend a progressive private school in New York. How astounding to discover that this bastion of liberal thought harbors the most sexist attitudes in class and library—unconscious, of course, and thus hard to see and painful to accept as one's own. From June 1970 to June 1971 a group of mothers of pupils at the Woodward School in Brooklyn found themselves struggling to bring about changes in the way their children were valued and treated—at the same time that they were struggling with themselves to decide what it was they were after, and how important the whole thing was. This is a paradigm of learning by doing. The Sex-Roles Committee found itself under a cabbage and just growed. It lurched from one dilemma to another. Was Black Liberation more vital than that of women? Should fathers be asked to join the effort? How flexible should a progressive school be? What do you do about liberating girl children who don't seem to want to be liberated? How much structure does an action group require? How many nonadvanced women do you turn off if you listen to the more advanced—even when you know their experience is needed and useful? It's a beautiful book, full of understanding of human nature and concise judgments. And because Ms. Harrison knows that thinking about education means thinking about the standards and procedures of our whole society, it's about a lot more than sexism in school.

Women in Prison, by Kathryn Watterson Burkhart, comes at women's position through that of the least advantaged in America, but it too reaches far beyond that. As Jesus told us, the poor we shall always have with us. Unfortunately we tend to deal with their presence by paying as little attention to it as possible. This study of women convicted as criminals (and of some of their female jailers and guards too) offers a bitter accounting of the price society pays for this inattention. Once more we are given an example of how the right to define one's own status, to value the importance of one's own lived experience, is and has been denied to whole categories of beings. To the powerful, the experience of the poor isn't interesting; their deviance raises no questions that seem to warrant exploring, and the trouble they make is dealt with by labeling it criminal; that's a simplistic summary, my own, not Ms. Burkhart's, but it seems to me the message here. Women and the weak (and especially women among the weak) are strangers to central, normative concerns of society; if they are alienated, it is because they are first labeled alien. "All the things you don't know about me would make a new world," wrote Ida Mae Tassin from Bedford Hills Penitentiary. Here are some of the things we don't know; and need to know if the world we have to make (remake) is going to have any strength and staying power.

Eminently practical, a mine of information and readable by the laity even though it is set up as a legal text is *Sex Roles in Law*

and Society by Leo Kanowitz. This is a compendium of cases dealing with sex-related issues, enlivened and illuminated by Professor
Kanowitz's notes and queries. I browsed longer than I meant to,
out of sheer interest, caught again and again by the vivid facts of
the dilemmas and entanglements that brought these hundreds of
humans to court, where their personal imbroglios could be worked
out for public judgment and the future guidance of others. Employment issues (running to more than 200 pages), abortion, contraception, marital status, women and the draft, women in
McSorley's, women *behind* the bar (OK if they worked for a
husband or father but not if they owned the establishment themselves!), Help Wanted ads and access to higher education—you'll
find it here, with good notes and an index of cases as well as of
issues. The Women's Movement owes this male a vote of thanks.

Looking back at where we've been, let me recommend the work
of another male sympathizer. Professor Vern Bullough, with the
assistance of Bonnie Bullough, has written as good a general history of woman's role and position as any nonhistorian can ask for.
The Subordinate Sex is subtitled *A History of Attitudes Toward
Women,* and Dr. Bullough is clear throughout that this is wom-
en's history as seen and felt and recorded by men. "All I am doing," he remarks, "is . . . indicating that what men said about
women only rarely reflected what women themselves thought or
felt." But since what men said defined the limits of what women
could do or be, this record is indicative of the public image of
women through the ages. Dr. Bullough's well-documented book
covers ancient history and China and India as well as Western
Europe and America. It ranges from ancient religious dogmas to
the effects on feminism of the advent of efficient sanitary napkins—
the product of new bandaging techniques developed in World
War I.

Dr. Bullough's book might be supplemented by a volume of
quotations recording men's views on women, *Not in God's Image,*
compiled by Julia O'Faolain and Lauro Martines. This book unfortunately does not stand by itself, for little historical context is
given and some of the dating of references is inaccurate.

Six centuries are spanned by women's own reports of their lives,
from Margery Kempe to Muriel Rukeyser, in *By a Woman Writt,*

edited by Joan Goulianos. Once more the view from inside, the private reality, overlooked because it was never named.

Contemporary voices resonate movingly against this historical background. An example of how we got (are still getting) from there to here is the record of the 1970 congressional hearings on equal rights in education and employment which Catharine Stimpson has edited in *Discrimination Against Women*. Facts and fantasies, myths and statistics confront each other in a telling demonstration of the human mind in the process of coming to terms with change.

So far I have dealt exclusively with books favoring the liberation of women, and the reader will surmise, correctly, that I advocate this position. I have however tried to find serious statements of the opposite view; and the fact that I've been signally unsuccessful in the search should not be taken as evidence of bias. Nor does it make my heart leap up. The reason why there are few rejoinders of any weight to women's liberation theses is that most opponents are calmly going about their business in a state of deep unconcern. The torpid eye of the Establishment finds little to arrest it in the gestures of angry women. Their experience is as unimportant as that of the poor, and their very vehemence permits their dismissal as "strident," which is convenient since it precludes the need to consider their case.

Three 1973 books by men viewing women's liberation are typical. The first is simply antediluvian: *The Inferior Sex,* by Wallace Reyburn, a 235-page put-down of women as giddy, brainless, incapable creatures who should be saved from feminist dupes intent on leading them into the wilderness out of egomaniacal delusions. It is worth noting only as a handy summary of one traditional male view, woman as pinhead verging on nut.

Steven Goldberg's *The Inevitability of Patriarchy* is a more literate exposition of a similar position: women are simply not capable of challenging male dominance. Biology, in particular the fortunate gift of the male hormone, testosterone, ordains woman's subordinate place in man's world and will always do so. It is interesting to note that hormones have succeeded to the voice of God in arranging this division of power, just as genetics have taken over from black skin and kinky hair to mark the race of

Ham as slave material. In fact, 200 years ago the argument of both these books could have been, indeed was, applied to uphold the legitimacy of slavery; it has always been this way. In short, these are the tomes of those who look upon change and, like Canute, opt to ignore it—for as long as they can.

George Gilder has at least got far enough to be worried by evidence of social change. Liberation will, he feels, lead to *Sexual Suicide:* if women refuse to be women, how can men be men? This is a much more serious reaction than those of the other authors cited, and one does want to sympathize with Mr. Gilder's emotions. But if his emotions must be respected, his reasoning cannot be. His prescription for dealing with the change that has shaken women loose from their traditional role is a purely mythic, indeed magic, one. Let them go back and play the old role, climb up on the pedestal again, resume the ancient pose. This will some-how (presumably by sympathetic magic) bind the world to its traditional place and recreate the loving family and the healthy society Mr. Gilder thinks prevailed in the past. A great putter of carts before horses, Gilder's view is that the Women's Movement is shaking up society and damn well ought to stop. A large igno-rance of historical process, economic trends and technological ad-vance allows him to imagine that one can banish change by attacking it head on and denying its existence: especially if it's women who do most of the attacking and act out the denial. Since the task of examining Gilder's fallacies would require ten times the space I have here, I shall leave readers to turn them up themselves, with all good wishes.

One last book, held to the end because it offers a view of a possible future. Carolyn Heilbrun's *Toward a Recognition of Androgyny* has met some misunderstanding in its reviews, partly because it has been taken as arguing a feminist position. What Dr. Heilbrun is doing, however, is looking for evidence in the past of viability for a society which has outgrown insistence on the immediacy and primacy of sex distinction in areas of life en-tirely apart from the sexual. Fully aware of change, she is won-dering what it may produce if we can reintegrate within ourselves the half of the psyche which each sex has denied itself, and been denied, by attributing limiting roles and characters to men and women. It isn't suicide she sees following this breaking of stereotypes, but instead a release of talent and energy within men and women who need no longer repress aspirations which are not "proper" to the physical sex they bear. This leads perhaps to a sympathetic fellowship that would replace the hostility and fear so long taken as normal between the sexes. This is a small and scholarly study, based on literary evidence; but since great literature, like all great art, is per se a revelation of truth about human emotions, it is an area where possibilities for future living may legitimately be sought. Dr. Heilbrun's book is modest, but her vision is large and it is rooted in the prophetic vision of artistic creation.

This is a good harvest of books for a movement still less than a decade old. The insight, the creative thinking, the breadth of interest shown by these writers are, in themselves, evidence of the strength of women's new energy and confidence. Too many books about women? Not really; though we could surely do without some of the hackwork that we must expect to surface in any new field. But the first task for any subordinate group is to be taken seriously, as *present:* with a space in the world and in the minds of others that is taken for granted.

Liberties and rights can only be defined in terms of such a status, such a known social place. The slow growth of women's rights during the last century and a quarter has accompanied our own ability to see ourselves as capable of demanding these rights; for one does not break one's heart by asking for what one knows to be unachievable. These demands have often been voiced on grounds affecting others besides women. When Susan B. Anthony, at her trial for illegal use of the suffrage, instructed the judge that "Resistance to tyranny is obedience to God," she spoke for all rebels struggling for the basic right to claim rights. In the Women's Movement today, we can witness the continuance of this primary, elementary process of definition by which oppression is sorted out as oppression; by which opportunities become accepted as present and possible. This is the stage past tokenism where the public repetition of actions makes experience normal and liberty real. I believe it is where we are heading today. New questions, new problems, lie ahead, but they will surface in forms we cannot predict, as the multifarious responses to innumerable individual pressures force them on us. The value of testamentary evidence, as offered in books such as these I have discussed, lies in their enlargement of the context we bring to the solution of real problems in the real world.

Civil Liberties
Spring 1974

XV

I have been wondering lately whether there is not a useful and revealing analogy to be drawn between the position of women today and that of the middle classes at the beginning of modern times. It was the bourgeoisie which embodied the expansive forces that ended the limitations laid on society by the feudal structure of the Middle Ages. There have been arguments aplenty among historians as to whether the bourgeoisie really represented a "progressive" force in this period or not. But if we leave aside the value judgment implied by the word "progressive" we can surely agree that the new class of merchants and traders and makers of goods for sale and heapers-up of capital for future investment did function as the instrument which smashed hierarchical feudal society at a time when feudal order, once sustaining, had become crippling. Of course the rise of this class was a response to social and economic trends already in being: to a growing population which, by the twelfth century, had accumulated enough wealth and enjoyed enough time off from necessary labor to build the cathedrals and to set powerful minds considering physical relationships in the actual world in a way that would, in time, produce true science. It was a response to existing, continuing technological advance. If we take only the three inventions which Lynn White cites in his *Medieval Technology and Social Change,* namely, the stirrup, the crank which improved wind- and watermills and fathered the lathe, and the harness for draft animals, which allowed them to pull ploughs heavy enough to turn wet bottomlands into fertile fields, we see that a revolutionary reprogramming of work had already begun. No longer was its motive force to be that of human muscles.

265

In the period of peace which followed the end of the Viking raids, trade flourished and traders with it. And so on.

The strength of this new social force can be judged by the fact that it survived the disasters of the fourteenth century and, having done so, began to build an internal organization and to find a name of its own. A vitality of its own, too. Huizinga, in *The Waning of the Middle Ages,* has told unforgettably the tale of the decline and growing despair of the aristocracy of the fifteenth century. Against this dying fall, the vulgar, shoving rise of the bourgeoisie displayed a rough and not very attractive vigor. Chekhov wrote it all out for us, in terms we can understand, at a time when nineteenth-century Russia was still straddling the divide between a feudal society and modern times. Those charming, ineffectual aristocrats whose cherry orchard grew a crop of dreams but not of fruit confronted Lopakhin, the bourgeois climber, and went down before him. We sympathize, we regret their fate—but should the world grow nothing but dreams? As Firs, the old servant knew, the fruit had once been sold profitably; the orchard had once fed its product into the real world. When it ceased to do so, other forces in the real world rose to reclaim the dream orchard and return it to use. A new use, be it noted, for Lopakhin had no intention of marketing cherries. He was planning a housing development.

The middle class, that is, not only took over power from the aristocracy of the feudal world as the centuries passed, but it invented new ways to do things, new ways to live, new connections among human beings—not simply new knowledge, but new kinds of knowledge. This didn't happen because of a sudden mutation in the human species though, if we believed the neo-Darwinians, we'd have to think so. It happened because a whole order of society was given an opportunity for the first time to use the minds and energies and imaginations of its members. If they smashed the old order, it was done in a fit of absentmindedness for the most part, just because it got in the way. They were building a new order in a new place. Trade. Money. Towns. Capitalism. Exploration; ruthless, inhuman, this nascent force discovered the unknown New World, exploited it, grew rich on it and founded new societies there, one of which, at least, imagined new human values. Indeed, new human values and ideals rose like weeds in the footsteps of the bourgeois revolution. We owe it the Renaissance and the Reformation and the Enlightenment and the ideas of democracy, science, the factory system, the modern world. It created a society that was unimaginable in the world that gave it birth.

One of the things it has created is a female sex that is ceasing to be second and subordinate, and that is beginning to come together. Around us a world seems fading toward a dying fall as its hope and its imagination fail. That is the world the bourgeois revolution made. So perhaps it is time for a new force to venture out. A female revolution? Not exclusively, by any means. But because women are the repository of the largest store of unused abilities they will surely be a primary source and resource of ideas and energy. We have been taught to be pleasing, yes, polite and deferential in public, properly reverent before the great male structure of ideas that governs the world. But in fact we have never been all that reverential inside our own heads. Good, devoted, loyal wives may see men's hierarchies as games. And when you tell a woman that her proper role is that of mother, its centrality will affect the way she looks at the world. "They're all like little boys, aren't they?" say those good wives to each other.

I think it very possible that the fundamental irreverence with which women regard men's world will, in time, provide the answer to those who deplore the tendency of women who are moving out into men's world to move also into men's roles. At the beginning, acting a male role is a learning process; but even today, women are modifying masculine ways of doing things within the business structure. It is extremely difficult for men, even men of great good will, to conceive of interpersonal relationships which do not incorporate an element of dominance. Someone, they assume, has to be top dog. Women find it much easier to imagine, to create and to work within relationships of shifting power and initiative; you're better at this, I'm better at that, but it won't hurt for each of us to know how to do all that we're responsible for doing. These attitudes come out of old, normative experience. We expect to be able to ask for help. The "best-friendships" we grew up with were more often flexible rather than one-way dominant. And, to a considerable degree, we are less hung up on issues of "face." We have never had much "face" to worry about.

In the end I suspect that we are not simply going to modify man's world, as the bourgeoisie modified the feudal world; we are also going to amplify it, as they did. Man's world, the power world, is impoverished and in need of emotional values which will restore to it true human significance. They can't be thought up and pumped in like a transfusion of idealism. They will grow with new activities and processes not yet conceived, but which will deal with areas of life now empty. "The Lonely Crowd" desperately needs new, functioning communities. There is an enormous amount of work for such communities to do, linking individuals together and supporting isolated families. These communities will coalesce to meet felt needs which are now unsatisfied and unsatisfiable. They will involve themselves in political action at all levels. They will begin to shape new structures of living and new connections between people. They will turn up rewards and pleasures we have no way of picturing. And they can begin anywhere, come together at any level to achieve any sort of goal, great or small. Perhaps some will start with a few women who decide to introduce neighbors to each other, either for a purpose or simply for social interaction; some of these have already started. Perhaps some denizens of the residential ghettos we call housing developments will set up meeting places within them for discussions or learning or gripe sessions—or who knows what? Energy shortages promote car-pooling, and car-pooling involves organization. High food prices and other consumer issues join housewives together for talk and protest. They get gardens started, and gardeners exchange advice, and produce too. Any aggregate can grow, under the right circumstances, into a snowballing movement.

Such a world of ordinary daylight, one that lies not only beyond old myths but beyond the rosy light of dawn too, is where women are going; not easily, not simply, not without making mistakes, some of which will be grievous, not without sacrifices and losses. We face struggle and setback and boredom. We will find our hopes overblown, our efforts ineffective often and often. But we have no choice, for this is reality and we can't live in fantasyland any more. "For the time being, here we all are," wrote Auden,

Back in the moderate Aristotelian city
Of darning and the Eight-fifteen, where Euclid's geometry
And Newton's mechanics would account for our experience,
And the kitchen table exists because I scrub it . . .
There are bills to be paid, machines to keep in repair,
Irregular verbs to learn, the Time Being to redeem
From insignificance. The happy morning is over,
The night of agony still to come; the time is noon.

It is not Utopia and never will be, but it is the world we have been given and can learn to change. And will change, according to human capacities and for common ends.

Bibliography

Adler, Alfred. *What Life Should Mean to You.* Ed. by Alan Porter. Boston: Little, Brown, 1931.

Bengis, Ingrid. *Combat in the Erogenous Zone.* New York: Alfred A. Knopf, 1972.

Bird, Caroline. *Born Female.* New York: David McKay Company, 1968.

Comfort, Alex. *The Joy of Sex.* New York: Crown Publishers, 1972.

Cosmopolitan Love Guide. New York: Cosmopolitan Magazine, 1972.

de Beauvoir, Simone. *The Second Sex.* New York: Alfred A. Knopf, 1953.

Decter, Midge. *The New Chastity.* New York: Coward, McCann & Geoghegan, 1972.

Dickey, James. *Deliverance.* Boston: Houghton, Mifflin & Co., 1970.

Firestone, Shulamith. *The Dialectic of Sex.* New York: William Morrow and Company, 1970.

Foust, Carolyn. Letter to *Time* magazine, June 15, 1973, page 4.

Freeman, Jo. *The Origins of the Women's Liberation Movement.* Included in *Changing Women in a Changing Society.* Huber, Editor.

Freud, Sigmund. *On War, Sex and Neurosis.* Ed. by Sander Katz with a preface by Paul Goodman. New York: Arts & Science Press, 1947.

Friedan, Betty. *The Feminine Mystique.* New York: W. W. Norton & Company, 1963.

Gilder, George. *Sexual Suicide.* New York: Quadrangle Press, 1973.

Ginzberg, Eli. *Life Styles of Educated Women.* New York: Columbia University Press, 1966.

Greer, Germaine. *The Female Eunuch*. New York: McGraw-Hill Book Company, 1971.

Horney, Karen. *New Ways in Psychoanalysis*. New York: W. W. Norton & Company, 1939.

Howell, Mary C., M.D., Ph.D. *Effects of Maternal Employment on the Child*. Part I, *Pediatrics*, Vol. 52, No. 2, August, 1973. Part II, *Pediatrics*, Vol. 52, No. 3, September, 1973.

Huber, Joan, Ed. *Changing Women in a Changing Society*. Chicago and London: University of Chicago Press, 1973.

Huizinga, Johan. *The Waning of the Middle Ages*. London: Edward Arnold, Ltd., 1924.

Janeway, Elizabeth. *Man's World, Woman's Place*. New York: William Morrow and Company, 1971.

Janeway, Elizabeth. *Women: Their Changing Roles*. New York: Arno Press, 1973.

Johnston, Jill. *Lesbian Nation*. New York: Simon & Schuster, 1973.

Jones, Ernest. *The Life and Work of Sigmund Freud*. New York: Basic Books, 1955.

Keniston, Kenneth. *The Uncommitted*. New York: Harcourt, Brace and World, 1965.

Kinsey, Alfred C., et al. *Sexual Behavior in the Human Female*. Philadelphia: W. B. Saunders Company, 1948.

Laing, R. D. *Self and Others*. New York: Pantheon Books, 1969.

———. *The Divided Self*. London: Penquin Books, 1965.

———. *The Politics of Experience*. New York: Ballantine Books, 1967.

Langer, Susanne. *Feeling and Form*. New York: Scribners, 1953.

———. *Mind: An Essay on Human Feeling*. Vol. I. Baltimore: Johns Hopkins, 1967.

Lerner, Gerda, Ed. *Black Women in White America*. New York: Pantheon Books, 1972.

Lundberg, Ferdinand, and Farnham, Marynia. *Modern Woman: The Lost Sex*. New York: Harper Brothers, 1947.

Masters, William H., and Johnson, Virginia E. *Human Sexual Response*. Boston: Little, Brown & Company, 1966.

Millett, Kate. *Sexual Politics*. New York: Doubleday & Company, Inc., 1970.

Minturn, Leigh, and Lambert, William W., Eds. *Mothers of Six Cultures*. New York: John Wiley & Sons, 1964.

Mitchell, Juliet. *Woman's Estate*. New York: Pantheon Books, 1971.

O'Neill, William. *Everyone Was Brave*. New York: Quadrangle Press, 1969.

Oppenheimer, Valerie Kincaide. *Demographic Influence on Female Employment and the Status of Women.* Included in *Changing Women in a Changing Society.*

Orden, Susan R., and Bradburn, Norman M. *Working Wives and Marriage Happiness. The American Journal of Sociology,* January, 1969.

Reuben, Dr. David. *Any Woman Can.* New York: David McKay Company, 1972.

Rogers, Carl. *Becoming Partners.* New York: Delacorte Press, 1972.

Rowe, Richard R., Director. *Child Care in Massachusetts.* A study for the Massachusetts Advisory Council on Education. February, 1972.

Schneir, Miriam, Ed. *Feminism:* The Essential Historical Writings. New York: Vintage Books, 1972.

Sherfey, Mary Jane. *The Nature and Evolution of Female Sexuality.* New York: Random House, 1972.

Sorenson, Dr. Robert C. *Adolescent Sexuality in Contemporary America.* Cleveland, Ohio: World Publishing Company, 1973.

Turner, Victor W. *The Ritual Process: Structure and Anti-Structure.* Chicago: Aldine Publishing Company, 1969.

White, Lynn. *Medieval Technology & Social Change.* Oxford, England: Oxford University Press, 1962.

Work in America: Report of a Special Task Force to the Secretary of Health, Education and Welfare. Foreword by Elliot L. Richardson. Cambridge: MIT Press, no date.

Index